THE FIRST COMMUNIST
IN FORT JAMESON

Doris Bailey

with best wishes

Nigel

22/3/19

Nigel Watt

THE FIRST COMMUNIST IN FORT JAMESON

RECOLLECTIONS OF AFRICA AND OTHER PLACES 1955-2018

Publisher: Books of Africa Limited
16 Overhill Road
East Dulwich, London
SE22 0PH
United Kingdom

Web site: www.booksofafrica.com
Emails: admin@booksofafrica.com
sales@booksofafrica.com

Copyright : © Nigel Watt 2018

ISBN : 978-0-9935036-7-2

A CIP catalogue record for this book is available from the
British Library.

Printed and bound in India by Imprint Press.

Cover design: Supriya Chaudhary

Page layout, composition and ebook production by Opteam
www.opteam-compo.com
contact@opteam-compo.com

Dedicated to the memory of my first meeting
with my dear late wife Edyth
in Fort Jameson in 1962

Contents

THE FIRST COMMUNIST IN FORT JAMESON

RECOLLECTIONS OF AFRICA AND OTHER PLACES
1955-2018

ANNEXES

Acknowledgements

I would like to thank many of the numerous friends listed in the index for their support and for filling some of gaps in my memory. I am also very grateful to Jean Ellis and Pauline Dodgson-Katiyo for their comments and suggestions on the manuscript.

Author's note

The title of this book came to me before I started writing. Fort Jameson, now Chipita is is small town in the east of what is now Zambia. I should point out that in Northern and Southern Rhodesia a communist was any white person who was friendly towards Africans and supported their struggle for independence. Although I really prefer Africa to be written about by Africans, I thought that my varied experience might fill in some corners of the historical record by evoking memories of people and places. I have also included in the annex the stories of some individual African friends. The book starts with my time as a young teacher and headmaster in colonial Northern Rhodesia as it was turning into independent Zambia. It includes accounts of several journeys in Africa and my later work with non-government agencies in Burundi and the Congo. Some of the travels are not in chronological order and there are countries I have visited often such as Kenya and Uganda that are mentioned frequently but have no chapter devoted to them.

As I started to write the project morphed into more of an autobiography. It therefore also contains a little about my early years and something about India and Palestine. I have also tried to sketch the history of the international voluntary service (or workcamp) movement and my part in it. This includes the promotion of African youth volunteer associations which is something I am still passionate about. Another part of the story is my seven years as director of the Africa Centre in London and later, in retirement, as editor for a small publishing company, Books of Africa, both of which provided different perspectives on the continent. I apologise for including an enormous number of people's names. As a historical record I thought that Zambian students, for example, were as worthy of recording as some of the better-known people I have met or who are referred to in the text. Have a look at the index and if your name is not included, dear reader, please accept my apologies.

My life has been unusual and quite a lot of fun, so this book is hard to classify. It is a mixed bag, and readers may like to dip into it according to their different interests.

THE FIRST COMMUNIST IN FORT JAMESON

Recollections of Africa and other places
1955-2018

1
Beginnings 1936-60

i) A family

I was born in what was then the London Borough of Paddington in 1936, the younger son of John Watt and Esme (née Holl). We lived in St. John's Wood on the corner of Abbey Road, a little beyond the famous pedestrian crossing on the sleeve of the Beatles' record.

I suppose there are interesting or eccentric characters in most families and mine is no exception. The Watt folklore was that our ancestor had come from Scotland and been a partner in the brewery, Courage McCorquodale and Watt and that he had sold his share in it. The official history of the brewery makes no mention of any Watt, but what is certain is that by the 1850s the Watt family was fairly prosperous and living in Blackheath, now part of London but then on the edge of the countryside. My grandfather, Richard Ernest, was a totally unflappable character, a lawyer who commuted to town every day. Although he was generous to others he would walk to the next bus stop to save a halfpenny on the fare. He loved children and would have liked to have more of them but the health of his wife (who was in fact his cousin) meant that my father was an only child. I knew Grandad when he was old and deaf. When asked why he had no teeth he would reply that he must have swallowed them.

At the time of my parents' wedding in 1927 hordes of elderly Watts were still alive. I will only mention three. Aunt Mabel was Grandad's bossy sister and she appears later in my story. Uncle Watty had only one eye, the other one having been poked out by his brother. He wore gloves, two pairs of trousers and an overcoat, even in summer. Aunt Eva, who always wore a bonnet, had married a rich brewer in a, possibly vain, attempt to save him from the evil of drink and in the process she had inherited a great deal of money which she proceeded to give to good causes and, although I was a baby when she died, she left a little of it to my brother and me. Luckily this money was protected in a trust – or my father would certainly have spent it. I am still indebted to her.

My father grew up in his family's gloomy Victorian house and he was a rebel from the start. He was sent to a public school and loathed it. He always said that his atheism dated from the day at school when he heard the news of bishops blessing the guns – it was 1914. He studied chemistry but never finished his degree. He had various small jobs including painting a frieze in a restaurant at the British Empire Exhibition at Wembley in 1924. He volunteered to drive a tram during the General Strike of 1926. His stint as a tram driver ended when, one night, he drove it off the rails and told the angry passengers to walk home. He was briefly a reporter on the Daily Express before landing the job of news reader at the new BBC studio in Northern Ireland.

This was the birth of radio and he had arrived at the right moment. He was excited by this new medium. He was full of ideas and energy and was soon producing plays and radio shows on very low budgets as well as doing the continuity. He was soon promoted back to London where his first big success was Music Hall where he pioneered the idea of having live audiences at broadcasts. He introduced the radio show that was always associated with his name, Songs from the Shows.

His successes continued and before war broke out in 1939 he was appointed the BBC's Director of Variety. He was what today we would call a celebrity. During the war he was responsible for many of the morale-boosting popular radio programmes including Happidrome, Workers' Playtime, Band Wagon and ITMA. He was known as Mr. Variety. He even featured as number one on a series of cigarette cards. As a man who swore, smoked and drank a lot he was not loved by the very rigid Lord Reith, the BBC Director General, but I do not think this was the cause of his resignation at the end of the war aged only 45. He was offered lots of good jobs but chose to run a summer show at Butlin's Holiday Camp at Skegness. That year the weather was hot, so few people went to the theatre. He lost most of his money and I know my mother was not at all pleased.

PIC 1) Nigel as an unhappy king in the nativity play.

He always had a nice sense of humour. He edited a book, *Radio Variety*, with the dedication: "To Miss Cushion without whose filing system this book would have been written in half the time." He never went into television, saying he had been a pioneer once and that was enough, but he continued to freelance with Family Favourites and Housewives' Choice and Songs from the Shows on BBC radio. I remember going to meet him and Gracie Fields at a shabby little studio by a bomb site off Baker Street where they were recording the Wisk Half Hour[1] for Radio Luxembourg. But he had really lost his energy. His health had never been good and he went on drinking plenty of "double gin with just a dash of Dubonnet." He used to come home with all three of the London evening papers.[2] I remember him muttering one such night after a few drinks that he wished he had been born black – and I know he was very friendly with the very popular black singer, Leslie Hutchinson (Hutch). His early death in 1960 at the age of 59 was mainly due to his heavy drinking. He was

1. Wisk was washing powder.
2. The Evening Standard, the Star and the Evening News.

14

not the sort of dad who spent a lot of time with his children, but I am proud of this tribute from Gordon Glover, a fellow broadcaster and neighbour who wrote in the local paper that he was a "one-hundred-per-cent radio man, probably the greatest all-rounder within his field which broadcasting has ever known or is likely to know again".

My mother's family, the Holls, lived opposite the Watts in Kidbrooke Park Road. Her father was a tea planter in India. I remember the names of two Darjeeling estates, Poobong, still listed today, and Palandong. The company he part owned, Stewart Holl, is still trading in Kolkata. He died when my mother was very young but she remembered him as stern and strict, a typical Victorian father. He had a daughter, Minnie, by his first marriage (whose letter in the Congo is referred to later). His second wife, my dear Granny, was the same age as her step-daughter and very beautiful. Born in 1860 she lived until 1957. I knew her well towards the end of her life. She was still handsome, combing her long white hair. She would talk of her youth when she would smuggle herself into the theatre under a lady's crinoline. She had an old-fashioned turn of phrase. I remember her saying: "Upon my soul I never did see such an ugly man in all my born days;" and she shared the prejudices of many of her generation. There was a synagogue across the road. She would look out of the window at the gathering Jews and say, "Just look at them." When the Prime Minister, Anthony Eden, divorced his wife she remarked, "But I thought he was a nice man."

She had one son and three daughters of which my mother was the youngest. Uncle Frank was an engineer who had worked in Burma and Kenya and in later life commuted from Welwyn with his bowler hat and Daily Telegraph. Like me he liked trains. Frank used to tease me for my support of Indian and African independence saying "Nehru, Kaunda, Nyerere, all scallywags."

Aunt Winnie (or Helen) Holl had lived in the literary world of Bloomsbury. She wrote some good poetry. She had worked as a kind of secretary to Rebecca West. H.G. Wells gave her a scarf. C.K. Ogden published *Basic English: A General Introduction with*

Rules and Grammar in 1930 and she worked with him on other publications and the campaign to make this simplified version of English into an international auxiliary language. Competition for Basic at that time came from Esperanto and French. Ogden's methods survive in EFL teaching, but today, with help from the Internet, English – sadly the American version – has no competitor. In later life Winnie became something of a hermit, devoted to her horse and to my mother. She taught me to ride and I used to go to tea with her. In contrast to her radical youth, she became progressively more reactionary.

Gladys, the other elder sister, married a man that everyone else in the family took against. So I never met him. They moved to Ireland during the war as he loved meat and wanted to escape rationing. After his death we became friendly with Aunt Gladys. She had taken up Christian Science which had made her hopelessly optimistic. When she drove the wrong way round a roundabout she said she was sure that God would preserve her. Luckily He did.

PIC 2) *Watt's Folly, Arkesden.*

PIC 3) *Nigel at school aged 13 in 1949.*

Granny Holl had taken my mother and her sisters to Germany to improve their education. They left for home just before war broke out in 1914. Gladys only just made it. She pretended to be Dutch and escaped through neutral Holland. My mother was sent to Parson's Mead, a boarding school at Ashtead in Surrey. She was not happy there and never passed any exams. Yet she always loved words and began to write verses and children's stories. She never gave up writing. Under her pen name of Angela Jeans she published ten novels, three children's books, a book about a tame owl and a biography of my father, from which I gleaned some bits for this chapter. She usually got good reviews but poor sales. Her best book was *Condemned to Life* which describes life after arrival of Grandad and Aunt Mabel into our household after they were bombed out. Many of her short stories were broadcast as "morning stories" by the BBC. She loved my father, but the showbiz lifestyle did not suit her. His infidelities and drinking finally caused a split two years before he died. She continued to live for many years in Arkesden, Essex in the picturesque cottage, Watt's Folly, which they had bought in 1936 for what was even then the bargain price of £140. The cottage has featured on calendars and tourist brochures and it still looks beautiful today. My parents had an old gipsy caravan in the garden and this was my bedroom when I was a teenager. My mother had strong principles, not least a profound hatred of war. After the bombing of Dresden she wrote a letter to the Daily Express deploring the destruction. She received hundreds of abusive letters blaming her for Nazi sympathies. She was especially passionate about animal welfare. She had hundreds of china cats as well as live cats and, latterly, Brussels griffons and other small dogs. She was a strong character, very efficient, consistent and a loving mother.

My only brother, Christopher, known to us as Chimp, was born in Belfast. He was six years older than me so I usually got bossed around when he was not away at boarding school. He left school at the age of 16 and got jobs in repertory theatres and was stage manager at several theatres including the London Palladium. He was a fan of Gene Kelly and wanted to be a film star. Emigrating from gloomy post-war Britain he started off as a ballroom dancing teacher in New York and ended up in Los Angeles as a Director at NBC television. He loved railways including especially model ones. In his retirement in Arizona he built a huge layout for his model trains. In between writing parts of this book I have been in Arizona helping Chimp's German-born widow, Roswitha, photographer son, Raymond, and accountant daughter, Frances, pack his thousands of models to ship to an auctioneer in England and listening to Roswitha's memories of her childhood in wartime and post-war Berlin.

ii) Young Nigel

My parents had bought a rather dilapidated house, No.1 Blenheim Road, on the corner of Abbey Road and modernised it in a very 1930s style. When I was born, a room in the basement was converted into a nursery. I was brain-washed with Disney: there were life-size cardboard figures of Mickey and Minnie Mouse and Pluto by the door and a clock model of the Big Bad Wolf. (My father knew Walt Disney personally and we used to receive Christmas cards from him with bits of film attached). A nanny was employed who apparently adored and spoiled me. To her I was "the lamb." My earliest memory was looking up at the sun shining through the fog, and I remember being taken to watch the trains on the bridge at South Hampstead station. The nanny had to return to Ireland in 1939 when war broke out. I missed being spoilt by her and I became impossible, refusing to speak or look at anyone. I remained shy and unsociable for years. Toys were rare at that time and to stop me playing with my grandmother's spectacles she bought me a set of Mickey Mouse bricks. I still have a few of them. Before leaving London we had a television set which showed BBC experimental programmes. These were stopped when war broke out in 1939 and radio had the monopoly until after the war. We never had a television set until after my father's death.

The variety and drama departments of the BBC moved to Bristol for safety in 1939 and we had to find somewhere to live nearby. We lodged briefly in Dunster, Somerset, where there were fleas in the bed and fish paste sandwiches every evening. Then we rented a house in Clevedon with a garden looking over the cliff to the Bristol Channel. I was sent to a nursery school in a convent. I remember the nuns praying as warplanes flew overhead. After a few months we moved to nearby Nailsea which was then quite a small village. I remember the sound of night raids. I fell into the duck pond in the garden and was dragged out by my brother, green with duck weed and choking. My mother used to take me on her bicycle to the primary school where, still as unsociable as ever, I refused to shelter with the other children when there was an air raid alert. They had to put me under a table in the staff room.

Air raids over Bristol soon led the BBC to move the Variety Department to Bangor in North Wales. On the day of the move I had whooping cough and I remember vomiting all over my grandmother on the long drive through Wales. We moved into a big, gloomy house across the Menai Bridge. This is where Grandad and Aunt Mabel arrived, as described in my mother's book. Aunt Mabel was constantly trembling with Parkinson's disease. They brought with them a neurotic maid and an overfed cat. When my brother came on holiday we played crazy games in the garden. Chimp made friends with the signalman at Menai Bridge station and we visited the next station up the line, Llanfairpwllg-wyngyllgogerychwyrndrobwll llantysiliogogogoch – and we learned to translate the name. We were taken one day to Beddgelert and got lost exploring the remains of the former Welsh Highland Railway. This line reopened in 2009. We were conscious of the war: the *Daily Express* was delivered daily and I remember looking at the black arrows on the maps showing the advance of the allied armies. On the radio I remember the announcement of the death of David Lloyd George, and also the Christmas broadcast of Disney's *Snow White and the Seven Dwarfs*. My father played the part of Bashful, so of course he hardly said a word!

iii) Fig

In 1943 we left Wales and settled at Watt's Folly. Chimp was already at the Friends' School in nearby Saffron Walden[3] and I followed him there. I was very happy there – and I became sociable at last. I was given the nickname Fig, a corruption of Nigel, and I was responsible for the nicknames of some of my fellows, names that some of them were keen to forget in adult life. On the morning of election day in 1945 we came down to breakfast and the dining hall had been plastered with Labour Party posters and "Down with Butler" banners. R.A. Butler, a future Chancellor of the Exchequer, was the MP for Saffron Walden. On this occasion he very nearly lost his majority.[4]

Together with my school friend, Kaye Whiteman – later to become a great Africanist – we had the hobby of collecting film advertisements from the papers and sticking them into albums. With Kaye and Brian Abbs, who was to become well known for revolutionising the teaching of English as a Second Language, we used to go to see the latest epic films during the school holidays and later we collaborated on writing songs and skits which were performed at the school. We wrote a musical version of Stella Gibbons' novel, *Cold Comfort Farm*. Kaye wrote the music and

---

3. Sadly the school closed in 2017.
4. See Butler's letter about the Suez crisis in annex 3.

we both worked on the lyrics and the dialogue. It was never performed.

Going abroad was something special in this post-war period. My first taste of it was a holiday with my parents on the coast of Belgium in 1950. We stayed in the Grand Hotel de la Plage in Heist and my father discovered what was then an unknown little local beer called Stella Artois. Then, a year later when I was in the sixth form several of us went on an exchange visit to Paris which included language lessons and visits to museums and chateaux. I stayed with a friendly family and improved my spoken French but the boy who was my "partner" seemed only interested in mending bicycles.

In 1952 I set off with my friend John Veit Wilson (Hanno) to cycle through Germany, from Düsseldorf down the Rhine Valley and through the Black Forest to Strasbourg where we took a train home via Paris. The war had only ended seven years earlier and there were many signs of this: strict border control; rusty signals, sidings overgrown with weeds and gloomy railway carriages; and many bomb sites. As a young child Hanno had narrowly escaped from the Nazis, but he still had family contacts in Germany and from them we learned a bit about the post-war situation in the country including some signs of the future economic revival.

At school I was always good at geography, history and languages. A charismatic Irishman whom we called BBJ taught geography and his method was to teach us to recite incantations. One example relates to this book: "The valley of the forested Belgian Congo, rich in oil palms and magnificent with its convergent waterways but hampered in its economic development by the paucity of its native population." He did not tell us about the many thousands who died under the rule of King Leopold II. When given the chance I jumped at the option of learning German and dropping Science, but I did not study seriously until major exams came in sight. Then I did well, ending up with a State Scholarship as well as a Minor Scholarship to St. John's College, Cambridge.

The first paid job I had was as an assistant at an archaeological excavation of the so-called Battle Ditches on the west side of Saffron Walden. This excavation proved that this trench was not a prehistoric earthwork but dated from the 13th century. This job gave me a taste for archaeology, to be followed up later in Zambia.

iv) Railways

Railways were my greatest passion. Saffron Walden was on a branch line from our local station at Audley End. I would ride on the little steam train as often as possible. I also took an interest in local bus services and at the age of twelve I wrote to the Managing Director of the local bus company, Premier Travel, suggesting a number of new bus routes. He wrote back in detail inviting me to meet the Area Manager, who would have been surprised if this small boy had turned up. In 1961 Dr. Beeching took charge of the railways and began closing lines as part of his Modernization Plan. I wanted to travel on all the lines that were going to close. After a journey around a lot of threatened railway lines with Adam Kendon[5] during the school holidays we created the Society for the Reinvigoration of Unremunerative Branch Lines in the United Kingdom (SRUBLUK). We formed a committee with classmates Tim Whitmore[6] and Elizabeth Paul, and we held a "conference" in the old carriage that served as the waiting room at Ashdon Halt, the next stop after Walden. Adam and I went on "ferroviations" on branch lines in the school holidays.

Some time in my last year at school I remember seeing the headmaster to ask if I could take a day off school to travel on the line from Haughley to Laxfield in Suffolk which was to be closed. He got out the timetable and started lovingly mouthing the names of the stations: Brockford and Wetheringsett[7], Aspall and Thorndon, Worlingworth… his heart melted and he said I could go. Shortly afterwards we wrote to British Railways to ask if SRUBLUK could rent this line. The answer unsurprisingly was no.

---

5. Adam and I also dreamed up a spoof academic discipline, Pemphthemerology, the study of the influence of Thursday over the other days of the week. Kendon studied psychology and became one of the world's foremost authorities on the topic of gesture.
6. Tim became a well-known expert on tropical plants and the rain forest.
7. Part of this line at Brockford has been reopened as a vintage steam railway.

PIC 4) The train to Laxfield, 1952.

However, soon afterwards we travelled on the Kent and East Sussex Railway and, realizing it was to be axed, we wrote to numerous newspapers proposing to save it.[8] We received so many responses that, as we left school, SRUBLUK started to become a serious lobbying association in the real world outside, with a mixture of older men joining our Executive Committee. We approached the poet laureate John Betjeman to be President.[9] He was very supportive but he proposed his friend Sir Arthur Elton. We would go flyposting, arriving in places like Monmouth and Brackley which were likely to lose their trains and sheepishly sticking up posters with our slogan "Use or lose your railway line." We also used the record the number of passengers on particular trains with the number getting on or off at each station. Our quaint acronym got us some publicity but it was too jokey for serious lobbying and, later on when I was no longer active, SRUBLUK amalgamated with the Railway Development Association and became the Railway Development Society. It still exists, more active than

8. The letter to the Spectator is in annex 2.
9. This letter can be found in John Betjeman; Letters Volume Two p.70

ever, as Railfuture. Congestion and environmental concerns have brought about a revival of rail travel and Railfuture's efforts have led to many stations being reopened and rail services improved. This first experience of campaigning may have encouraged me to be involved later in issues of race and peace.

v) Non-military service

In 1954 two years military service was compulsory for eighteen-year-olds in Britain. Influenced by my education at a Quaker school and by my parents' loathing of war, I registered as a conscientious objector (C.O.). This involved writing a "statement" to explain my reasons. I did not claim religious grounds as I was not a convinced Christian.[10] I had to go before a tribunal in Fulham Town Hall and face three stern looking magistrates, quite an ordeal at the age of eighteen. It seemed as if the Quaker influence did the trick because two of the other would-be "conchies" were Jehovah's Witnesses who refused to fight: they wanted to devote their lives to spreading the word. When asked if they would fight if God told them to do so they said yes, so they were declared not to be real pacifists and were rather unfairly turned down. Six years earlier, Chimp had also not been able to convince his tribunal and, when he refused the call up, he spent a few months in Wormwood Scrubs and Lewes prisons, where he was with real criminals including John Haigh, the notorious acid bath murderer. When he later emigrated to the US he reluctantly accepted being drafted into the American army. He was lucky that this was after the Korean War and before Vietnam. He got into the entertainment corps and managed to avoid having to fight.

Having got through my tribunal I was allowed to work in agriculture or forestry or in a hospital. Some of my Quaker friends ended up serving in the Friends' Ambulance Unit but I responded to a small ad in the Farmers' Weekly and went off to work at Clent Grove, a farm in Worcestershire at a wage of £4,7shillings a week less lodging and national insurance. This was no ordinary farm.

---

10. The text of my Statement is in annex 1.

It was attached to Sunfield Children's Home, run by *anthroposophists*, followers of Rudolf Steiner. Chimp had been educated at Michael Hall, a well-known Steiner school where my mother complained he never learned to spell correctly as they concentrated so much on art and music. Clent Grove contained an interesting collection of residents, some of whom were middle aged German ladies who had sought refuge from Hitler's Germany. The widow of the famous cellist, Pablo Casals also visited, as did the actress, Valerie Hobson,[11] whose son was at the home. I learned a bit about biodynamic farming and the wonders of compost, often called "muck and magic", about Steiner's ideas on architecture (no square corners) and dance (eurythmy) and Goethe's theories of colour and science.

When I was free I spent weekends visiting home or travelling on some of the railway lines which were shortly to close. I also fitted in a visit to Ireland with the fellow founders of SRUBLUK. Ireland felt more like the 1930s with few cars on the roads, numerous nuns on the trains and the evening meal always "rasher and egg". We travelled on some memorable railway lines: the Hill of Howth Tramway, the Cavan and Leitrim Railway, the County Donegal Railway, the Sligo, Leitrim and Northern Counties Railway, the West Clare Railway, the lines from Cork to Courtmacsherry and Bantry and from Farranfore to Valencia Island. These lines are all now distant memories. We took the horse-drawn tram from Fintona Junction where the horse had to hide in the stable as it was frightened of the noise of the steam train. We stayed in Tummons' Temperance Hotel in Enniskillen and in the Cork Establishment for Anti-Social Protestant Youth. One night in Donegal we slept next to a hearse in a barn on a stack of hay and we slept twice, with permission, in trains standing in sidings. It was all very friendly and laid back.

I quite enjoyed the farm work at Clent Grove. It consisted of market gardening, mostly weeding, looking after chickens, sheep,

---

11. Valerie Hobson had married the politician, John Profumo, and she stood strongly by him as he faced the scandal for which he is famous.

cattle and pigs and occasionally driving the tractor. Jim Harper who managed the farm was not an anthroposophist but a pacifist and a socialist. My other colleague on the farm, Frank Wheatley, informed me that I was allowed to take part in international voluntary workcamps as part of my alternative service so, after over a year at Clent, I applied to International Voluntary Service for Peace (IVSP) and became a "long term volunteer" attending one workcamp after another and receiving pocket money and travel costs. My decision to be a volunteer was to influence much of my future career.

To get to my first IVSP workcamp I took the non-stop Elizabethan express from London King's Cross to Edinburgh and continued to Glasgow where I was one of a group of twenty volunteers who slept and cooked in an old church hall in the city. Each day we would take the tram and go to grim tenement flats, tear down old wallpaper and paint the walls and window frames – and chat with the elderly tenants. They seemed to appreciate our work while being somewhat amazed at all these foreigners who had problems decoding the local accent. A letter I wrote at the time records that the volunteers were, apart from me, Indian, Pakistani, white and black African, German, Yugoslav, a Polish refugee, Swedish, English, Swiss, Austrian and Spanish. After my fairly sheltered childhood I was shocked at the living conditions in the tenements where we worked but I took immediately to the communal life the international ambience of the workcamp.

After two weeks in Glasgow including a few more rides on railway lines I took the overnight boat to Belfast, for my second workcamp. My only knowledge of the politics of Northern Ireland was the memory of having to show our passports at some not very friendly border crossings during our rail tour in 1954 and a book I had seen in the school library showing how the constituencies had been gerrymandered to favour the Protestants. On the bus to the workcamp I was amazed to see union flags everywhere. It was July. It was a peaceful time in the province and our project was not at all political. We painted the rooms in Childhaven, an orphanage run by the Belfast Central Mission set in a wood within earshot of the sea at Millisle, County Down. We stayed in a cottage in the garden and we got to know the orphan children, taking them out rowing and fishing.

I reported back to the IVSP office in London and was then sent to SCI workcamps abroad. IVSP (now IVS) is the British branch of the international movement, SCI, described below. I set off to my camp in Austria, first by boat and train to Paris where I slept in the SCI France hostel in Clichy. The next two days were on trains to Zürich and then to Vorarlberg in the west of Austria. Here we stayed and worked for five weeks in a typical mountain village, Bartholomäberg, which was not accessible by road. In fact our job was to build a road, just wide enough for a vehicle, and we did this by moving rocks and earth, working with pick and shovel, supervised by the local *Bürgermeister*, an elderly villager called Lorenzi. I sent a postcard home reporting on the mud and rain asking for my leather boots to be sent urgently. The volunteers came from twelve countries. There were two Egyptians who brought with them propaganda material about President Nasser and a loyal Israeli Arab who unfurled the Star of David at the summit of one of the mountains. We cooked and slept in a couple of the old farmhouses and there was little chance to wash. The panorama of mountain peaks speckled with snow was memorable when the sun shone, but it seldom did and we were often enveloped in dank, vaporous cloud and soaked with rain. At workcamps in those days volunteers used to arrive and depart on different dates, so after a few weeks I had become senior enough to become the camp leader. This involved persuading the volunteers to get out of bed – and they were all older than me. I was also responsible for communicating with Lorenzi and my German improved a lot. Bartholomäberg was very different when I visited it in 2013. I found a wide tarmac road, an hourly bus service and under every house where they used to keep the animals was a carport, but the mountain panorama was as stunning as ever.

From Austria I travelled by way of a few minor railway lines through the Black Forest to Metz, in Lorraine, France. Both here and in the subsequent camp at Worms in Germany we were working with local associations of families known as *castors* (beavers) to build houses to replace their homes lost in the war. After twenty years they got ownership of the homes they had helped build. At Metz we worked in a field at the edge of the town digging foundations for new houses and at another site where the houses had already been built where we dug trenches and laid water pipes. It was hard, boring work. The leader of the camp was the General Secretary of SCI France, Etienne Reclus, another railway enthusiast, who was a hard taskmaster but he used frequently to rush back to his office in Paris. Then we could lean on our shovels and relax a bit.

At the Worms camp the work was more interesting as we were involved in all the building process, barrowing sand and cement, mixing the cement and bricklaying; and the team included three notable volunteers: Ben Korley from what was still the Gold Coast (now Ghana), the first African volunteer to be invited to workcamps in Europe and a founder member of the Voluntary Workcamps Association of Ghana (VOLU); Sam Bala Sundaram from Ceylon (now Sri Lanka) who ended up in the Soviet Union; and Devinder Das Chopra, a future leader of SCI in India and Asia.

PIC 5) Coffee break at the Bartholomäberg workcamp, 1955.

In between camps I hitch-hiked with Bill, a German friend I had met at Metz, across northern France living mainly on bread and chocolate. I went on through Belgium, Luxembourg and the little railway along the bank of the Moselle to join the workcamp at Worms. After my six months as a workcamper I returned to London and finished my alternative service as a hospital porter at the Gordon Hospital for Diseases of the Colon and Rectum in the Vauxhall Bridge Road, London where I became a member of the then mighty Transport and General Workers Union. The morning shift was hard and often disgusting work but on the night shift when there was nothing to do I just sat at the switchboard learning Spanish and reading The Times which I retrieved from the waste paper basket.

There were several months before I was due to go to Cambridge. With school friends we had a crazy plan to buy an old London taxi and drive to Italy in it. The deal fell through so I sailed to Holland and hitch-hiked to Germany and worked as a volunteer at a Lutheran study centre beside the River Ruhr, weeding carrots and onions, often in the pouring rain. I attended some of the church services and decided that religion sounded better in German. Bill came to visit me and we went off for a few days and many beers at Münster University. I then hitch-hiked back to Calais to meet up with the school friends and we hitch-hiked to Sweden and Norway. Hitch-hiking was popular and fairly safe in those days. We usually displayed the Union Jack – the British were still well liked after the war – but even this was of little help on the main road, not yet tarmac, between Oslo and Stockholm, where there was almost no traffic.

vi) Cambridge

I finally took up my place at St. John's College in October 1956 and, after toying with the idea of studying languages, I read history. I love Cambridge but I was much less happy in the bigger university world, full of noisy, sporty public school types, than in my small, friendly boarding school. My friends were mostly people I had known at school. But there were good moments. While at school I had supported the Liberal Party but in the Suez crisis I reacted to Prime Minister Anthony Eden's attack on Egypt by joining the Labour Party. I remember the high drama at the Cambridge Union where the Tory supporters were in full voice against the young Anthony Wedgwood Benn, later known as Tony, who, when he could be heard, made a brilliant attack on Prime Minister Eden's foolishness and won the motion against the government. There was a protest meeting the following evening at which some rowdy Tories were shouting, "We want war" and later there was a huge anti-war meeting on Parker's Piece. I wrote a letter to R.A. Butler, then Lord Privy Seal, condemning the attack on Egypt. His reply is in Annex 4.

In the first long vacation in 1957 I hitch-hiked with Brian Abbs to Stockholm and earned some money washing up at the (unfortunately named) SHT Restaurant. I stayed in the Badminton Hall Youth Hostel and later in a flat with two Austrians who were doing the same job. I earned a little over £1 a day, most of the time loading and emptying the dishwasher. The restaurant was not doing much business so the work was not too tiring. Then Brian and I hitch-hiked via Strasbourg, Geneva and Andorra to Spain, for which in those days a visa was required. The reality of Franco's dictatorship was reflected in the heavy presence of police on the buses and trains – and the poverty of most of the people was striking. We had a kilometric ticket which gave us cheap travel on the railway and we took slow steam trains on narrow gauge lines as well as slightly faster trains to Barcelona, Madrid, Toledo, Cordoba and Seville. I remember being on the train from Girona to San Feliu de Guixols and eating my first water melon peppered with smuts from the steam engine.

From Seville I took my first ever flight on a small plane across to Tetuan in Morocco which cost less than £3. We found a bus to Ksar El Kebir and then a very crowded train to the beautiful ancient city of Fez, returning to Tangier and a ferry to Algeciras in Spain – my first three days in Africa.

In 1959 after leaving Cambridge I took a temporary job teaching at my local Newport Grammar School. At the same time I applied to do a postgraduate education course paid for by the Colonial Office which would start in September 1960. I was in the Cambridge public library when I discovered the wonders of Thomas Cook's Overseas Rail Timetable. This inspired me to plot a journey to India where I planned to spend the eight months before the course began. I asked IVSP if they had any suitable place for me in India. They had nothing that fitted my dates and suggested that I ask Voluntary Service Overseas (VSO), then a tiny organization that had just sent out its first volunteer school leavers. I climbed up to their tiny office in Grand Buildings, Trafalgar Square. Here I met Mohan Singh Mehta, the founder of Vidya Bhavan, an educational institute in India. He sounded interested and asked me to come for an interview in Geneva. I told him I could not go to Geneva but that I was going to India anyway and I would happily meet him when I got there. So he told me just to turn up at Vidya Bhavan and he would arrange for me to be met when I got to Bombay.

vii) A passage to and from India 1960

India, and especially the Gulf, have changed enormously in the last sixty-eight years. Fortunately I kept a diary and I wrote many letters home and these have helped keep the experience of my journey alive.

It was a week before my twenty-fourth birthday in January when my mother saw me off at London's Victoria Station on the train to Dover. I had planned to go via Istanbul and take the Taurus Express through Turkey and Syria to Baghdad and Basra. I had even bought a Bulgarian visa, but at that time Syria was linked to Egypt as part of the United Arab Republic and had had no diplomatic relations with Britain since the Suez attack of 1956. I had therefore to travel via Athens and Beirut. Getting off the ferry boat at Ostend I was alone in the one coach labelled Athens. I was soon joined by a talkative English military man who was with me all the way to Greece. He had worked as an adviser to the Greek army during the civil war (1944-49) and to him England was always Blighty. At Brussels the compartment filled up with "a Belgian with a square face and a square body, and five Germans, one a very old widow with teeth missing." The population of the compartment changed at each stop. The first night took me through Germany, into daylight in Bavaria and Austria and, after fierce frontier formalities to enter Yugoslavia, overnight again to Belgrade. Two hours there, long enough to have an incredibly cheap breakfast and to notice that there were no cars on the street, only a tram and a horse and cart. I wrote about Yugoslavia in my letter: "Many of the roads were nothing but mud and water... the soil was poor, the grass sickly, the hills utterly barren... people fighting to get into a local train." Overnight again and on the third day "Blighty" and I finally reached Athens.

I had booked to sail on Olympic Cruises to Beirut but I had to wait one night before boarding the ship. I climbed up the Acropolis as the sun came up and shone brightly on the marble. A vivid rainbow appeared on the nearby hill. The only other thing I remember seeing in Athens was an escalator from the metro to the open air, an unusual sight in those days. The next morning, waiting in Piraeus for the ship, I watched the ceremony of blessing the water. A procession of Orthodox patriarchs bearing silver crosses advanced to a temporary podium. A Rolls Royce drove up and a group of military men got out, one of whom apparently was the King of Greece. All the ships in the harbour responded by hooting and bells rang throughout the town.

My ship, the s/s Achilleus, was pleasantly luxurious and the meals were enormous. The few other passengers included an English Quaker with an IVSP badge who was going to a workcamp in Sudan, a Greek music teacher and his wife going to Beirut, a little Iraqi with a big moustache, and an unshaven German off to study community development in India.

It was night when we sailed into Alexandria and the famous lighthouse was flashing. An evangelical American missionary got on board. He was on his way from the pyramids to the Holy Land but he seemed ignorant of anything that was not in the Bible. That night, with so few on board and little freight, the ship rolled drunkenly. I think I was the only passenger who did not look green in the face. I gorged myself alone in the restaurant. The ship stopped outside the port of Limassol, Cyprus (still British but to be independent in eight months' time). On the final day the sea was calm and the mountains of Lebanon rose up on the clear horizon. You could see steep valleys and little towns and a line of white matchboxes which turned out to be the hotels and luxury flats of Beirut's glamourous *corniche*.

The ship was eleven hours late. It was already evening and the plane I had booked for Kuwait was due to leave at 1.00 am. All the taxis were large American cars. I took one to the home of Mr. Holmes of the British Embassy who knew I was coming. He very kindly drove me to his office, gave me my Kuwait visa and dropped me at the airline office. I still had a few hours to wander in the city. The streets were busy with an endless stream of mostly ancient buses with exhaust pipes pointing upwards. There were parked cars all over the pavements and lots of palm trees. *Hole in the Head, They Came to Cordura* and several films with Arabic titles were showing at the many cinemas. A Lebanese friend at school had told me a little about the country and he taught me the Arabic script which was also useful for reading Urdu later in Pakistan and India.

PIC 6) *With new Arab friends on the ship to India, 1960.*

There were only five of us on the plane to Kuwait, and a lot of boxes of oranges. I dozed off as we flew out over the sea to gain height over the mountains. I woke up over a strange wrinkled sea. It was of course the desert. My schoolmate Jennifer Edwards (known at school as "Spiv" as she dressed so smartly) met me at the airport and took me to the British India Steamship Company to buy my passage. I chose Intermediate Class with its wooden beds as Jennifer had offered to lend me an inflatable mattress. It took time getting a health certificate, joining a queue of Arabs. We went for a drive in the desert, past oil tanks and a Bedouin tent. We had a drink with a group of bored American wives living in luxury and leading totally American lives. We got up at dawn the next morning, Monday 11 January, only to find the boat was delayed so I had some time to see Kuwait. It was already a modern city with motorways, handsome mosques and a secondary school so grand that it was dubbed "the university" where all the students arrived in their own cars. Newly rich Kuwaitis had built themselves grand villas and there were, I noted, more mosques than trees. At that time Kuwait supplied 60% of Britain's oil and the ruling Sheikh had created a paternalistic little welfare state.

Finally to get on board the *Santhia* I piled into a dhow, crowded with passengers and their bedsteads, radios and trunks. One man laid his Taj Mahal prayer mat on a tin trunk, faced Mecca (which in fact was not very far away) and prayed. The only gangway was for the first-class passengers, all two of them, while the rest of us waited our turn to clamber up into the ship. There were eight bunks in Intermediate Class occupied only by me and Abdulla, a friendly Adeni who was also going to Bombay (now Mumbai). Two large Hindu ladies and another couple joined us at Bahrain the next day where the sea was quite rough: women and children had to be thrown into the arms of "coolies" or relatives at the foot of the gangway. I heard a white woman complaining that she had be ferried in the same boat as "locals." While our ship waited overnight for some sheikh to arrive, Abdulla introduced me to a group of young Omanis travelling in the bunked section, the cheapest. They were happy to find a European who was not cocooned in first class. There were also a number of Bahrainis on board, a cheerful lot who had a gramophone which played non-stop Arabic pop songs.

We must have stopped at Doha and Abu Dhabi in the night as I made no diary entries about them. On the Thursday morning we reached Dubai. Given the metropolis that Dubai has become, I have to quote my exact description: "Dubai... another sheikhdom but without oil... we anchor, as always, out at sea and only the tiny line of ant-sized houses can be seen, and a row of date palms lining the sea front." I wish I had had a camera! We also stopped at Sharjah, also just a tiny fishing village.

On the Friday we woke up to different scenery: weird rock formations, small jagged islands, the bare mountains of Persia (Iran) in the distance. This was the Straits of Hormuz where the Gulf – Persian or Arabian according to your allegiance – becomes the Gulf of Oman and where both coastlines are visible at the same time. The Persian town of Bandar Abbas is (or was) built entirely of the local stone and was invisible from a distance against a background of hills. The sea was utterly calm and the evening was especially beautiful. As the sun went down the rocks stood out black against a sky "first burnt yellow, then very burnt custard, then burnt orange, almost for a few minutes a pale mauve... The huge sun has gone leaving a pink wash behind it in the sky. The moon comes up just as suddenly. It looked like a headlight... really superlative Cheshire cheese throwing its path across the sea. Calm and silver – only clichés will describe it."

Early on Saturday we are hugging the rocky coast of Muscat, the capital of Oman. My diary comments: "Ruled by a bad Sultan, also protected against his subjects by us."

Muscat was a proper town, squashed into a cavity between rocks and sheltered by a rocky island. On these rocks were several picturesque castles and round watch towers. The commercial centre, Matrah, could be seen in the next bay. People and goods were ferried ashore by very light canoe-shaped boats painted in an almost African style. As we churned away from Muscat I spent the day chatting about politics with a Bahraini called Ahmed. He was for democracy and against sheikhs (which probably meant he was one of the *shia* majority). In the evening he invited me for coffee with some aged Bahrainis who were going to India for medical treatment. An imposing Pakistani sheikh came and sat with us and questioned me about Christian beliefs. I am not sure that my attempt to describe the nature of the Trinity was very convincing.

The next morning we arrived outside Gwadur in Pakistan. The scenery was like the moon, with weird white cliffs around a small bay and no vegetation to be seen. This place had belonged to the Sultan of Muscat and Oman but he gave to it Britain in lieu of a big debt and Britain handed it on to Pakistan. The people here were Baluchis wearing woolly Russian-type hats.

A week out from Kuwait we reached Karachi. Abdullah and I went ashore, past appalling slums, riding in a *tonga* (a horse drawn taxi) to the National Museum, a dignified Victorian edifice complete with a statue of the great queen. Abdullah then found he needed some sex. It was hard to find a brothel open on a Monday afternoon. It looked very unattractive so while I waited for him I went and dined on a large *biryani*. Karachi was otherwise unimpressive. Camels were pulling little carts along narrow, dusty streets. There were donkeys but few cars.

PIC 7) *With Indian friends at Udaipur station, 1960.*

After another night the ship finally berthed beside the very British looking harbour terminal in Bombay. A small, shrimp-like man sent by the British Council came to hustle me through customs, a difficult task as everyone arriving from the Gulf was expected to have gold secreted on their person and most were carrying large, shiny radiograms, cameras, watches and other items which required payment of import duty. He took me in a taxi to a hotel on the Marina. It was hot and humid. The next morning it was a surprise to wake up cold in the overnight train going north towards Udaipur.

I was to stay only six months at Vidya Bhavan school. It had been established as a truly Indian project before independence when this was the princely state of Mewar, not under direct British rule. It was part of a complex of different colleges including a teachers' training college, a training school for *mukhya sevikas* (social workers), a rural institute and a basic school run on Gandhian lines and concentrating more on spinning and craft, but free and thus accessible to the poorest children. Vidya Bhavan was in a lovely setting surrounded by hills dotted with little bushes and small temples. It was a short walk from Fateh Sagar, an artificial lake built by one of the Maharanas with pretty little white shelters along the dam wall and a palace in the middle which has now been converted into a luxury hotel. Udaipur's sumptuous City Palace had stables for the late Maharana's ninety elephants, the remaining one of which could be seen going for its walk through the streets. It was available for hire for wedding parties, one of which was in progress for three days soon after I arrived with a loud, squeaky band playing non-stop. The royal stables for the cavalry were equally enormous. This lovely old city has since become a tourist attraction and it was good to live there when it was just itself.

My work was to improve the English of the secondary school pupils who had few opportunities to speak the language. Class picnics were organised where everyone had to sing. I had to dig up my repertoire of workcamp songs in various languages. My lessons did not stop one boy from saying "Bread eat monkey" when we cycled to visit the famous temple at Eklingji. This visit was one of the most vivid of my experiences in India. The entrance to the temple is guarded by two painted elephants and, gazing inwards towards the shrine of the god, Shiva, are two cows, one black and one bronze. Women were frantically worshipping in one corner and there was a buzz of children's voices. Only the inner sanctum of the temple had not been left undamaged during the Mughal invasions in the 16th century. Police stopped me at the door but my friend Sood explained that I was not a foreigner but a pale-skinned Hindu from Kashmir and I was allowed inside – a confused memory of coloured cloth, paper hangings, erotic carvings and the four faces of Shiva.

I stayed in the teachers' college hostel, defeating bedbugs and mosquitoes, and adapting to the diet of *dal* and vegetable curry served in the college canteen. I made many friends among the college students and several anglophile families and learned quite a lot of Hindi. I earned a bit of extra pocket money teaching the children of an American family. Staff meetings were a trial. I was not good at sitting cross-legged on the floor and my Hindi was not up to it, so I would hide in the corner reading the Observer newspaper which my mother mailed to me each week. On Sunday mornings we used to go to "English picture" at the Chetak cinema. The films were mostly American and people came to see kissing which was never quite allowed to happen in Indian films. They did not understand a word and talked all the way through.

One weekend I was invited to visit Mayo College at Ajmer, a night's train ride away. It was founded in 1876 as a school for princes and it claims still to be the best school in India. It was a contrast to Vidya Bhavan: a Victorian bathroom, a school museum, residential boarding houses and housemasters, even whisky to drink. I met four English public school boys who were there, like me, as volunteers. The one who showed me round the school I later realised was David Nobbs who was to become a great writer of comedy and creator of *The Fall and Rise of Reginald Perrin*. It was the weekend of *holi*, the spring festival which celebrates the triumph of good over evil. Normally coloured powder and water is thrown around but because there was an epidemic of mumps the schoolboys were limited to coloured powder which was less likely to transmit the infection. The scene in the city streets would probably have been more exciting. As I was about to leave, the current Maharana of Udaipur who happened to be visiting Ajmer gave me a lift to the station in his old Rolls Royce.

After a little over three months it was time for the long school holidays. and I set off to see India, first to Mount Abu in the north of Rajasthan to see the amazing white carvings at the Dilwara Jain Temples. Then a long train journey south including a lot of bedbugs in the waiting room at Bhopal and my first experience of trying to eat *dosa* and *sambar* with either very dirty hands or an equally dirty spoon. Reaching Madras (now Chennai) I got a cycle rickshaw to Cherian Nagar, where I was to attend a workcamp. For two years Indian and foreign SCI volunteers had been working in this fisherman's neighbourhood helping to build nearly 200 mud houses for people re-located from slums. At first sight the place looked rather like a slum, but in fact each cottage had a bathroom and latrine behind. We distributed milk powder and sometimes wheat, ran a dispensary every afternoon and bathed the children on Sundays.

I moved on to visit some of the stunning temples of Tamil Nadu. I also stopped in the former French city of Pondicherry with its puce and cream houses reminiscent of New Orleans, featured in *The Life of Pi*. France had only recently handed its small enclaves back to India and the place still felt very French. Back in Madras I visited the world headquarters of the Theosophical Society outside which stands the most amazing banyan tree with its many drooping branches forming new trunks. I returned to the workcamp where I succeeded in burning two cauldrons trying to cook a "European" meal of spaghetti followed by stewed mangoes!

Back north on a comfortable 3rd class air-conditioned train, I visited the famous painted caves at Ajanta, spent a couple of days in Delhi and continued to Punjab where I was invited to stay in the small town of Dera Baba Nanak by my friend Bedi from the Teachers' College. Bedi is a descendant of Nanak, the first

Sikh guru. I gave talks at two local schools about the UK and the English language.

Kashmir was peaceful at this time. I arrived in Srinagar on bus, twisting and turning on the mountainous road. I stayed on a houseboat on the shore of the lake and spent the little money I had on some of the very fine local handicrafts and a tailor-made over-coat which was to be useful on my journey home through Russia. I went in a bus up the mountain to Gulmarg. Indian tourists came there to experience snow. I took one look at it and just cowered shivering in the nearby hotel.

Back to the lowlands I stopped in Chandigarh. This is the strikingly modern capital of the Indian province of Punjab, built because the original capital, Lahore, ended up in Pakistan. It was designed by the great French architect Le Corbusier. From there I took the little steam railway which climbed the mountains to Simla, a cold and misty, very British hill station with mock-Tudor houses and hotels. Final stops on the way back to Udaipur were at the Taj Mahal in Agra, which I reached just as the monsoon burst. You have seen so many pictures of it but you are still stunned as it comes into view. I stopped at the extensive Mughal ruins of Fatehpur Sikri on the way to the lovely capital city of Rajasthan, Jaipur, where I caught up again with Dr. Mohan Singh Mehta, who had given me the job at Vidya Bhavan and was Vice Chancellor of the university there.

Life returned to normal for my final two months at Vidya Bhavan and it was good to be back among so many friends and the schoolboys and girls who seemed to like me. The most excit-ing event was the *shia* festival of Muharram. We watched from a balcony a procession of *tizias,* replicas of Hussein's tomb, some as tall as the houses, snaking through the narrow streets. Young men beat themselves, shouting, "Hussein, Hussein!"

I had word that I had been accepted for the postgraduate educa-tion course in London and therefore had to be home by the end of September. My journey home took me to Delhi but first I diverted to visit the very aged Vinoba Bhave who had been a lead-ing follower of Mahatma Gandhi and had initiated the *bhoodan* movement which urged landowners to make gifts of land to the poor peasants. We arrived just in time to follow the old man and his followers up the hill for prayers. He was living at Kasturbagram, the ashram named after Mahatma Gandhi's wife, and he gave me time for a short interview where we talked about how SCI had introduced international voluntary service to India when Pierre Cérésole had come to Bihar in 1934.

In Delhi I struggled through the bureaucracy to get permission to take money out of India, to get visas for Afghanistan and the USSR and to get on the one daily train that crossed into Pakistan. In Lahore I saw Jehangir's tomb and the Shalimar Gardens, a city of faded glory. Two more trains on, arriving in Peshawar I had a morning to wander round the bazaar and negotiate Afghan currency and a visa.

The Khyber pass, dry and rocky, seemed peaceful enough. The little bus was full of burly Afghans with huge trunks full of goods they had bought in Pakistan. The new customs building on the Afghan side boasted a waiting room for foreigners with magazines and free cigarettes. I slept so well in the government hostel in Jalalabad that I delayed our departure in the morning. Our little bus climbed and zigzagged through the mountains. This, the only road to Afghanistan, was narrow and not yet tarred. It was just becoming the hippy trail to and from India.

Arriving in Kabul I had a meal of meat and spinach and found a cheap hotel. The next morning I was driven to the airport where the terminal consisted only of tents. I boarded a small Aeroflot plane which flew near to the Hindu Kush, capped with parcels of snow on the north side. We dipped low over the Amu Darya river which forms the frontier with the USSR (Uzbekistan) and over small irrigated fields to land at a deserted airstrip where, in a rather cosy waiting room warmed by a big ceramic stove, we went through immigration procedures. On to Tashkent where I changed on to my first ever jet plane overnight to Moscow. In those days tourists were strictly controlled and you had to buy a tourist "day" for £10 (with a guide) or £5 (without). I had bought two of the former, one for Moscow and one for Leningrad, but apparently my Russian visa was only for Moscow and I spent hours getting it extended for Leningrad. As I had little money I was angry and almost in tears. The lady in the agency said, "Why are you so nervous?" The Moscow deal included a guide, a mousy woman wearing a red cardigan. She was friendly but seemed to think demolishing old buildings was a good idea. She kept saying rather obvious things like, "Well, we are in Moscow, the capital of the Soviet Union." She reluctantly took me to visit a working church, and we toured the Kremlin, saw the city from the twenty fifth floor of the university and rode on the metro where I noticed that the mosaics of one or two disgraced leaders had been bricked in.

I took the train to Leningrad, having paid my extra £5 for a day there. I wandered around the beautiful city and looked at the famous Finland Station where Lenin arrived in 1917. However, my train to Finland left from the Moscow Station and I was one of only four passengers. Most of the houses on both sides of the border were built of wood but in Finland they were painted in bright colours. I was suffering from some kind of rheumatism and I hobbled around Helsinki before taking the overnight ferry to Stockholm. Here I was welcomed by my school friend Brian Abbs, who was developing his English Language Teaching expertise in the excellent Swedish adult education system. More trains and ferries brought me finally to England. I had no money left and could only gaze at the spread of *smörrebröd* on the boat. Landing at Harwich I had to call my mother, reversing the charges, to ask her to meet me at Bartlow station with enough money to pay my train fare!

The notes I made on 1960 India are fairly obvious ones. Thirteen years after Independence British influences were still strong These included tomato sauce on the table, toast and tea for breakfast in government rest houses, the magnificent railways, especially Bombay and Madras stations, the hill stations which felt like British seaside resorts with mountains instead of sea, schools such as Mayo College, double-deck buses and trams, the Times of India and other newspapers and a passion for English Literature among the educated. It was Nehru's heyday. The Congress Party was totally dominant and it was the year of the second five-year plan. A tradition of popular demonstration had developed during the struggle for independence. During my time in India there was a campaign for a Punjabi-speaking (mainly Sikh) province; there were riots in Assam and demonstrations in the south against the imposition of the Hindi language. In fact there were two Indias; the educated, modernising, polluting, industrialising minority and the masses living in terrible poverty in villages and city slums, bound by unchanging tradition and culture. I thought that the obstacles to modernisation would never be overcome but it seems today that the middle classes are winning – but the poor are still the majority.

In later years I visited India a number of times for my work, usually for meetings. My father had died during this first visit and it happened that my mother died when I was at meeting in Nagpur in 1994. I visited Afghanistan once more, also for work, in 1975. Kabul was still peaceful and the hippy trail was still busy. On that occasion time I was looked after by the British Council and the Embassy. We went for a picnic on the road towards Pakistan, now fully tarmac but with no insecurity. I also went north to Kunduz by bus through the tunnel through the Hindu Kush. I had omitted to put a film in my camera so I had to buy every postcard I could find! I was researching a possible volunteer programme in Afghanistan but nothing came of the idea.

2
Northern Rhodesia / Zambia

i) London 1960

My personal discovery of Africa began in 1960. As a child I remember being quite proud of the British Empire. My stamp collection consisted only of stamps from countries marked in red on the map. However, as a student in the 1950s I learned something about the iniquities of colonialism. At school I remember a talk by Reginald Reynolds, a Quaker who had travelled from Cairo to the Cape. He vividly described the segregation he found all over southern Africa and I got interested in the idea of volunteering in Cape Flats, a township outside Cape Town.[12] The Observer newspaper covered Africa brilliantly in those days and some of us joined the Movement for Colonial Freedom, led by the redoubtable Labour MP, Fenner Brockway.[13] In May 1957 I remember seeing a group of Ghanaian students jumping up and down in Trinity Street, Cambridge shouting "FreeDOM" on the day of Ghana's independence. We read about the impressive leaders of the struggle, Kwame Nkrumah in Ghana, Nnamdi Azikiwe in Nigeria, Julius Nyerere in what was then Tanganyika. Yet elsewhere oppression continued: Jomo Kenyatta was still in detention in Kenya where the war against the Mau Mau rebels showed its worst brutality when 11 of the "hard core" were clubbed to death and 77 injured at Hola camp in 1959; and, as I was later to witness, the white settlers of the Federation of Rhodesia and Nyasaland were still trying to resist the inevitable. This Federation had been set up in 1953 as a

---

12. Reg Reynolds' book, *Beware of Africans* (Jarrolds 1955) describes his journey. The title refers to a sign on the main road at Broken Hill (now Kabwe, Zambia).
13. The Movement for Colonial Freedom had been founded by Fenner Brockway in 1954. It later changed its name to Liberation and for a time Jeremy Corbyn was its chairman.

British attempt to create a new Dominion linking Nyasaland and Northern Rhodesia which were both protectorates where "native interests" were to some extent protected, with Southern Rhodesia where the white settlers were more numerous and the Africans marginalised. The settlers who effectively ruled the Federation were "Rhodesians" mostly of British origin, many of them recent arrivals, but their attitudes were not much different from those of the Afrikaners who dominated South Africa where the policies of *apartheid* and separate development had been imposed from 1948 onwards. While I was in India I tried to follow the African news, especially the rise of Lumumba and the independence of the Congo and of many French-speaking countries. I also met up with some Kenyan students in Delhi who talked of their independence struggle and complained of racism in India.

In those days you could apply to teach in the colonies. The Colonial Office, housed in a rambling Victorian edifice, since demolished, in Great Smith Street near Westminster Abbey, paid for postgraduate training with fairly generous pocket money at the Institute of Education in London. The deal required you to serve in Her Majesty's colonial service for three years. I thought it would be interesting to learn Arabic and opted to go to Aden but, happily, was selected to go to Northern Rhodesia. The Education in Tropical Areas course was fairly boring. The tropical bit included a section on health where we had to study things like the anopheles mosquito and the hookworm, an annoying creature which apparently entered your feet and then travelled systematically to all corners of your body. One bit of orientation for the colonies which I missed, but Edyth, my future wife, was to experience was the introduction to the Women's Corona Society. Kate McRae recalls some of the typical advice handed out to women heading for the colonies: "Matching linen table napkins should be folded into water lilies, which is something easily taught to an African"; and "When exporting a grand piano make sure it is fully tropicalized." I did, however, buy an ant-proof trunk from an old-fashioned firm which supplied everything a colonialist could possibly want from pith helmets and mosquito boots to hurricane lamps and paraffin cookers.

African politics were more enthralling than the hookworm. The Belgian Congo became theoretically independent on 30 June 1960. Its leader, Patrice Lumumba, wanted real independence and he was captured and killed six months later. The Belgians and Americans were both implicated. An angry crowd of us, including the African students on my course, joined a big march and shouted slogans outside the Belgian Embassy. There were not many black people in London in those days. West Indians, as they were called then, the Windrush generation, were working on the buses and the tube. Calypso and ska (but not yet reggae) could already be heard on the streets of Notting Hill and Brixton. Africans from Africa were a rarer sight. They were usually well-dressed and most were students on British Council scholarships or sent by rich parents. Ghana and Nigeria were already independent. Sankoh, a fellow student, took me to a Sierra Leonean dance where I first met Iye Kabia who was on a nursing course. We spent a lot of time together until I left for Africa in August 1961. Through Iye and her friends I got learn a bit about the frustrations of African and Caribbean people in London, faced with blatant racism when trying to find a room or a job. Yet there was an atmosphere of hope and determination among the African students. The liveliest African place at that time was WASU, the West African Students' Union which had been founded as early as 1925. The Ghanaians had also set up a centre in Collingham Gardens, Earls Court. The Ghana government, led by Kwame Nkrumah, was planning to develop this as a beacon of Pan-Africanist ideas. Shortly afterwards some British Roman Catholic friends of Africa had decided to counter this by establishing the Africa Centre in Covent Garden, where I much later served as Director.

Northern Rhodesians were even rarer than other Africans. The first one I met, Joe Mweemba, one of the country's first graduates, was on a sponsored visit and the British Council wanted someone to show him round London. I later met him in Zambia when he had become an Inspector of Schools. Five of us on the course at the Institute of Education were going to Northern Rhodesia: Joy Orr had managed to penetrate the London group of Kenneth

Kaunda's UNIP party and I went with her and met the future Vice President, Simon Kapwepwe, the future Attorney General, Fitzpatrick Chuula, and my unforgettable future colleague, Carpenter Kafumukache, in a dingy basement in Upper Gower Street. Apart from Carpenter they seemed a bit suspicious of these nosy whites, as well they might have been, given the attitude of the colonial regime towards UNIP at that time. Another memory I have is of a group of African girls singing at a party at WASU. The soloist was Gwen Konie who will feature later in my story. She became Zambia's first woman ambassador and even stood for the presidency in 2006.

Most of the Africans on my course stayed at the British Council hostel in Hans Crescent, just behind Harrods, and to their credit the Colonial Office people had urged us to stay there too. I rather regretted I did not take their advice as there was a lively African atmosphere there, with a brilliant group of Ugandan students among whom I made friends in particular with Jozef Muwanga, who was later involved with the ground-breaking journal, Transition.[14] However, I had a good time sharing a flat facing Primrose Hill with Kaye Whiteman, later to be editor of West Africa. We saw a lot of Keith Henry, a Trinidadian friend whom I had met at Cambridge and we went to more plays and films than at any other time in my life. A highlight for us that year was the production of the South African musical, *King Kong* with Peggy Phango in the lead. This was a show which defied apartheid. The music was by Todd Matshikiza whom we later met in Lusaka when he was in exile and whose daughter, Marion, was to be my colleague in Christian Aid in 1998 – and we produced *King Kong* at Kalomo Secondary School in Zambia in 1969.

ii) The voyage out

Northern Rhodesia (now Zambia), landlocked and shaped like a rather lopsided butterfly, is a huge territory which ended up British in the scramble for Africa, although the Portuguese had

---

14. See Annex 7 for Jozef's letters in 1961-2.

made an unrealistic claim for all the land between Mozambique and Angola. Cecil Rhodes, who founded the De Beers diamond mining company and became Prime Minister of Cape Colony, was ambitious to extend British control north from the Cape. He made (often fraudulent) treaties with African rulers for mineral concessions and this was followed by white settlement. The Litunga (king) of Barotseland, in the west of Northern Rhodesia, agreed to such a treaty in 1890, and in the same year Rhodes established the British South Africa Company (BSAC) and the first white "pioneers" arrived in Fort Salisbury (now Harare, Zimbabwe). Rhodes wanted empire but he did not want control from London. He established a kind of colonial franchise whereby the BSAC ruled the three territories named after himself, Southern, North Western and North Eastern Rhodesia. The latter two merged in 1911 as Northern Rhodesia with its capital next to the Victoria Falls at Livingstone. From 1904 the railway was extended over the amazing bridge over the Zambezi gorge to serve the mines at Broken Hill and those in Katanga which was part of the Belgian Congo.

Southern Rhodesia became self-governing, by the white minority, in 1923. Northern Rhodesia remained a British protectorate ruled from London. However, it had a small but influential population of white farmers and businessmen whose political ambitions, along with the desire of the Southern Rhodesian whites to enjoy the wealth of the copper mines in Northern Rhodesia, were the reason for the creation of a Federation of Rhodesia and Nyasaland in 1953. Nyasaland, now Malawi, had even fewer settlers but it seemed logical to include it for geographical reasons. Africans in Northern Rhodesia and Nyasaland rightly saw Federation as a plot to give land rights and control to white settlers and as an abdication of Britain's protection. They opposed it bitterly and their voice was ignored. By the time I set off for Africa this bitterness had boosted nationalism: the original Northern Rhodesia African National Congress led by Harry Nkumbula had been outflanked by the even more nationalistic United National Independence Party (UNIP) led by Kenneth Kaunda. There were a number of violent incidents, known as the *chachacha*. Federation had promised "partnership." Lord Malvern, the Federation's founding Prime Minister, had described this as the partnership of a rider and a horse. The Africans were determined not to be the horse any longer and the British government belatedly began to understand that its duty to the populations of Northern Rhodesia and Nyasaland was incompatible with the continuance of the Federation. One of independent Zambia's first actions in 1964 was to remove the statue of Physical Energy, in fact a rider on a horse, which had graced the roundabout in front of Lusaka's High Court, to drive it through the streets and send it to the Department of Antiquities in Salisbury, Southern Rhodesia (now Harare, Zimbabwe).

In August 1961 I waved good-bye to Iye and my mother as the boat train steamed (yes steam!) out of Waterloo station and I entered a strange intermediate world mainly populated by white South Africans sailing home on R.M.S *Pretoria Castle* to Cape Town. "Bilious Afrikaners and pipe-chewing planters" was how I described them in a letter home. They seemed to grow whiter as we moved south and when they saw you were coming to Africa for the first time they rushed to defend their colour bar. "A pity you're going to the wogs." There was the traditional Crossing the Line ceremony when we crossed the Equator and everyone joined in the chorus of the favourite Afrikaans song, *Sarie Marais*: "*O bring my trug naar die ou Transvaal, Daar war my Sarie woon.*" Three of my fellow recruits to teach in Northern Rhodesia were on board too and these ten days of reading, eating and not doing much else were a good way of preparing for life in a new world.

Conversations overheard on the ship were a preparation for apartheid but Cape Town station brought it home. You went through a *slegs blankes* (whites only) entrance past the "white parcels" office and your bags were carried by a white porter, but once you were through the entrance the platform was not segregated. Our train climbed up into the mountains, blue and pink in the evening light, the few trees throwing heavy shadows. We woke the next morning on the Karroo, a huge flat plain covered with scrawny grass, passing occasional untidy settlements beside the passing loops on the railway, with a water tower (for steam trains), several general stores, a few cottages for white workers and segregated huts for blacks. The craziest bit of segregation was at Kimberley station where the footbridge had a barrier down the middle but once in the street you were free to mix again. Most of the passengers in the train were white but the front coach, where most of the soot from the locomotive landed, was reserved for blacks. This was winter and the nights in the train were cold.

The train stopped at Mafekeng, famous for being besieged in 1899-1900 during what the British call the Boer War. This town was still the capital of the Bechuanaland Protectorate in 1961, although it was just inside South Africa. The capital moved to the small town of Gaborone just before the Independence of the new state of Botswana in 1965. Seen from the railway Bechuanaland was still a wide open plain but broken up by funny little hills and covered by "bush" resembling an immense wild apple orchard. The country had just been suffering from exceptional drought, rather than its usual dry semi-desert climate, and the development of the country had been totally neglected by the British, who controlled it, along with Lesotho and Swaziland, from their High Commission in Pretoria. The result was very evident poverty: poorly dressed women were selling handicrafts at the little wayside stations. Visiting booming Botswana today makes it hard to imagine what it was like before Independence.

As we entered Southern Rhodesia the vegetation changed to the twisted, leafy trees of typical of the African plateau and then to the freight yards and the busy junction at Bulawayo. Here we had time for a much-needed shower at the station, still whites only, and a short walk into town with its wide streets and buildings that would not be out of place in a Wild West film. After a third night we crossed the iconic iron bridge over the Zambezi gorge with the spray of the Victoria Falls in the distance – and into Northern Rhodesia. The sun shone on the tall grass and the patchy savannah forest. We passed Kalomo where I was later to spend five years, continued along the plateau, crossed the wide Kafue river and climbed up to Lusaka. The capital of Northern Rhodesia had moved from Livingstone to Lusaka in 1935. Chief Lusaaka's village had been chosen as the site for the capital because it was in the centre of the country and it was on the level so the trains could stop and start easily. It had – and has – few interesting features and, in tune with the colonial mindset, residential and trading areas were segregated and separated. There was a main shopping centre, Cairo Road, a short stretch of Cecil Rhodes' dream of a British road and railway from the Cape to Cairo; a "second class" shopping area where the shops were run by Indians and the customers were mostly African; a zone for government offices, cheap single storey constructions with green roofs; some "white" suburbs with spacious bungalows and manicured lawns; and some townships for the blacks with rows of small identical houses. The only buildings of note were the state secretariat, built in brown stone, and the red brick high court, in front of which stood the rider and the horse, the fine statue erected in honour of Cecil Rhodes, referred to above.

I was welcomed at Lusaka station by a beery white civil servant and taken to the Longacres Hostel, a typical colonial building, also with a green roof, set in an undemonstrative garden. The evening was cold and it was good to find a log fire ablaze on my first night on the ground in Africa. I spent a couple of days in Lusaka. A moustached official in the Ministry of African Education (there was a Federal ministry for the whites, coloureds and Asians) advised me that colonial civil servants needed to find something to do in their spare time such as playing bridge or tennis, or, for the really eccentric, indulging in anthropology. He probably guessed I was one of the latter. He also reminded me that the uniform was a white shirt and shorts with long white socks. I was taken on a visit to Munali Secondary School, the leading government school, indeed the only one with a sixth form; and also to Chalimbana Teacher Training College. I was then put on a plane to Fort Jameson and to my posting at Chizongwe Secondary School.

iii) Fort Jameson

The usual way to get to Fort Jameson was along the Great East Road. It was nearly 400 miles from Lusaka. In 1961 the first 140 miles was a wide dirt road with extensive views over the bush

51

landscape, past the Chinyunyu hot springs which were surrounded by a type of palm tree the fruit of which reputedly made elephants drunk. There were a few bloated baobab trees too. At Manenekela the road climbed dramatically along the edge of a deep valley where before the road was widened many vehicles had fallen into the gorge below. Half way to Fort Jameson was the neat government hotel at Kachalola with roses and poinsettias in the garden and even a swimming pool. The view over thick green woodlands to the grey hills across the border to Mozambique is still stunning today though the hotel is closed and dilapidated. A little further on was the long metal framed bridge over the Luangwa river, a major tributary of the Zambezi. Then there was a sign saying "Diversion. Danger – bends for next 73 miles." It wasn't a diversion but this narrow, winding stretch was only open for half a day in each direction. Then there was a final 130 miles of wide dirt road to the little town of Fort Jameson, the capital of the Eastern Province, surrounded by wooded hills with no fort to be seen, Its name was changed to Chipata at Independence in 1964. I had looked it up in the handbook on the Federation before I left England and it claimed there was a population of 400. This referred to Europeans. The thousands of Africans did not get a mention. It also told me that the nearest railway station was 150 miles away in Nyasaland (now Malawi), a great disappointment for a railway enthusiast like me.

Like most towns in southern Africa "Fort Jimmy" had developed on the basis of segregated housing and schools for whites; coloureds[15] and Asians; and blacks. The town centre was a crossroads of two tarmac streets boasting a modern Barclays Bank and a post office. Nearby was a red brick replica of an English Anglican village church; Camco, a "European" general store, and several shops run by Indians. Some distance from the centre there was the so-called second class trading area, a busy street of shops run by Indians with a mosque at one end. Fort Jameson's Indians were, unusually for this country, Muslims. There was an open-air market

---

15. The standard southern African term for people of mixed race. They tend to be culturally like the whites and have little in common with Asians apart from the fact that they are brown rather than white or black.

where the vendors would squat on the ground and sell the plentiful local vegetables and fruit which were arranged in little heaps priced *tickey* or *susu* (threepence or sixpence), as well as twists of tobacco and various herbal remedies. The town boasted four clubs, the grandest being the Victoria Memorial Institute where there was a plaque on the wall declaring that this was to be a memorial to the great queen for all time. No Africans apart from the barman, waiter and cleaners were seen in the place – until we teachers started inviting our friends to sneak in to watch the amateur dramatics. There was a MOTH club, and a Police Club where fireworks would be let off on 5 November, a ritual that the local people found very strange. A few African police officers were later to be allowed to join this club. There was also a very small multi-racial club. In the 1950s there had been a prosperous community of white tobacco farmers in the area. One ruined farm where the land was returning to bush had a dried-up swimming pool and the remains of a private plane rusting in the yard. By the 1960s the main agricultural export was high quality peanuts, grown by African peasant farmers and exported to Canada.

Looking through letters that I wrote home at this time it is possible to piece together the atmosphere of these strange times – the tail end of colonialism. The Provincial Administration was a small hierarchy which ruled the African population of Northern Rhodesia. When I was there its head in the Eastern Province was D.C. Goodfellow, the Provincial Commissioner *"with his fierce moustache, his one arm – he had lost the other as a young officer in India – he looked like some battle-scarred colonel."* The quote is from *African Sunset* by Robin Short, who praises the PC as a man of old fashioned views, fair but firm and sometime fierce, but well-liked by the older villagers. The flavour of the PC comes across in a well-known remark of his: *"The nigpigs are alright if you give them something to pull on."* Robin Short was a District Commissioner, on the next level of the hierarchy. He invited me for lunch a couple of times. In his paternalistic way he loved "his Africans," the docile villagers who saluted him, and he loathed and feared the change represented by the newly educated ones who led the freedom movement and were cheeky enough to read the African Mail, a weekly paper which supported African aspirations but could hardly be called subversive. Short was fairly typical of the colonial rulers – some very public school, some mildly eccentric, quite a number Scottish. They had a lot of power. One District Commissioner in Lundazi, 100 miles north of Fort Jameson, found he had a big stock of bricks so he designed and had built a replica Norman castle as a government rest house. You can still stay there. Officers in more technical roles such as agriculture and education tended to be more in sympathy with the changes that were starting to take place. Although in fact a teacher, I was a colonial civil servant too. Africans filled the junior administrative levels, though a few were starting to be promoted to officer level. Although part of the partially self-governing Federation of Rhodesia and Nyasaland, Northern Rhodesia was still a British protectorate and the provincial administration looked after most African affairs while the federal government was responsible for many common matters and all those affecting the non-African population, including education – and we were to experience the last gasp of this type of education in Mufulira in 1965.

The churches and the missionaries were part of this colonial picture. One Sunday I went on a visit to Msoro, an Anglican mission station about eighty miles away along a very bumpy road. An odd group of white men were sitting in a summer house eating cutlets when we arrived: Father Mudford, a sinewy man in his 60s, much-loved by the locals and in whose honour a library in Chipata is named, a healthy looking lay missionary and a rather intense young Franciscan monk. After an interminably long service in the huge barn of a church, with incense, a choir and the lot, we called on three ageing spinsters housed at a safe distance from these decidedly undangerous men and were invited to sherry and a very English Sunday lunch. A year later I attended an African wedding in Fort Rosebery (now Mansa) at a mission belonging to the Plymouth Brethren where the ambience was even more old-fashioned than at Msoro. There were withered texts in Gothic script on the walls, an aged washstand and a four-poster bed.

Eccentricity took many forms. One of my best memories was visiting Mrs. Jerominsky on her farm near Katete. Like most farms its name was painted on an old plough blade at the gate and you went up a long drive, two ruts with grass in the middle. The farm house was one of the oldest in the country, dating from 1903. We found Mrs. J sitting on the ground outside the tobacco-curing barns, busily sorting groundnuts, a short woman with very white legs under a large straw sun hat. She was a fascinating survival from pioneering days. Born in Silesia, Germany in around 1884, she worked as a child in Berlin. The man she was eventually to marry had come to North Eastern Rhodesia as it then was and established the farm. He then advertised in the German press for a wife. When he received a photo he sent for the lady in the picture. He went to meet her, making the long journey by bicycle and boat down to the port of Beira in Portuguese Mozambique and looked in vain for the girl in the photo. A woman came up to him and explained that her sister had had cold feet and that she had come instead. Judging by the rather faded sepia photo she showed us, taken in Berlin in 1913, she was a good substitute. We learned about this story later, but she did describe to us her honeymoon journey. This consisted of going by boat from Beira up the Shire River into Nyasaland and then being carried in a *machila* (a kind of hammock attached to two poles) for the 350 miles to Katete. They covered about twenty miles a day with a changing supply of "natives" to carry it while her husband cycled in front.

She lived on the farm for the next fifty or so years. She went once to Germany in 1920 and hated it. She longed to get back to the farm. Much later, after her husband had died, she was persuaded to go as far as Lusaka to be presented to the Queen Mother who, she proudly recalled, put the sugar in her tea. When she first arrived at the farm she had planted a huge orange orchard: she always served visitors with enormous juicy navel oranges with their tops sliced off and a sprig of leaves on top. Her husband had been a hunter rather than a farmer: there was a picture on the wall of him shooting an elephant. She herself had a baby leopard as a pet and it used to sleep in her bed, along with her husband. (They had no children.) After the man's death she slept with a machete for self-defence. I visited her again later with my fiancée, Edyth, and with our colleague Elias Chipimo. By this time her mind was becoming hazier: she asked Elias if the natives were quiet. He told her tactfully that they were. They were not! A year or two later the nephew who helped her run the farm moved her off to a farm outside Kalomo where we were later to live ourselves. By then she was in her dotage, sitting at home eating Sugar Puffs. Meanwhile the beautiful orange orchard had fallen into decay and been partially burned.

Racism was blatant in "Fort Jimmy" in 1961. The post office had only recently been de-segregated. The butchery still advertised "boy's meat" at 1/4d a pound. Africans were not allowed to buy anything stronger than beer. I used to go and buy gin and whisky at Camco Stores for my friends. This, and our attempts to invite our students to drama productions at the club and to have Africans in choral performances including Handel's *Messiah* were enough to get me labelled, as I proudly learned later, "the first Communist in Fort Jameson." Throughout the Rhodesias anyone seen as too friendly with Africans had to be a communist.

Here are some examples of the atmosphere. A white American couple came to work in the nearby game parks and they had brought their servant with them from Lusaka. The servant fell ill with VD but was later diagnosed as having bilharzia. The wife went to visit him in the African hospital, taking him magazines to read. The next thing was that the gossip in town was that she was having an affair with her servant. Her family was shunned by all the whites. Their suspicions were increased when an official leaked that she had also innocently enquired at the government offices about the procedure for taking this excellent servant to the US. The happily married couple felt victimised and went back home.

Another example was the day we called in on a farmer's wife whom Edyth knew from the church. She looked into the car which was crammed with some of our students and said that since there were just two of us, would we like to come in for tea. Again, an Anglican vicar, knowing our views, felt he had to justify that he felt his children "had an inalienable right to sleep between sheets," as if some people didn't. On another occasion our very well-spoken colleague, Carpenter Kafumukache, ran out of fuel and went to the nearest house for help to be greeted with shouts of "dirty Kaffir." At the agricultural show at Ndola (entrance fee for all 5 shillings) free samples of *Nesquik* were being handed out – only to whites. Andrew and June Kashita were the first mixed couple to return from England where they had met. Andrew was a brilliant engineer who later served as a minister under Kaunda and Chiluba. He was the only black person on the ship and they faced rudeness and hostility on the journey and even after arriving in Northern Rhodesia. June used to enjoy leading the ladies on in the hairdressing saloon with their tales of Africans "down from the trees" and then shocking them by saying she was married to one.[16] The sight of Anna Chipimo, the first African woman to be seen driving a car, raised a lot of eyebrows in Fort Jameson.

iv) Chizongwe Secondary School and the new politics 1961-64

I taught at three secondary schools in Northern Rhodesia-Zambia: Chizongwe in Fort Jameson from 1961 up until Independence in 1964, then Mufulira High School on the Copperbelt (1965) and finally as Head of the new Kalomo Secondary School (1966-70). Chizongwe in 1961 was one of only six government senior secondary schools for boys. This is how Cyrus Undi (Form IV) described it in *Aurora*, the school magazine: "*We come to the crest of our watch dog Chizongwe Hill. From here Chizongwe scenery is a semi-paradise. Immediately below the crest, green painted solid looking corrugated iron roofs stand among lots of flat topped green trees.*" The original plan had been to make this a co-educational boarding school, but Kaizore, the headman of the nearby village, protested successfully that if the school was enlarged it would disturb the place where his ancestors were buried. Chizongwe was combined with a Trades School teaching woodwork and metalwork. The boys came from

---

16. June has just published her story, *This was my Africa; Living with changes.*

all over the Eastern province and even beyond. There was stiff competition in the final year of primary school and so the boys who were accepted were very bright – though a few exceptions somehow got through the net. They were also old, some almost my age and I was 25 at the time. Registration of births had not long been introduced so short boys often pretended to be younger than they were to get into school. Later they needed to be a few years older again when they wanted to vote in the pre-Independence elections!

The staff at the school were very talented, as there were few jobs open to educated Africans before Independence and teaching was one of them. Even driving a train was a job reserved for whites, rather to the amazement of the black engine drivers who took over the trains as they entered the Belgian Congo. Carpenter Kafumukache, whom I had first met in London only to find he was to be my neighbour at Chizongwe, had been the star pupil at his primary school in the North Western Province. He had the ability, as was later proved, to go to secondary school and university but the missionaries were determined he should teach in their schools and they made him attend their college for training primary teachers. He later escaped from their clutches and went for further study.

Those Africans who persisted in their studies were outstanding individuals. Elias Chipimo was one of them. Around the time of Independence in 1964 they were creamed off to become senior civil servants, diplomats and senior managers. Elias was soon to become Zambian High Commissioner in London and later the Head of Standard Bank. I interviewed Elias shortly before he died and his remarkable life story is in Annex 5.

Dalson Nkunika was our science teacher and he later became head of scientific research in the country. Wesley Nyirenda, whom I replaced as history teacher, had gone off to be the head of a new secondary school at Monze but soon ended up as the Speaker in the National Assembly.

The headmaster was Alf King, a liberal-minded product of the colonial education service, a warm-hearted man who was always a great support to all the staff. Then we had a rather bored and boring American whose house I shared for a short time. He did not like me much but was not used to unsliced bread, so he tolerated me and my breadknife. Menna Roberts was a very popular teacher of English who lived in the town, as did our excellent maths teacher, Ann Williamson, the wife of the local butcher. There was also a paranoid black South African, Jones Siyo, a victim of the *apartheid* system who found it hard to trust any white person and believed he was being spied on all the time. Worse, he reported to the UNIP office that our African teachers were traitors, which was far from the truth, and on one occasion he stirred up some of the students whose slogan was "Down with Watt. We want Siyo and Mrs. Roberts." The storm passed quickly and the students reverted to being very friendly. The bad name given to the Zambian teachers led me to write to Kenneth Kaunda, who was visiting the area, and he came to my house to hear our colleagues' side of the story. Siyo soon left the school and the country.

A year after my arrival my social life brightened up with the arrival on the staff of Edyth Hitchens to teach English and French. She came from a village near Cambridge, close to my home, and we got on very well from the start. It was kind of the Colonial Office to place us in the same school. As Education Officers we were supposed to remain at our posts during school holidays but we managed to travel together a bit – to Blantyre in Nyasaland (Malawi) officially to visit the dentist where, to the amusement of Ann Williamson, we saw Ingmar Bergman's film, *A Lesson in Love*. We also had a memorable visit to the north of Nyasaland to the beautiful Nyika Plateau where it was cold enough for a log fire in the rest house. I proposed to Edyth one weekend on the shore of Lake Nyasa (Lake Malawi) and we arranged to get married when my home leave was due in 1964.

Other arrivals on the staff included Timothy Holmes, a poet who had fled from South Africa, having buried his "subversive" books in the garden so as to avoid arrest as he left the country. He had worked on *Contact*, the anti-apartheid journal run by Patrick Duncan in Cape Town. Another South African who joined us was the large and very friendly Livingstone Ngqobongwana who had been working in Nigeria and who ended his life in Manchester. Later we were joined by a highly politicised teacher from SWAPO's liberation struggle in Namibia, Ottilie Abrahams. She successfully set up a students' union which radicalised some of the boys who organised a strike as a result of which some boys were expelled. Years later I visited Potphar Kabandama, one of the most revolutionary ones, by which time he had become head of a secondary school himself and had a different perspective. Edyth and I also met Ottilie again in Namibia in 2003 and I met her in 2015 when she was still running her own school and was as lively, politically active and critical as ever. Local churchmen came to teach religious knowledge, the most notable of whom was Emmanuel Milingo who was to become the Roman Catholic Archbishop of Zambia. A charismatic man, he became extremely popular, though not at the Vatican, by performing exorcism and faith healing. He resigned and moved to Rome. He caused greater shock when he married the leader of the Moonies. He founded a movement to allow priest to marry. Unsurprisingly he was excommunicated by the Church.

By this time John Nelson, a Scottish former missionary, had become head and his wife Elizabeth taught English. She put together the successful production of Shakespeare's *Macbeth*, described below. Tulsiram, an Indian South African also taught English. He was fanatical about English literature. He organised a Shakespeare evening at which the boys, deprived of girls, got very excited by quotations from Romeo and Juliet. Another Indian arrived but his high caste apparently prevented him from eating food prepared by a local cook, so he informed Mrs. Tulsiram that he would kindly allow her to cook for him. His rapid departure was a clear indication of Mrs. T's response!

Chizongwe School had originally opened in 1955 and in 1960 there was a riot. The African population had been against the Federation from the start and the reality of it had proved even worse than they had feared. The British government, hoping to save the Federation in some form, had set up the Monckton Commission in 1959 to collect the opinions of the people. Africans assumed that this would simply be a whitewash. The students, politically very aware, decided to strike. Elias Chipimo had just started teaching at Chizongwe and he told me: *"It put me to tears because I had just been teaching for the first time in my life and I loved the children and I just couldn't bear it; I tried to talk to them, but they would not listen… There was an atmosphere, a resentment of anything pertaining to Federation. The politicians had brewed it up and the students were burning with it in their hearts. The Monckton Commission was going to sit at Chizongwe and the students would not accept that."*[17] The school closed. 218 boys were expelled.

When I arrived in 1961 the political temperature was still high and some rural primary schools were being set alight as part of the *chachacha*. The rebellion by the charismatic Lumpa Church led by the prophetess Alice Lenshina was also creating a lot of tension further north. For a few weeks we had a night patrol at the school which consisted of a teacher and a few students armed with torches walking around the premises.

Chizongwe was a different world from Fort Jameson town, though even at the school colonial planning had resulted in a few spacious houses up the hill, meant for white teachers and some more recent "African graduate houses" where I lived. The latter had more bedrooms and gloss paint half way up the walls – African families were deemed to be larger and their kids might mess up the walls. I employed a cook called Gordon. I did not like the idea of employing someone but I accepted that domestic service was a major source of employment – and I was not used to cooking on a wood fire. Gordon insisted that we also hire Baidon, a "garden boy," to chop firewood, polish the floor and help with the washing up. In a letter home I wrote: *"My cook and garden boy are paid by me at appallingly low rates – the cook gets £5 a month and the garden boy 30/ –… The cook gets a free house: at the moment he is living in a round brick hut with a thatched roof, but as soon as a proper tin-roofed house is free he will move there… The garden boy I would not have employed at all except that cooks think it below their dignity to chop firewood."* The garden was small but we cultivated

---

17. My complete interview with Elias Chipimo is in Annex 5.

pumpkins. Baidon sat around most of the time but came into his own when Gordon had drunk too much beer, a traditional brew made from maize, or *kachasu,* a much stronger drink, distilled often using rusty cans.

In 1962 the country was more than ever in a state of political excitement and our students were infected by this. Relations between Sir Roy Welensky, now the Federal Prime Minister, and the British government had grown worse after the visit of the British Prime Minister, Harold Macmillan, to Zambia in 1960. (Carpenter Kafumukache had been among the educated Africans presented to him.) He went on to make his famous speech in South Africa where he said: "*The wind of change is blowing through this continent. Whether we like it or not, this growth of national consciousness is a political fact;*" and he referred to "*our own deep convictions about the political destinies of free men to which in our own territories we are trying to give effect.*" This signal from Macmillan along with the fact that the Monckton Commission's report was not in the end a whitewash, meant that federation could no longer be imposed on the population. It therefore became likely that in the end Britain would respect the protectorate status of Northern Rhodesia and Nyasaland despite the strong pressure in the Conservative Party not to let the settlers down. Insistence from Africa and at the UN led to agreement to hold an election in 1962 to try to square the circle. Complex electoral rules, described as a "dog's breakfast" were concocted, with an upper roll of voters (mainly whites) and a lower roll of Africans with a certain level of education or wealth or status, voting in 15 constituencies each. Then there were seven national constituencies where there had to a certain proportion from both rolls for the seat to be filled. One further seat was reserved for Asians (mostly the Indian shopkeepers and businessmen and their families). The total number of registered voters was only 130,000.

I volunteered to be a registering officer for the 1962 election and the government provided me with a pile of registration forms. Chiefs and headmen were allowed to complete the form in a local language, in this case Nyanja. I was sent to Chief Jumbe's area in the Luangwa valley to register villagers. I was provided with a

Land Rover, loaded with deck chairs, tables and camp beds, and two messengers. They wanted to provide me with a cook but I took Gordon. I was not accustomed to behaving like a big white bwana and when the messengers would stamp their feet and salute me I just smiled weakly back at them. We camped at a small thatched government rest house. The would-be voters had to have tax receipts and be able to complete the registration forms by themselves, though we were advised to be helpful. Even in the local language the form was complicated and these people were not used to filling forms. I helped three delightful elderly chiefs complete their forms. This area was just outside the game reserve. In those days there were many more animals around, and we met a colossal snake which straddled the road and the two messengers jumped out of their skins. Back in Fort Jameson I spent many evenings at the local UNIP office registering supporters, continuing to be extra helpful. Literacy is a senseless criterion for the vote. Many of these illiterate people were politically highly aware. I remember one poor woman who sat up all night to practise writing the magic words and finally copying the letters one by one on to the form. By the end I had registered 128 voters. I have a letter from the Electoral Officer congratulating us on exceeding the target. He might have been surprised how it was done!

Four national parties contested the election: the almost entirely white United Federal Party (UFP); the African National Congress led by Harry Nkumbula, the original nationalist party which was strong only among the Tonga and Ila people of the south; UNIP, led by Kenneth Kaunda; and the multi-racial Liberal Party led by Sir John Moffat. I attended two election meetings. At the VMI club some slightly drunken white men were taunting Mrs. E.F.M. Randolph, a white candidate who was standing for the ANC on the Upper Roll. She tried to explain that the reason Africans opposed the Federation was that its capital was Salisbury. "Why not move it then?" bawled somebody. The Liberal Party meeting was even odder. Sir John was leaning on the bar at the scruffy multi-racial club and exuding pessimism. He addressed us as "Lady and gentlemen": the crowd comprised Edyth, me and three others. Before the election the ANC had done a deal with the UFP which allowed it to win four seats in the national constituencies which, added to their three on the lower roll in the Southern and Central Provinces, gave them the balance of power. They could collaborate with UNIP which won 12 seats on the lower roll or with the UFP with 13 seats on the upper roll. The multiracial Liberal Party, intended in the electoral law to hold the balance, won no seats and very few votes: many of the more liberal whites voted UNIP. After the results were announced, UNIP managed to persuade the ANC to break its pact with the UFP and join with them to form an African majority. My friend Alan Jarvis happened to be at Harry Nkumbula's house that day and he was very proud of his ballpoint pen which was used to seal the deal which brought Kenneth Kaunda to power as Prime Minister. This deal, together with the earlier triumph of Dr. Hastings (Kamuzu) Banda in Nyasaland, meant that the Federation was now doomed. It was brought to a quiet death on 31 December 1963 after only ten years of life. Africans celebrated. The Chizongwe boys happily sang, *Yatha fedulo. (*The federation is finished.)

That was not the end of politics. Before Independence there had to be another election, and this time there was no literacy or property qualification and everyone could register to vote. There was an air of excitement. Edyth (not quite yet my fiancée) and I were both polling officers for which we were paid an extra £6 6s. I first collected ballot boxes and other equipment from town in my old Peugeot 203. Each party's symbol was pasted on the box so that illiterate people could simply put their voting slip in the box of their choice – a hoe for UNIP, a lion for ANC and an alarm clock for independent candidates. There was indelible red ink into which each voter's finger had to be dipped; Pond's Beauty Tissues to dry the ink; a Bible for the swearing in of the polling assistants; and sealing wax for sealing the ballot boxes. The ballot boxes were placed inside the polling booth and, in spite of some civic education programmes, some voters had no idea what to do with the ballot paper, trying to push it under the lid or calling out, "Will someone come and open this box for me!" Voters were supposed to have a registration form or some other form of identification. Husbands were allowed to identify their wives, which could be a problem when they had several. Edyth wrote to her parents: "*I had a very small polling station with 475 voters on my roll. Only 20 didn't vote! We had a 96% poll and this is general all over the country. Everybody looked happy and important as they came in to register their vote and everybody came early. On the morning of the first day there was a queue of about 100 nearly all the time... after 1pm only 40 more people came. In the bigger stations the rush lasted all day on the Monday and people had to be turned away in the evening to come again next day. The polling lasted two days because some stations are in areas with a very scattered population. In some areas, rivers have flooded (it was the height of the rainy season). A friend called in to say that he had to wade through a river shoulder high with his ballot box on his head.*"

The Chizongwe students were at a pitch of excitement as the results came in. Each time UNIP won a seat (55 of them) a big cheer would go up. When the ANC won 10 in the Southern and Central Provinces there were sniggers or silence. There were 10 reserved constituencies for voters with higher qualifications. The National Progressive Party, the UFP under a new name, won all of them. Kaunda and his youthful but impressive cabinet were sworn in shortly afterwards.

Chizongwe was a typical colonial school with many of the aspects of a British boarding school. The boys' dormitories formed four "houses" which competed on Sports Day. The houses were named after two African heroes, Aggrey, the famous Ghanaian educationalist, and Chuma, who worked for David Livingstone and helped carry his body to the coast when he died; and two colonialists, Rhodes and (Gilbert) Rennie, a former Governor of Northern Rhodesia. Prefects were appointed and became quite powerful, supervising punishment, which was usually hard work in the school grounds, slashing the tall grass or digging holes to plant trees. Food was always a sensitive subject: one boy was elected as Minister of Food and he would negotiate with the Boarding Master to get the best deal. At Chizongwe meals generally consisted of either *nsima* (maize porridge) and beans or, less frequently, rice and meat. Cocoa, *masokoni* (scones, or rather bread rolls) and fruit were also provided. In fact it compared reasonably well with what the boys would have eaten at home.

There was little chance for most of the students to leave the school premises in term time. The vanette, a small brown Bedford lorry, would take a few boys to town to do shopping on a Saturday. It would also carry football teams to play at Katete, the Dutch Reformed Church school 50 miles distant, or even further to the Catholic one at Chassa. When the school holidays came, boys who wanted to stay with relatives on the "line of rail" had to apply for a government pass. There was no free movement from the outlying provinces to the main towns. Some students stayed at school over the December holidays if their homes were too far away or were liable to be cut off by floods. January was the height of the rainy season. Since at first most of us had no car, the staff would also ride to town sitting in deck chairs on the back of the vanette.

During term time we organised a film show at weekends – often documentaries from the British Council such as one about the royal children, then Charles, Anne and Andrew, or from the French Cultural Centre such as *Giraffe à Paris*. I remember laughing one day when the students were served with *The Life History of the Cockroach* while at the white club in town they were showing *Brides of Dracula*. On another occasion I remember hearing loud cheers coming from the classrooms that served as a hall to find that it was a film about ballet. The boys assumed that lifting up the ballerina was a prelude to sex. Feature films were sometimes shown. Laurence Olivier's *Richard III* went down very well – boys limped around the school with their backs hunched for weeks. It also gave them some ideas for the school production of *Macbeth,* which was performed in our open air amphitheatre on an evening as cool and drizzly as it ever was in Dunsinane. Our feisty Scots teacher of English, Elizabeth Nelson, unlocked a lot of acting talent among the students. The part of Macbeth himself was shared between two players and, as in Shakespeare's time, Lady Macbeth had to be performed by a boy. (It was whispered that the boy in question was already married). The students loved it and quotes from the play were heard around school: "Macbeth has murdered sleep"; "Is this a dagger which I see before me?" We spent long hours recording sound effects and I trained myself to do the stage lighting. Another play we put on in 1964 in the new assembly hall was Bertold Brecht's *The Exception and the Rule*.

The students organised regular concerts at weekends and they were brilliant. The best group was the Mad Kids, featuring five juniors including Kafumukache's son. The songs were interpretations of songs they had presumably heard over the radio ranging from Roy Orbison to Carmen Miranda and Miriam Makeba. Kwela, a jazzy sort of street music played on the penny whistle of Spokes Mashiyane was also very popular. Some of the staff joined a choir in the town led by a very charismatic priest from Québec. The first performance was of Handel's *Messiah* and the students were invited to St. Anne's Catholic cathedral for it. They were very impressed and all came back to school singing the Hallelujah Chorus. The choir later performed Haydn's *Creation* and Mendelsohn's *Elijah*. Around this time a visiting charitable optical service arrived at the school. A majority of students claimed they needed glasses which were the sure sign of being an intellectual. We managed to whittle the numbers down to 15 who had real eyesight problems and they received free spectacles.

I enjoyed teaching at Chizongwe. The students were very keen and, with exceptions, very intelligent. In another letter home I wrote soon after my arrival: "*I have to keep ahead of the classes in all the subjects and in geography I cannot always babble on unless I have vaguely prepared the subject… Civics is even worse… as I am dealing with agriculture without ever having lived in an African village… History I only teach to the Remove – equivalent of English 14-year olds in academic attainments but rather more adult in outlook. Some of them must be getting on for twenty… They have so far had the French Revolution and the agitation for Parliamentary Reform in England, so they have learnt plenty of subversive ideas.*"

I learned a huge amount from our outstanding African colleagues before they were creamed off to top jobs in the new

Zambia, and also from our students, many of whom have remained friends. Chizongwe produced some high flyers: Dennis Chirwa (Deputy Chief Justice), Yobert Shamapande, (expert at the UN Institute for Namibia, head of UN information Office in South Africa and professor at Columbia University), Alfred Sakala (Senior Manager at ZCCM mines), Permanent Secretary Austen Mweemba, Ambassadors Bizwayo Nkunika and Solomon Mumbi, and many others including the writer, Gideon Phiri, who covered the Nigerian Civil War as a journalist and wrote a popular novel, *A Ticklish Sensation*. Although I was happy to move elsewhere after three years, my first posting is the one I remember most fondly. In 2009 Edyth and I revisited Chipata, taking the Post Bus along the greatly improved tarred Great East Road and over the Luangwa Bridge, rebuilt in 1968 after it had been sabotaged as revenge for Kaunda's stand against the racist regime in (southern) Rhodesia. It was sad to see that the hillside which Cyrus had praised in 1961 was now bare of trees. The school had become Chizongwe Technical High School and it was still one of the best – and the Head was amazed to learn that we had taught there before he was even born.

PIC 8) *Fanuel Mapfuwa and Alfred Sakala (Form 2 at the time) with my car and the "African Graduate House", Chizongwe School, Zambia, 1963.*

Although life at a boarding school was a step away from African reality, we had opportunities to learn a bit about the culture. The one year old baby of Paul Gondwe, one of the trades school staff, died. The funeral was to take place at the nearest village and the school vanette was used as the hearse. I joined the crowd of mourners as the tiny coffin was loaded on the back of the lorry. Paul and his wife, who was howling with grief, climbed in and the other women followed. The growl of the lorry's engine in low gear competed with the higher pitch of the wailing women as we moved along the muddy path to the village. The sun came out and we were surrounded by green maize, tall grass and trees – but we were infected by the spirit of the dead child. Kaizore, the garrulous old village headman, was master of ceremonies. The men stood at one end of the pit and the women sank to the ground at the other and Paul crouched by the grave. Carpenter Kafumukache read from the Bible and gave a short sermon (in Bemba which the locals would not have understood very well). In spite of this and the little white cross on the coffin it did not feel like a Christian occasion. Kaizore was like a second priest, indicating when the baby's bottle should be pierced with a hoe and thrown into the grave, along with a jar of Vaseline. He stuck little sticks in the ground once the grave had been covered and at his bidding the women went off to collect stones to cover up the mound. It was a moving experience for me. Such rites prolong grief but bring out tremendous solidarity from all the community.

v) Zambian Names and Zambian English

One of the many strange effects of colonial and missionary influence has been the grafting of European sounding names on to African traditions of naming children. We asked students at Chizongwe in 1963 and at Kalomo in 1969 how they got their names. Alice Mulwani, a student at Kalomo, wrote: "*In our tribe, the Tonga, names are given by your grandmother... and she is the one who will take you out when you are about three weeks old. While you are a child you will be called by that name you are given until you start school or when they baptise you they give you a Christian* name." Gilbert Hibeenzu, also Tonga, wrote: "*The name given to the first born if at all he is a boy… is his grandfather's; a girl is given her grandmother's. All the others that are born after are named after a thing that happened when they were born, or the season when they were born… or what the father did when the wife was pregnant.*"

Samson Namadula was given the name *Samson* by his father, *Shasha*, meaning handsome, by his mother and *Kungubala* meaning lazy by his grandfather. He said he stopped using *Kungubala* "because I am not as lazy as 13 years ago." Zambian families often keep a family name, which is not the case all over central Africa. Children were often named after someone, often a missionary, a pastor or the doctor at the child's birth. One boy's father insisted he had to be called *London*. The parents – and the children when reaching school-going age – would choose names that sounded European and then they invented similar sounding names. Thus, at Chizongwe we had *Jackson* but also *Frackson, Lackson, Mackson* and *Waxon*. Girls could be *Eneless, Loveness, Fatness, Fednes* or *Etiness*. Some of these types of names were hard to take seriously: we had *Hilarius, Billius* and *Beltt*. Of course at baptism many children were given biblical names or saints' names: *Francis, Elias, Elijah, Joshua, Benignus, Jeremiah, Solomon*. I remember once calling *Goliath* into the staff room and Edyth was surprised to see a rather small and not very muscular boy come in. (He went on to become Director of the Central Supply and Tender Board). My favourite sad tale was of a bright boy who lined up to be baptised at the Anglican church in Fort Jameson and when he reached the font the priest asked his name. "*Sunboy*", he replied. "I can't baptise you as *Sunboy*. You are *James*" After the service Sunboy was in tears. "My brother is called James". There had never been a Saint Sunboy!

English is the common language in Zambia today, although Bemba and an urban version of Nyanja (*Chitauni*, town language) are widely used. Before Independence fewer people used English but those that had been to school usually spoke it well, often better than their first teachers in primary school. Chad Kawamba writes in *Aurora*, the Chizongwe magazine: "*English is composed of so many rhyming words that it is sometimes difficult to make the whole difference of either being understood or not. I know when most of us began to learn to speak English we found some peculiar type of pronunciation which we had never had to make in our mother languages."*

Pronunciation, and therefore spelling, is of course influenced by the local languages which are members of the huge family of Bantu languages. Zambia theoretically has 70 languages but most are very close to the seven major ones (Bemba, Nyanja, Tonga, Lozi, Kaonde, Lunda and Luvale). The letter r usually becomes l, and the vowel sounds are very pure compared to some of the English ones and this has its effect on students' spelling: the tool shed inventory at Chizongwe read: "Hard blooms, soft blooms, small garden folks, large garden folks and muttocks." So cows ate glass, beds flew into their nests and people sat in the shed under a tree. "He riched a reach man's house."

As Zambian words usually ended in a vowel, the clipped ending of English words was difficult, so you could hear: "Iti isu a goodu road" but the ends of some words such as "dignity" and "custody" posed problems. The police held some of our Kalomo boys "in custard." Generally our students had very good English but of course there were some howlers and we noted some of them in a book in the staff room at Chizongwe. Quite understandably the students resented being laughed at and sometimes removed the book. The students also got their revenge by mimicking the foibles of the staff. I was known as Gaucho and boys used to imitate me walking with my thumbs in my pockets.

The recommendations of applicants for secondary made by the primary school heads sometimes needed decoding: among the Special Peculiarities of one highly recommended boy was "hideous character." The Head was about to reject him when Dalson Nkunika worked out that it meant shy, one who hides! Some other gems from Mufulira: "He claims to possess a fractured leg"; "It appears he has been brought up loosely"; "He plays truancy at its uttermost… very good at football but fond of dodging."

The use and quality of English has increased greatly since the time I worked there, especially in the towns but there are some distinctly Zambian usages. For example, the time is always given in the 24 hour clock and if someone was late it meant he was dead. The downside is that the main national languages, although spoken, are written and read much less while some of the smaller languages, as all over Africa, face a threat to their survival. Before Independence books were published in some of the local languages. This is rare today. Since culture and language are inseparable this has to be a matter for concern.

Other things changed quite fast after Independence. The country started feeling African. Africans filled most jobs at all levels. Those who did well, the *apamwamba* (top people), built houses, bought cars and many grew fat. I remember the satirical columnist in The African Mail suggesting that beer should be piped into these peoples' houses as well as water. This letter also appeared in the African Mail:

A stern warning to Zambian women

This business of women Prime Ministers is a threat to stable marriages… I must warn Zambian women not to divorce their husbands with the hope of kissing their way to premiership. We in Zambia will not tolerate it.

CHISENGA Y. KOBILI, Chingola

---

vi) Independence for Malawi and Zambia

I was due to go home for six months leave in late July 1964, and Edyth and I were to be married in October. As her contract was with the colonial government, Zambia's imminent Independence meant she could break it and go on leave. We were going to miss the festivities in Lusaka so we went across the recently re-created border to experience Malawi's Independence celebrations on July 6. It was a memorable weekend. A friend dropped us at the railway station at Salima on the shore of Lake Malawi, the same place where we had decided to get married a few months earlier. The train was overtaken by a man on a bicycle but it eventually speeded up slightly and got us to Balaka where the line crosses the main road. We hitch-hiked from there to Zomba, the small, sleepy and rather charming town on the side of a mountain, very much like a hill station in British India, which was then the capital but is now Malawi's university town. We stayed with Anthony and Anne Wilson. Anthony was head of the Community Development Department. He took us to Blantyre to watch the Independence ceremony. The loudspeakers kept proudly trumpeting the arrival of the "Duke of Edinburgh, husband of the Queen." The Union Jack came down and, as the new rising sun flag of Malawi reached the top of the flagpole, the face of the new Prime Minister, Dr. Hastings Kamuzu Banda lit up in fireworks and a big cheer went up. The following morning we took a little bus from Zomba to Blantyre for our flight back to Fort Jameson. Half way along the road all traffic was stopped to wait for the Prime Minister and the Duke to pass. As the cortege passed we must have looked like a couple of local farmers. We missed the plane but were very lucky to hitch a lift back in time for school the next day.

Sadly, things turned sour in Malawi within weeks. The leading members of the Malawi Congress Party had built up Dr. Banda as a dominant leader to create national unity before Independence without realising they had created a monster. When six members of the cabinet dared to raise issues with the Prime Minister (soon to be President for Life) they were accused of treason and had to escape into hiding or into exile. Anthony Wilson wrote in November 1964: "… *friend no longer trusts friend, families are divided, people 'disappear' – over the Zambia border or into restriction… Dr. Banda incites violence in his speeches and his youth groups respond, feeling secure against police interference… while the ministers who resigned seemed to want to do no more than spark off a debate, the Prime Minister has regarded this as a slight to his leadership and, therefore, treason.*" A little later, on our honeymoon, we met the Malawian Ambassador, David Rubadiri, in Washington and he offered us the use of his flat in New York. The wall was decorated with a huge photograph of Dr. Banda. The following year David, an academic and one of Africa's best-known poets, was also branded a traitor and he has spent most of his life in exile.

Edyth and I spent a day in Malawi in 2009. We were shown around the new capital city at Lilongwe, built with aid from the apartheid regime in South Africa. It's a fairly undemonstrative place – and the old capital on the hillside at Zomba would have been difficult to develop into a modern capital. Dr. Banda, who created the new Lilongwe, still has admirers, one of whom is the custodian of the rather ugly mausoleum which many regard as a tribute to the Father of the Nation while opponents see it as a monument to a dictator and a waste of money. More recently I spent Christmas 2015 in Malawi with Fetson Kalua, who as a Tumbuka from the north of the country, found no work in Malawi and has ended up as a Professor in Pretoria. We stayed on the lake shore at the home of Chimunthu Banda, who had been Speaker of the national parliament.

Zambia was to be much luckier having as its first leader Kenneth Kaunda (KK), a more modest, sincere man. On 24 October when KK became President of the new Republic of Zambia we were on our honeymoon and were in Los Angeles. Some Zambian contacts there invited us to a rather strange party in a hotel in Santa Monica. The Americans present had little idea where Zambia was, so the hosts had organised a map ceremony to fill that gap and everyone had a few drinks to toast the new country. Meanwhile in Tokyo the team that entered the Olympic Games in the name of Northern Rhodesia left it on Independence Day proudly carrying the new flag of Zambia.

vii) A year on the Copperbelt, 1965

After our wedding and a long honeymoon in the United States and Mexico Edyth and I returned to Zambia, as it had now become, in January 1965 and were posted to Mufulira High School. Mufulira is one of the four copper mining towns which, together with the administrative and industrial centre, Ndola, form the Copperbelt. Mufulira mine was the largest and deepest of the mines. The town was segregated into four parts: the mine township and the "town" both had low density (originally all white) and high density (all black) sections. The copper company was paternalistic and provided a good hospital, schools and reasonable housing for the black mining families. There were a lot of whites, many of them miners and many from South Africa. We were given a spacious house in a leafy street of comfortable bungalows guarded by fierce dogs whose licence tag read "European owned dog" and which tended to attack anyone on foot. (Whites generally moved in cars.) Behind the houses there was a "sanitary lane" which linked the servants' quarters.

Mufulira High School had been all white until 1963 and we arrived with the first large intake of black pupils in Form One. We had resisted being posted to this school as we would have preferred a boarding school and we found, as we had feared, that the culture of the place was that of the old Federal Ministry of Education. The teachers' uniform was long trousers and a tie. The colonial white shirt and shorts were thought shocking, Prepared lesson notes had to be shown to the Head and Afrikaans was on the syllabus (taught by Mrs. Van der Walt, generally dubbed "Mrs. Fond o'Homework"). John Harker, the Head, had grown up in Natal and thought he was a liberal but he had evidently never met any Africans socially. So when Simon Maonde, later to be Zambia's Ambassador to China, joined our staff, Harker was pleasantly surprised to find one who could speak good English. Then Joe Mweemba came from the Ministry to inspect the school. That made two of them. Alan Jarvis, Edyth and I who had moved in from African Education were part of a creeping black advance that Harker seemed unhappy with.

Integrating the pupils did not come easily. Most of the black kids had walked miles to get to school with little or no breakfast. The relatively few white kids in the first year were driven to school or lived nearby and they were mostly younger and well fed. The result: the blacks were quiescent and wanted to study; the whites bounced about with excess energy and disturbed the class. Harker had to be persuaded to provide bread rolls (*masokono*) at break and each time he announced this he felt he had to point out that they were "totally without flavour." The African pupils enjoyed them anyway.

We quickly got depressed. It was very boring teaching the same lesson to six streams in Form One. The Head treated the staff like bad children. One day we took President Kaunda's advice to display maximum festivity for the state visit of Emperor Haile Selassie of Ethiopia and we went off to Kitwe to wave at the great man, thereby failing to complete some students' reports on time. I was reprimanded by the Head and I rudely stormed out of his office. On another occasion I had spent the evening in the pub across the Congo border and when I got home found our bedroom door lock broken. I had to explain humbly why I was wearing dirty clothes and no tie in school. Edyth had been at a meeting that evening and was wearing high heels and a smart dress.

In the school stock cupboard we found a booklet first published in 1946 entitled *Understand the African,* used by the Federal Ministry of Education to teach white children about African life and culture. The author, J.M. Winterbottom, describes visiting a village and writes about chiefs and traditions. He may have meant well but the booklet really exposes the prejudices of the time. Here are some examples: "*Africans can be educated to do the same jobs as Europeans but if the European, with centuries of civilization behind him, cannot do them better than the African, then it is right that the African should get the job. But what people who use this argument are afraid of is not that the African will do the job better, but that he will do it for less money... because he does not want so many things as a European; he is content with fewer and cheaper clothes, he eats cheaper and less nourishing food, he lives in smaller and worse built houses.*" And again: "*the African looks for guidance to the European. Even when he is insolent and rude he realises that the European has wisdom and power and wealth...*" And the very last words in the book: "*Tell the truth. Even if most Africans tell lies, you should know better.*" That generalised individual, "the African," is described in his quaint cultural context and the young European has his imagined superiority confirmed, though the author might wish him to be a little less arrogant.

Being only a few miles from the Congo border was a boon for burglars, but the local police were often able to retrieve things – but not in the case of our neighbour's car which was found one morning propped on bricks with all its wheels missing. One good thing about being close to the border was the chance to go across to drink Simba beer in Mokambo with some very friendly and often drunken Congolese as on the night when our bedroom door was locked. Edyth and I also had a weekend in Elizabethville (now Lubumbashi), still an elegant town then. Another weekend we crossed the Congo Pedicle to Fort Rosebery and Samfya, where the wide, sandy beach looks at what appears to be the sea. It is in fact Lake Bangweulu, so wide and flat that the far side cannot be seen. This Pedicle is another colonial absurdity. If you look at a map of Zambia you will see this strip of land in the shape of a foot which effectively cuts off northern Zambia from the Copperbelt. The road across it was theoretically, but never, maintained by the Congo and was a mass of mud in the rainy season and deeply rutted when it was dry. Worse, drivers were supposed to change over to driving on the right for these 42 miles. The crazy demarcation of this frontier was the work of the King of Italy who had mediated between the claims of King Leopold of Belgium and the British South Africa Company in 1894. Of course, neither king had ever visited Africa.

To keep myself sane I began teaching an adult evening class, we joined the town branch of UNIP and I applied for school headships all over the country. One day, visiting the amateur theatre in nearby Kitwe, I saw they were advertising for a news reader for Zambia Television which at that time only broadcast from a little studio in Kitwe, just two hours' work a week for a fee of £3. I got the job. They tested me reading commercials but I was too bad an actor to sound convinced of the wonders of soap powder. However, I had a good BBC-type voice and for a couple of months I read the news every Thursday. I still have a continuity sheet dated 8 June 1965 with Chou en-Lai visiting President Nyerere, the Vietcong blowing up a bridge and two students in Rhodesia fined for heckling Prime Minister Ian Smith. Then one Thursday I broke a tooth eating some dates and worried that this would be the end of me on ZTV. We studied the faces of other newsreaders and were relieved to notice that their teeth, or lack of them, did not show. 11 November 1965 was also a Thursday, the day of Ian Smith's Unilateral Declaration of Independence (UDI) in Rhodesia. Edyth set up a tape recorder at the house to record me announcing the event, but my boss wanted to read the big story and I was left the small stuff: a new open-cast coal mine in the Zambezi valley. Shortly after this, ZTV decided, quite rightly, to appoint an African to read the news and that was the end of my very brief broadcasting career.

viii) Kalomo Secondary School 1966-70

My search for a headship bore fruit. I was first told that I would be sent to Mpatamatu, a new day secondary school in the nearby Copperbelt town of Luanshya. Happily the Ministry of Education changed its mind and I ended up as Head of Kalomo Secondary School in the Southern Province.

The lack of educated manpower in the new Zambia was shocking. At Independence there were fewer than 100 Zambian graduates and less than 1,000 people who had completed secondary education. The government's big plan was to build a large co-educational secondary boarding school in each district and new day secondary schools in all the towns. By 1971 the number of pupils finishing Form 2 would increase from 2,700 to 17,500, the number passing O level from 500 to 9,000 and the University of Zambia would open. This lack of qualified Zambians meant that a 29-year old like me could be selected to run one of these new schools.

Kaunda's new government was ambitious. Building and equipping so many new schools, as well as plenty of other development projects in a land-locked country with a hostile regime in Rhodesia to the south and fuel supplies rationed, was bound to cause immense logistical problems. We visited Kalomo a month before the school was due to open, the very weekend when Zambia's fuel supplies were being cut by Rhodesia, whose illegal regime was now being targeted by international sanctions. We left the car in Lusaka, continued to Kalomo by train and hitch-hiked back. Most of the school buildings had been erected but it was clear that the school was not going to be ready to open in the New Year. Edyth then went on a visit to her family in England and in January 1966 I drove south with Zulu, who worked for us, a load of luggage and a cat. Sure enough there were no desks in the classrooms, no beds in the dormitories and no electricity.

The first task was to hire labour: a queue of 200 applicants formed and there were only 9 jobs. I set up a temporary office, using the only two chairs I had. The removable back seat of our little Renault 4 car had to serve as the furniture in my house. When the school finally opened in February we had 140 pupils, all boys, all boarders, six classrooms, four storerooms, four dormitories and a huge unfinished dining hall; 140 beds, 139 mattresses, 48 desks, 50 chairs plus some tiny ones borrowed from a primary school. Electricity arrived on opening day though the wiring was all mixed up. To cook meals we had to borrow two colossal cauldrons and buy firewood, using one of the dormitories as a dining room. Yet because we were on the railway and the main road we were much better off than other schools in outlying places. Gradually things got sorted out, including the arrival of sophisticated oil burning cookers and the completion of enough buildings for the eventual roll of over 1,000.

Kalomo was the sort of place that in South Africa would be called a *dorp*, a small township with a few stores, churches and a police station and not much more. T.R.R. Nayar, a new teacher who had worked in Aden, described it as "an uplifted village." Its most attractive feature was a large green open space in front of the row of shops known as the village green (or more often the green village) with a huge fig tree in one corner. There was an old hotel where we had stayed on our earlier visit run by the aged Mrs. Horton who had arrived in a covered wagon as a young woman. The hotel was scruffy: bed but no breakfast. "There isn't the demand," she said. It is still scruffy today and the bar is even seedier than I remember it. Alan Franks joined the staff in 1967. When told he was going to work at Kalomo he looked in his father's ancient encyclopaedia. It contained a map of North Western Rhodesia with the capital city, Kalomo, in bold type. I drove him down from Lusaka when he arrived. We passed though the other small towns and each time

I had to tell him that Kalomo was even smaller. But it had truly been the capital. The old Administrator's House, built in 1903, and the Pioneer Cemetery are at a distance from the small modern town. Both are listed as National Monuments.

When the railway was extended over the Zambezi to Kalomo in 1905 – and on to Ndola and the Congo by 1909 – a wide strip on each side of the line was declared Crown Land and made available to immigrant European farmers. In 1907 Kalomo lost its status as the capital to Livingstone but it remained a commercial centre for the farmers – with a couple of churches, a primary school for whites and, later, one for Asians and another for Africans. A memorial beside the main road commemorates the Kalomo Culture (800-1300 C.E.), of which more later. Kalomo was also the driving test capital of Zambia. People from all over the country came for this: there was nowhere for a hill start and the rather beery white man who administered the test rarely failed anyone. I hope this was not the cause of the high number of accidents on the "hell run" along the Great North Road to Dar es Salaam, the lifeline of Zambia's trade when sanctions were imposed on Rhodesia. A bizarre event in Kalomo in 1966 was the arrival of a really old-fashioned circus, marquee, trapeze artists, lion tamer and all. It was during the school holidays but the local people crowded in. The weirdest thing was to see this white South African band playing the Zambian National Anthem. This was the last visit of the circus to Zambia.

Edyth edited a history of our five years at Kalomo, based on weekly letters home that her mother had preserved (along with some from me to my mother) and much of this chapter is based on this detailed record. In those days even to telephone Lusaka meant booking a call and waiting hours to be connected. In these days of texts, tweets and skype it is extraordinary to think that in ten years in Zambia we never once called home on the telephone. The post was efficient and we just exchanged regular letters. We were able to travel during school holidays and visited Malawi, Tanzania, Rhodesia (as it was) and South Africa as well as most parts of Zambia. We also had some practice as acting parents when

Arthur Maonde, aged 7, stayed with us so that he could attend the English medium primary school. His father was head of a similar school in the more isolated town of Namwala.

Each of the first 140 boys to come to the new school had to struggle to get there. Scriven Masole writes: *"Competition to get into secondary school was so great that when the results of the entrance exam were announced those pupils who had been accepted had to hide in the teachers' houses because the less fortunate ones were so jealous they wanted to stone them."* We were seven teachers, all British, and all apart from Edyth and me new to the country. The boys were excited to be there, happy that there were no fees – even soap and toilet paper were government issue. Edward Sakufiwa noted that *"one of the advantages of being the first pupils at a new school is that we did not go through what is commonly known as mockery."*

Although the boys who made up the first intake had to rough it, they soon formed a happy community. Yet it could be mind-blowing for students first arriving in secondary school, especially for those coming from other parts of the country. Instead of a Zambian class teacher pronouncing English in a familiar African way they were faced with seven or eight foreign teachers with their different accents – and they loved taking us off when we were out of earshot. They were convinced that Bill Bleeks had some speech defect. In fact he just came from Northern Ireland. After that first year the origins of the Kalomo staff were more diverse. They used to keep asking Ramesh Sharma a question which would make him repeat words they thought he could not pronounce. One Indian teacher at another school was dubbed "Pisics and Tchemistry Patel." Our own Mr. Patel was famous for exclaiming: "If I would be in Nigeria I would hammerer you!" We had a variety of South Africans: both Coloureds and Indians (Christian, Hindu and Muslim), all happy to escape from teaching under the *apartheid* system. Other teachers were part of the aid programmes of Denmark and Norway as well as the large number of British. Our Russian science teacher had to report to his embassy at regular intervals. His wife was also a highly qualified scientist but she had no English and was bored out of her mind with nothing to do. They managed to communicate with the only other Russian speaker in Kalomo, an eccentric elderly Armenian dating from before the revolution who had Orthodox icons all over his house. A strange friendship, probably best not reported to the embassy. When we needed a teacher of Tonga, the local language, we head-hunted Joshua Cheelo from a primary school and soon had him promoted to be Deputy Head. At Kalomo out of a staff of over 30 we never had more than four Zambians during my time there. One of these was Naomi Sikumba who taught domestic science. Her husband, Cox, was later Zambian Ambassador in Mozambique and tragically he died in the air crash that killed President Samora Machel. Another was Rajah Kunda who went into politics and later held several ministerial posts.

As at Chizongwe food was always a sensitive issue. In the first year when we had no African staff, Rosemary Derwent Crowther who was a trained Home Economics teacher was asked to organise the "boarding." Her idea of a meal was not the same as that of the boys, nor was she used to having food cooked in huge cauldrons in the open air. We had to adjust the portions to respond to the boys' reasonable complaints. Equally the domestic science syllabus took little account of African tastes. When we asked a girl if she would serve at home the onion soup she had prepared in class, she just laughed.

The word food normally meant *nsima,* the solid maize staple known as *ugali* in East Africa, *sadza* in Zimbabwe and *papa* in South Africa. Telling the students about the multi-racial Outward Bound course he attended, Romey Luchen reported to the other boys' amazement that he had eaten no food for two weeks! The special meal which we sometimes provided on Saturdays was very popular. Edward Sakufiwa recalls: "*We were served with delicious meals (at least by school standards). The meal included a good relish – meat or chicken – which was a break from the less popular relishes such as beans. Sometimes well-buttered bread and tea with lots of milk was served...*" On one occasion the school was offered a whole buffalo. We thought this would be a treat but it was rather tough, and after a week of non-stop buffalo the students started complaining.

The University of Zambia

President Kaunda was installed as the first Chancellor of the University of Zambia in July 1966. We attended the ceremony which took place at a temporary campus located at a stone's throw of the British High Commission. (This suited the students who were keen to throw stones at the British High Commission to protest against what they saw as British complicity with the illegal Smith regime in Rhodesia.) In his address Kaunda recalled discussions which had begun as early as 1948 about provision of a university college in Lusaka on the lines of those established at Ibadan in Nigeria and Makerere in Uganda. The need became more urgent when the recently elected *apartheid* regime in South Africa refused to admit any more Africans from Northern Rhodesia or Nyasaland to Fort Hare, where the earliest graduates had studied. In 1953 the plans were going firm, but, in Kaunda's words: *"Unfortunately this great project was killed by the creation of the Federation of Rhodesia and Nyasaland six months later. The plan for a university college primarily for Africans became confused with a parallel proposal by Rhodesian Europeans to build their own university."* The resulting University of Rhodesia and Nyasaland was built in Salisbury and, although it was racially mixed (and dubbed by most whites "the Kremlin on the hill"), it was not always a place where African students felt at ease. Zambia remained, again in the President's words, *"Economically... one of the most developed countries on the continent but educationally one of the least developed."* Zambia had to wait another thirteen years for its own university which moved to its own campus a year after this inauguration. An impressive campaign had been organised to make the university a popular national project. Small fundraising events were held all over the country, including Kalomo, and voluntary donations came from Zambians in all walks of life, even from lepers! We went to the university again to attend the very first degree ceremony in 1969. President Nyerere of Tanzania was the guest of honour. We were proud in 1975 when we heard that the six students from our first intake at Kalomo all received their degrees, two of whom, Samuel Zilombo and Shamutiba Kanyanga, going on to teach at the university.

January 1967 saw Kalomo's school roll increase from 140 to 501 and the staff from seven to twenty-three. Many of the new arrivals were girls and it was not easy for some of those who came from other parts of the country. Venus Nang'amba wrote: "*At first I was very unhappy. There was a tree in the school compound that I climbed into and cried because I thought I could see my parents' home from the top.*" Gabriella Mtonga wrote, "*I remember my terrible journey to get there. I was alone on the train with a heavy suitcase… I had no idea where Kalomo was and asked at every station if it was time to get off. I fell over several times with the suitcase on my way up from the station. At school I was given a bed in the dormitory but I could not speak a word of Tonga and was so unhappy that I did not even go to the dining room for three weeks. Fortunately one of the girls, Edna Ngoma, could speak Nyanja and looked after me and brought me food. After three weeks I said to myself that I would just have to face up to my difficulties and from then on I played a full part in school life, eventually becoming a prefect.*" Herbert Haamucenje wrote: "*My parents were poor villagers and could only give me enough money to pay my train fare to and from school. Without the free education provided by the Transitional Development Plan I would not have been able to go to school at all. I did not know what to expect on arrival. The newcomers were 'mocked'… I did not mix freely and kept out of trouble. I read a lot and was a serious student, finding consolation in books as I had few other resources.*" A brilliant student, Herbert ended up as the Chief Executive of Unilever for Southern Africa. Bates Namuyamba, who later held several ministerial posts in the government, recalled, "*Another aspect of school life that would surprise present day students was that everything was provided free of charge: transport to and from school, boarding costs and uniform.*"

As Gabriella's story suggests, the train played an important part in life at Kalomo in those days when there were few bus services. Almost every school in the country opened and closed on the same day and the conditions on the overcrowded trains were terrible. Lameck Banda, a former Chizongwe student, described his journey from Ndola: "*… about 200 were to go into 4th class. I was scared because I knew I could not enter as I had heavy luggage… all* *the people rushed inside. It was survival of the fittest... I was about to cry when I thought of going to 3rd class. I tried to enter but some very undisciplined railway workers refused to let me enter. I had no alternative but to enter through the window after putting my katundu* (luggage) *inside the coach"*. At Kalomo the steam train was often hours late but we could telephone to check when it was expected. Diesel trains came in in 1967 and they were more punctual, but the daily train often arrived at night. When the term began in 1968 it came in at 11.30 pm and the students staggered up the half-mile from the station in the pelting rain with their tin boxes on their heads – through the puddles and the long grass straight into the dormitories.

The new teachers arriving from Britain had been impressed at first by the neat new houses where they would live, but they were rapidly confronted with the reality of faulty wiring, cockroaches – and worst of all – a shortage of water. Kalomo's water supply came from a small dam owned by the railway. The dam was silted up, and what little water came from it was pumped up into a water tower and then used both by the steam trains and the local population. The arrival of a huge boarding school put an impossible strain on this meagre supply. Taps ran dry most of the time and we used to store the rather muddy looking water in the bath and channel the dirty bath water to irrigate our bananas. In April1967 the health inspector advised closing the school and I advised the Ministry, unsuccessfully, that at least the school's expansion should be put on hold until the problem was solved. The local Catholic priest was a water diviner: he swung his stick and located a good spot and raised funds to dig a new borehole which led to some improvement. Then the town council paid a consultant to investigate the problem who advised that a second water tower be built – when there was not enough water to fill the existing tower! Things gradually improved, perhaps due to diesel engines taking over from steam on the railway, but in 1969 the system broke down again and one day at school assembly I demonstrated drinking water from a barrel of water mixed with alum to persuade the students to drink it. They refused.

During our stay in Mufulira we had attended a short course on archaeology at the National Museum and we had taken part in excavations in Livingstone and at a site near Mkushi in the north. The plateau around Kalomo had been inhabited by Early Iron Age people from 300 to 1300 C.E. who first introduced agriculture and this period was known as that of the Kalomo Culture. There was evidence of earlier Stone Age people too. Edyth wrote to her parents: *"I took about thirty pupils down to the riverside… when I gathered the group together I asked cheerfully, expecting the answer 'No', 'Has anyone found a hand axe?' There was a chorus of 'Yes' and they had found about eight good specimens."* This set the Archaeological Society off to a good start. A group of us climbed the jagged Siakaunda Hill to photograph the only rock painting in southern Zambia. Then in 1967-68 we undertook a proper dig at Matobo, near Kalomo, and unearthed a hut floor which could be dated by radio-carbon to around 1,000 CE. Edyth wrote this up for the Zambia Museums Journal.

TEACHER: Prehistoric man ate uncooked food.
STUDENT: Just like Europeans.

The students later enthusiastically took part in an oral history project, making contact with elderly people in their home villages. We had by this time bought a Land Rover and we took members of the Historical Society to their home villages where they recorded interviews with a remarkable selection of old people. The interviews were collected in a cyclostyled (later printed) booklet entitled, *Busongo bwa bapati bufwa ambabo* (The stories of old people die with them). The memories, even if occasionally inaccurate, revealed a lot about rural life in early colonial times. Syatwiinda was a well-known herbalist who claimed to be 108 years old. He had worked on the construction of the railway and remembered seeing the first car. Mukwenda had a Lozi[18] name

---

18. The Lozi were the dominant people in the Western Province or Bulozi, formerly known as Barotseland. They were descendants of the Makololo invaders

which she was given as a slave. She was taken from her mother when she was about five years old. "*This was during the last of the slave raids. The Lozi did not kill the parents. They just wanted to take the children... The people who had taken them said, 'Stop crying. We are taking you to your mothers'. When they reached Sesheke, meat was cooked and the children were also given some meat. At this time the railway was not yet built... At Sesheke spears were used for killing animals and for dancing. They used decorated pots for storing food, holding water and as cooking pots. They were forced to go to Sunday services and since this is the first time they had seen churches it was very strange for them. They had to pray and sing songs about God... After some time before she had breasts she ran away... they walked the whole day and slept in the forest where there were a lot of hyenas. They could hear them roaring angrily all night long but they were not attacked. The next morning they started off again and came to the railway line. They were afraid because they had not crossed it when they were taken away.*" Siankusule was one of the first teachers, from 1927 to 1946. He described Tonga life: "*The Tonga people wore bark of trees and skins of animals such as sheep and goats, covering only the front and back parts. Blankets were also made from skins of animals. They also knew how to trap animals by using fall traps and spring traps. They grew sweet corn and water melons and gathered wild fruits... Tobacco was sent to the parents before marriage. Lobola* (dowry paid to the parents of the bride) *was 15 sheep and 10 beads which were given to the parents of the girl. They usually got married at a very young age.*"

We started a small museum at the school which was much appreciated by Vice President Simon Kapwepwe, a keen promoter of Zambia's heritage, when he visited Kalomo. We also took three members of the Historical Society to visit the Western Province, Bulozi. Scriven Masole remembers: "*At Muoyo we had an audience with Mulena Mukwae Makwibi* (the king's sister) *who talked with*

---

who came from the south at the same time as the Zulu empire was expanding. The Lozi king was the *litunga* and the *mulena mukwae* is the king's sister who has a separate court. Both courts move by royal barge during the annual floods in the impressive *Kuomboka* ceremony.

us and served us with tea and biscuits. We also had an audience with the Litunga (king), Ngambela Sikota where we were also served with tea and biscuits. The Chief Minister instructed us in the formal behaviour required in the Litunga's presence. We had to kneel and clap as we approached. Mrs. Watt appeared to have some difficulty in getting down far enough and the Litunga indicated that she could remain standing. He was very pleasant and pleased to have a visit from his Southern province cousins". The Tonga and Lozi have a joking relationship where they call each other cousins.

Many other clubs and societies were organised at Kalomo with one member of staff acting as sponsor. Joshua Cheelo sponsored the traditional Tonga dance club, Ngoma ya Maanu (drum of wisdom) which was always on demand at Independence celebrations and national competitions. The Science Club (JETS, Junior Engineers, Technicians and Scientists) won a national competition and led some students into careers in science or engineering. The Young Farmers Club raised chickens and took part in agricultural shows. The Ballroom Club was an occasion for boys and girls to mix without breaking school rules. There were Scouts, Guides, a Debating Society, a School Band, a World Welfare Association, a Chess Club, one of the members of which, Charles Namushiya, became the national champion, and a French Club. Clubs blossomed and withered. The members of the Mechanics Club hoped to be able to service cars under the supervision of Brian Lundall, one of the South African teachers. He was a perfectionist and got the members to construct an extremely solid inspection pit. This took so long that they never got around to servicing cars – and the empty pit still stands as Brian's monument.

The Student Christian Movement was quite strong in Zambia and the Kalomo branch was proud to host a conference in 1967 with large numbers of students from other schools representing the variety of Protestant and Evangelical churches in the country. Many of these were the result of American missionary activity: in the Southern Province we had schools run by Pilgrim Holiness, the Church of Christ, Seventh Day Adventists and the Salvation Army as well as the Methodists, Anglicans and Roman Catholics. As ours was a state school the Catholics built a small convent nearby and provided us with two exceptionally good teachers.

Some clubs promoted particular sports – football, volleyball, table tennis, badminton, hockey and netball. We created a large sports field but the facilities were never ideal. Nonetheless Kalomo built up a formidable reputation in athletics at provincial and national events and produced some star performers. Hildah Mweene was the first woman to win the national Women's Cross Country and Ambrose Miyanda represented Zambia in the East African Championships in 1972.

Overheard: TEACHER: What is Zambia's national slogan?
BOY (after much thought): Things go better with big, big Coke.
CORRECT ANSWER: One Zambia, One Nation.

At Kalomo – as at Chizongwe – we staged some good theatre. In the first year we put on a Zambianised version of Molière which I had written, *The Unwilling Doctor*. Other plays included a Nigerian play, *Obadzeng goes to Town* by Saka Acquaye, Bernard Shaw's *Androcles and the Lion*, Wole Soyinka's *The Trials of Brother Jero* and the South African township musical, *King Kong* which I had first enjoyed in London. Darius Bubala remembers helping the art teacher to paint the township scenery on the back of the stage and the painting survived for many years.

We had one major crisis during our years at Kalomo – and it revealed some of the tensions inherent in co-education. I was away that day and I got word that trouble had erupted. The Deputy Head had caught a boy prefect with a junior girl in the prefects' room with the windows blacked out. He sent all the girls to their dormitories and some of the boys started plotting how to react. They began by tearing down the fence around the girls' dormitories and they threatened the Deputy Head. Rather unwisely he called the police. They over-reacted and took 38 boys to the police station. Unrest continued overnight. Misheck Munguza described things well: *"I think one of the problems had been the bar that had* been put up at the tuck shop so that girls and boys had to queue up separately. It was pulled down that night before the boys began to try to destroy the fence round the girls' dormitories... and there was no weekend entertainment that Saturday." Simon Mudenda recalls: "Some of the boys ran to the Young Farmers' Club and climbed into the chicken houses to sleep. They broke under the weight and the boys fell out... On the following day the boys called for a strike and forbade anyone to eat in the dining hall. Mr. Watt effectively broke the strike by going up to each student one by one and inviting him or her to go in with him."

Occasional eruptions like this were not unusual in Zambian boarding schools but it was a profoundly depressing experience because we had such good relations with the students. Edyth asked some of the women ex-students in 2003 what they thought of co-education in retrospect. They did not condemn it. They said it was true that boys bullied the girls, but the girls did learn to stand up to them. Nor did they think that girls tried not to shine in class for fear of provoking the boys, which is what some of the teachers suspected. After this riot various sanctions were imposed on the whole school for a month or two. I decided that some of boys who were proved to have been seriously at fault should be expelled. The Provincial Education Officer opposed this and I offered my resignation. In the end I was persuaded to stay on. I am glad I did, as the final two years at Kalomo were happy ones.

Leaving Kalomo in December 1970 was an emotional affair. The District Governor spoke appreciatively of our service and the way in which we had identified with Zambian society: "To me Kalomo is like a child born in the morning, walking at noon and performing all the duties in the afternoon. It has taken no time for Kalomo to grow and it is already ahead of some of the secondary schools that have been in existence for about twenty years, and this is because of your untiring efforts." Local people saw the school as a symbol of post-independence development and were happy that it was doing well. There had of course been tensions. The influx of a lot of new expatriates into this tiny community occasionally led to misunderstandings and one or two of our staff exploited this. The Southern

Province, and most of our students, supported the opposition ANC. Students would refuse to buy party cards when aggressively approached by members of the local UNIP Youth. They would also sing the National Anthem in school assembly with a distinct lack of enthusiasm. Some local politicians wrongly believed that we encouraged such things. Relations with the Ministry of Education also had its rough moments, especially after the riot in 1968, but I left with the impression that they would have been happy if I had stayed on longer. It was in fact a hard decision to leave. We both loved Zambia and especially Zambians and I was offered quite a good job at the Mindolo Ecumenical Foundation at Kitwe on the Copperbelt, but we both had elderly parents and England was still home.

I have been back to Kalomo several times since. I found the school in bad shape in 1982 and 1991 with the toilets out of use and windows smashed. Things were starting to improve in 2003. There were some computers, the toilet blocks had been restored and there were new bunk beds. In 2011, however, it was looking better still. The buildings were painted, the classrooms looked smart, with more computers and a smart school bus stood in the yard. The government was not able to be generous as it was in the early days but support has come from parents and from the Kalomo Old Students' Association which had finally been established. Prominent former students included, from our time there, ex-minister Bates Namuyamba and India Musokotwane who had been regional director of the International Union for the Conservation of Nature. The Environment Resource Centre for Southern Africa has been named in his honour. After our departure Kalomo educated, among others, Hakainde Hichilema, twice runner up for the presidency and the governor of the Bank of Zambia, Dr. Denny Kalyalya.

Back in England, Edyth began a project collecting the stories and reflections of expatriate teachers who worked in Zambia during the immediate pre- and post-independence period. She was not aiming to write a book but to create an archive which might be useful to future students of educational history. This material is available for researchers. We also renewed contact with Francis Makambwe who ran the Boy Scouts at Chizongwe. He had become an Anglican priest and moved to London where he was an extremely popular vicar. He set up a charity, Fighting Poverty in Zambia, with the aim of supporting development in his home area, Petauke in the Eastern Province. He brought me onto his committee and I have visited the two villages where we have financed water projects. The charity continues after his death, mainly funding education for young people in the Northern Province. The creation of a voluntary service movement in Zambia is described in chapter 8.

Reflections on ten years in Northern Rhodesia / Zambia

Boarding schools in Africa, based loosely on the British public school tradition, were of course a tool of colonial cultural domination and teachers like me were part of the system even as we supported liberation from it. All over the former empires the policy of removing children from their culture has provoked controversy, the cases in Australia and North America being the most shocking. In Zambia no children were forced to go to boarding schools – though sending children to school was seen as a way of creating wage earners who could pay colonial taxes. But as elsewhere modern education created divisions in society. Sometimes these were harmless such as when Kalomo students insisted on dressing in their smart school uniforms and polished shoes when visiting their village. Members of the urban elite created by education became estranged from their relatives still living in the villages. Some students suffered from psychiatric problems trying to bridge the gap.

Whatever problems it may have created, African leaders and African people wanted development – and schools and universities were the means of achieving this. They jumped on the westernizing bandwagon: farmers wanting tractors when they were not necessarily appropriate; churchmen rejecting African drums. This was all part of the very rapid change which speeded up after Independence.

For me it was a fantastic privilege to experience the rapid change in Zambia over these ten years. School syllabuses had to be made relevant. Edyth and I contributed to changes in the teaching of French, history and geography. I had arrived in the country when the racial segregation typical of the British Empire, exacerbated by the presence of settlers who wanted political control, was starting to break down. The rise of nationalism meant that the African population could no longer be marginalised as before. In Northern Rhodesia, as in Nyasaland, the political influence of the white settlers dissolved in the course of my three years at Fort Jameson. The new government of independent Zambia relied a lot on some of the more liberal colonial civil servants who remained and, thanks to the high price of copper, was able to recruit many foreign advisers as well as personnel vital for the ambitious development strategy of the government. The large expatriate staff at Kalomo Secondary School was replicated in nearly all the government secondary schools and in many other fields; and, as we saw, it could lead to tensions, but most of the teachers were excellent and did help to multiply the vitally needed number of educated and trained Zambians with impressive speed. The new state got off to a good start.

The copper mining company, Anglo American Corporation, produced a film, *Zambia 64* which captures the optimism of Independence. It features Alick Nkhata singing an ABC of all aspects of the country: Africa, birth, copper, death, education, food, game parks, health, Independence, Kaunda, Lusaka, marriage, news, overseas links, politics, relaxing, subsistence, the twist (which was all the rage), unemployment, Victoria Falls, water, youth and Zambia. J represented the agony aunt in the African Mail's column, *Tell Me Josephine*[19], who responded to all kinds of personal problems. Alick introduced clips showing aspects of traditional culture (Lozi Makishi and Ngoni dancers) contrasted with modern life and music (Q for the Bartholomew Bwalya Quintet and the Congolese-style band led by Baba Gaston).

---

19. "Josephine" was actually Barbara Hall who in her retirement produced the crossword in the London Sunday Times for very many years. Her husband, Richard Hall had co-founded and edited the African Mail and wrote a number of books about Zambia and Africa.

The first ten years of Zambia were full of hope and progress. Money was spent – perhaps a little too freely since everything cost more due to the sanctions against Rhodesia. The major roads to the north – the "hell run" to Tanzania, to Chipata and Malawi in the east and to Bulozi in the west were tarred; hundreds of schools were built and education was free; the university started to grow fast; Zambia Airways took off; health provision improved; embassies were opened; the new currency (100 ngwee = 1 kwacha) was launched at the rate of K2 to a British pound – and it even rose higher briefly. President Kaunda kept his nerve in the face of threats from Rhodesia and South Africa.

It was good to leave Zambia when things were going well, although the tensions we saw back in Fort Jameson between the militant grass roots of UNIP and the intellectuals and technocrats who would be the leaders of the Civil Service still rankled. I had experienced this at a seminar attended by President Kaunda, party members and top administrators in 1968. Valentine Musakanya, then head of the Civil Service, wrote: "... *the President's intention... was the total politicisation of the administration to ensure the Party's and his own continuity in power. My motives were to... ensure the eventual creation and stabilisation of a national administration to serve the people impartially, so the politicians might come and go.*" After we left the country the price of oil rose in 1973 and the copper price started to fall in 1975 and Zambia had to face much tougher times. As Musakanya feared, Zambia became a One-Party State in 1973. During this period Kaunda tended to be heavy-handed and suspicious of all opponents but he was at heart a decent and moral man. The weakening economy and the ambitions of increasingly vocal educated people – and political changes elsewhere in Africa – led to pressure which forced Kaunda to agree to a multi-party constitution in 1991. The election of that year sent Kaunda and UNIP into the political wilderness. I was visiting Zambia just before these elections. Everyone I met, apart from one former student from the Eastern Province (which UNIP was to win), forecast Kaunda's defeat. Sadly, his advisers had only told him what he wanted to hear and he got quite a shock when he heard the results. Nevertheless he handed over power gracefully to the Movement for Multi-Party Democracy (MMD) and the trade union leader, Frederick Chiluba, became president. My friend Elias Chipimo served as Chair of the MMD for five years and he served Chiluba as an ambassador but I think his support waned towards the end.

Under Chiluba's ultra-liberal economic policy the country lost most of its industry and corruption prospered. I recall a slogan on a wall in Lusaka: "MMD – Movement of Mandrax Dealers." His attempt to change the rules and stand for a third term in 2002 was defeated and he left office mired in corruption scandals. The MMD provided two more presidents, the popular Levy Mwanawasa who was replaced on his early death by Rupiah Banda. A second change of ruling party occurred in 2011 when Michael Sata of the Patriotic Front won. Michael Sata died in 2015 and in a close but peaceful election his colleague Edgar Lungu became Zambia's sixth president. The atmosphere became very sour and confrontation became more ethnic than before when Lungu won again in 2016 and Hakainde Hichilema, the Kalomo boy, was briefly imprisoned and continues to be harassed. Zambia had become something of a model democracy where governments could be voted out and political violence was very rare. I hope this tradition will not now be lost.

I have been back to Zambia many times. Some of the visits are recorded below. In the villages, there has not been much change, though communications are better, thanks especially to mobile phones. The towns have grown bigger and more socially, rather than racially, divided. Lusaka has glossy shopping malls while the old main street, Cairo Road is run down. There have been traffic jams for many years and they have got worse. Traffic on the main road north to the Copperbelt is now seriously heavy. Visiting Chipata in 2015 the town was big and bustling, a contrast from the small and sleepy Fort Jameson where I first arrived to work in Zambia. There are fewer internal flights than in colonial days, but most of the roads have improved since then and many bus companies, some "luxury" and others far from it, compete for customers. Arriving at the bus station you find a bus which appears to be half full and promising to depart soon. In fact many of the people sitting in the bus are not travelling but are there to fool you. It can be a very long wait till the bus is really full and sets off.

When we were at Kalomo the railway had a monopoly on the route from Lusaka to Livingstone. Now even the Zambezi Express with its comfortable coaches, originally from South Africa, takes 17 hours from Livingstone to Lusaka. Understandably most people go by bus. However, the government seems finally to be taking railways seriously. It has announced that heavy and bulk goods would be compelled to use rail and was making a feasibility study on the rehabilitation of the main line which runs from the Copperbelt to the Zimbabwe border. A line from Malawi to Chipata opened in 2010 and a contract has been signed with the Chinese for a huge project for a 400 mile extension to link up with the Tanzania Zambia (TAZARA) line. This is only one example of the numerous Chinese projects in Zambia which are useful for the development of infrastructure, but Zambia should beware of allowing the Chinese to buy too much land or other assets or this risks becoming a new colonialism.

3

Travels, mainly in West Africa

i) Sierra Leone and back 1963

Dis ting you like so, it belongs to me
Show your money, pay as you go into.

(*A big hit in Sierra Leone in 1963*)

In 1963 I flew from Northern Rhodesia to Sierra Leone, Salone as it is known to its friends, to visit Iye, who had been my girlfriend back in London. Crossing Africa by air was in some ways better than it is today. I started on the skybus from Fort Jameson to Lusaka and flew on to Salisbury (now Harare). From there to Brazzaville it felt like luxury on the French colonial airline UAT (which four months later changed its name to UTA). There was a smell of *cuisine* as we boarded the plane. A hot night in a hotel with a noisy air-conditioner at Brazzaville was followed by breakfast among the bougainvillea on the terrace with a view across the Congo river to Leopoldville (now Kinshasa). I changed planes at Douala in Cameroon, the wettest city in Africa. It was pelting with rain when the plane landed and a long line of hostesses walked up to the plane carrying umbrellas to conduct us to the terminal building. The next stop was Lagos where I was welcomed at the Ghana High Commission by a friend of Iye's and we went to a press party to promote films about Ghana. The next stop was Accra where I found myself at another party, hosted this time by the Sudanese Ambassador and ended up eating a kebab in a strip club.

The flight from Lagos along the coast was a vivid geography lesson. The plane was a Fokker Friendship, a very user-friendly small plane which had its windows under the wings and it flew very low as it had to make short hops to Cotonou (in Dahomey, now Benin) and Lomé (Togo). Along this part of the coast we looked down on the tropical sandy beach fringed with coconut palms and small fishing settlements and, just inland much of the way, a parallel lagoon.

Coming to Nigeria and Ghana from Northern Rhodesia in 1963 was like bursting into a new, liberated world. Here people were proudly wearing *agbadas*, *kente* cloth and topknots, and hotels served African food. This was a wonderful contrast to the claustrophobic atmosphere in colonial-settler states in southern Africa with their regimented African townships and an apparent lack of confidence in African culture. Stopping in Accra I went to see Kwame Nkrumah's new Volta Dam being built at Akosombo with Jenny, a friend of Edyth's. The Volta Hotel was already open so we had a drink with a view of the half-built dam wall and drove back in the rain to Accra. Jenny then took me to a party at the Sudan embassy: a strange mixture of people mostly talking French and at one point having a passionate argument as to whether Paris was more beautiful than Beirut. Nkrumah was still in power in Ghana but security was tight. It was only six years after Ghana's Independence but there was tension in Accra. In spite of his many achievements the president had a lot of political enemies.

Leaving Accra and after touching down at Abidjan and Robertsfield (Liberia) I reached Lungi Airport in Sierra Leone where Iye and her friends were waiting to take me over the ferry to Freetown. "De man tire," they remarked, and truly I was exhausted from the journey.

Sierra Leone had been independent for just two years and the popular and moderate Prime Minister, Sir Milton Margai, was still alive. Tension was to build up later when his half-brother Albert Margai came to power and ran a harsher régime. Freetown is blurred in my memory: the lovely old wooden houses, the steep hill up to Fourah Bay College, the ancient cotton tree in the city centre. My two weeks involved meeting Iye's numerous friends and relatives; the wedding of our hosts with a speech from Banja Tejan-Sie who was the Speaker of the parliament; a play at the British

Council theatre; much chewing of kola nut and lots of jollof rice, sweet potatoes and fufu. One meal I could not recommend was meant to be a special treat, the Sunday breakfast of cold fufu with spicy palm oil sauce.

The narrow-gauge railway was still running in 1963, operated by steam trains. Our first trip out of town was on the "express" train from Water Street station. My only bad moment was when the train was pulling out of the terminus. I had my arm on the window ledge and my watch was ripped off. After that we settled down to an incredibly slow journey through places with evocative names like Hastings and Waterloo, typical villages in the original colony peopled by freed slaves. We called on Iye's mother at Rotifunk, the railway junction in the centre of the country. She fed us an omelette and we jumped on another train to Bo, the country's very small second city. Sankoh had first introduced me to Iye in London. Now he was a teacher at Bo School, a boys' boarding school dating from 1906 and one of the country's most prestigious. On our return to Freetown the train took twelve hours to do 150 miles. It is understandable that as soon as the roads were improved the railway had to close. On another day we hired a car and went inland to visit Iye's aunt. We returned past the iron mine and slag heap at Marampa. We turned off the main road to following the tortuous narrow road with thick forest on both sides, circling Freetown's peninsula, passing through the villages of York and Sussex.

We went to a party, the significance of which only became evident later. We were invited by David Lansana and his wife, Komeh. We got there very late. He struck me as a very charismatic person in his flowing blue boubou and woolly hat and she, I wrote in my diary, was "thin and delightful." We drank quite a lot of beer. Lansana went on later to become commander of the army and, when Siaka Stevens narrowly beat Albert Margai for the presidency in March 1967, Lansana staged a coup and arrested Stevens. Weeks later he was himself overthrown and both he and Sorie Forna, the brilliant former finance minister and father of the well-known writer, Aminatta Forna, were executed for treason.

99

It was sad to leave Iye but I knew my future would be with Edyth. My journey home took me for a few hours to Conakry in Guinea where I found a mammy wagon[20] to go into the city. Guinea, led by Sekou Touré, had voted No to President De Gaulle's neo-colonial referendum in 1958 and the French left in a huff, cutting off telephone wires and trying to make the country ungovernable. Kwame Nkrumah immediately invited him to join a union with Ghana which Mali later joined. E.K. Mensah's song, *Ghana, Guinea, Mali* was a big hit.[21] In the streets of Conakry in 1963 there was plenty of evidence of Sekou Toure's socialism: banners proclaiming power to the people, slogans from *La Voix de la Révolution* booming from a loudspeaker van and shops selling badges, t-shirts and records. I never visited Guinea again but my Malian friend, Diapy Diawara, tells the beautiful story of his encounter with Sekou Touré in Annex 6.

I had a day back in Accra with Jenny, visiting the old town and Legon University, Ghana's rather self-conscious version of Oxbridge. Another day in Lagos was followed by a further stopover in Brazzaville which allowed me a quick ride on the ferry to Leopoldville (now Kinshasa) where I found the legendary Ngoma record shop and stocked up on 45rpm records of the Congolese music I had been listening to on Radio Brazzaville back in Fort Jameson.

I was to visit Salone again in 1991 as a guest of the Voluntary Workcamps Association of Sierra Leone. By then the country was really going downhill: the uninspiring President Momoh would be overthrown four months after my visit and civil war would follow. The economy was in bad shape and power cuts were long and frequent. Edmund Kamara invited me to stay in his family's handsome old wooden house in Waterloo. There had been no electricity in Waterloo for six months but on my second day there was a sudden crackling sound and lights flickered on. Before people had time to celebrate there was a small explosion and fire began to move along the overhead wire. People ran to throw water up at

---

20. A mammy wagon is a lorry converted into a bus with a painted wooden structure on the back and benches for seats They are found all over West Africa
21. You can hear it on YouTube.

the flames as they advanced towards the house next to Edmund's. The village returned to candlelight.

We went to visit the creek where slaves had once been loaded on to ships going west. A huge rusty chain for holding the slaves still lies by the water's edge. From the first arrival of the Portuguese at the end of the 15th century up until the mid-18th century slaves were taken from this area; and only after 1792 was the flow reversed and Freetown become a haven for the liberated ones.

We also visited an old airfield converted into a camp for Liberian refugees. There were neat rows of huts with walls made of banana leaves and the ubiquitous blue UN tarpaulin sheets as roofs. A makeshift primary school and a mosque had been constructed too, and young men were playing volleyball in a clearing in the bush. A few miles further on at Mabuveh we called in at the Workcamps Association's long-term project, a farm with pawpaw and mango trees and a small house where volunteers could stay. This place was to be attacked during the civil war.

ii) Who knows tomorrow? 1971

Edyth and I returned from Zambia to England in 1971. The journey took three months and took us through eighteen countries, to nineteen museums, on twenty-four trains, sixteen buses, sixteen shared taxis, seven lorries and mammy-wagons, six boats, five short flights, seven lifts in private cars, three canoes and a hovercraft. These statistics require some definition. What is the difference between a bus and a taxi if the taxi has sixteen people squeezed inside? Does a canoe with one passenger count as a boat? Several countries on our route have subsequently changed their name. Zaire, the former Belgian Congo is now the Democratic Republic of Congo, Dahomey is Benin, Upper Volta is Burkina Faso, Spanish Sahara has been occupied by Morocco.

It was New Year's Day and the journey began disastrously. We turned up at Ndola station for a Zairian railcar due at 13.30 to take us to Lubumbashi, the former Elizabethville. A station official told us it was not running. Then he made a phone call and said it was on the way. A few hours later some tired people appeared on the railway line. They had walked from where the railcar had broken down. It was dusk when Zambia Railways tried to shunt a passenger coach on to a goods train which was due to leave for Zaire. A goods wagon came off the rails before our eyes. I should point out that Zambia is a heavy drinking country and perhaps New Year's Day is not the best day to choose to travel. Finally, after a customs official on a bicycle had checked our luggage, a special one coach steam train finally took the small group of hopeful passengers to the Zaire border station at Sakania. Here a Zambia Railways official assured us that a platelayer's trolley would come for us in three hours. We bought tickets and immigrated. We shared the bread and cheese we had fortunately brought with us and waited. There was a heavy rainstorm which turned most of the platform to mud. Then came the news that the promised trolley had also broken down. They would send another one, but in the meantime would we like to sleep in the *maison de passage*, the hostel for engine drivers? There were seven of us, a British volunteer working in Botswana, an African American with his two sons, a Zairian with no passport and ourselves. We got one of the two beds – and there was even a bathroom and a fridge.

In the morning the sun came up and the trolley arrived. It turned out to be a smart little green inspection car with seats for the seven of us. The once a week train onward from Lubumbashi was due to depart at 09.00 when we were still far away, racing along the track. It was a relief to find the train still waiting for us when we arrived after midday. Chatting later with some of the other passengers brought the response: "So it was you, was it?"

We spent the next three days in this train. Some people had commented that we were travelling home the hard way. Yet for these three days we travelled First Class in the kind of luxury that existed before the advent of air travel: a cabin for two, clean linen every night, a shower and enormous well-cooked meals. Sparkman, the African-American, was a sports instructor travelling with his two sons, born of Somali mothers in Ethiopia. They were on their way to settle in Liberia, where African-Americans reputedly got citizenship within twenty-four hours. We had interesting discussions with Sparkman about blackness and colonialism. This southern part of Zaire, the province of Katanga (which Mobutu named Shaba), was much like Zambia – bush country, scrubby woodland known in the trade as *miombo*, peppered with tall brownish red anthills. Like Zambia this is the Congo/Zaire's copper producing area. For the first part of the journey the line is (or was) electrified. This was no express but it moved at a reasonable pace. At Likasi (the former Jadotville) crowds of children cheered as the train went past. The next morning as we got up to a view of open grassland we crossed the River Congo and the forest began to get thicker. Still three hours late, we stopped at Kabondo-Dianda where the sellers of cassava and fish on the station seemed to be doing bad business. At Kamina there was a scheduled stop of ninety minutes and here steam replaced electric traction. The food sellers here were corralled outside a security fence and had to sell their snacks though the wire mesh.

On Day 4 arriving at Kaulu we were puzzled to hear a regular thumping sound. It turned out to be wooden logs being thrown into the locomotive's tender. We were entering one of the world's greatest forest zones and the train was wood-burning from here to the terminus at Port Francqui. We were only two hours late when we reached Luluabourg (now Kananga), the capital of Kasai Occidental province, and it reached Port Francqui (now Ilebo) at 0810 on Day 5, only ten minutes late.

The Belgians had devised a workable transport network in the Congo, as I had learned from my geography teacher at school. This consisted of river steamers and freight barges on the navigable rivers run by the state company, OTRACO, connecting with stretches of railway. Only in the south of the country could this be called a rail network. Our 1,400 kilometre line from Sakania to Port Francqui was the backbone, with a main line running west from Likasi to Dilolo, continuing to the port of Lobito on the coast of Angola and another substantial line branching off northwards to Kamina and splitting at Kabalo to reach Albertville (now Kalemie) on Lake Tanganyika and Kindu on the Congo River. The oldest line in the country had been built to avoid the rapids on the Congo River between Leopoldville, the capital, and the coast. This was in the days of King Leopold's notorious regime where local people were treated worse than slaves and many lives were lost during its construction. Another tiny stretch of line ran from Stanleyville (now Kisangani) to Ponthierville (now Ubundu) to by-pass another set of rapids. Katharine Hepburn and Humphrey Bogart travelled on this line to the location where they filmed *The African Queen* in 1951.[22] Finally there was the isolated Haut-Uélé line in the north from the Congo river at Bumba to Isiro. The last two sections are now closed and overgrown. The line from Kabalo to Kindu also fell out of use. The story of its reopening and my small part in it is described in chapter10.

Port Francqui (Ilebo) was named after the Belgian soldier, diplomat and business man, Emile Francqui, who spent time in the Belgian Congo and became the first president of the Prince Leopold Institute of Tropical Medicine in Antwerp. In 1971 Port Francqui was one of the country's main interchanges, with two huge cranes for transferring freight between trains and river steamers. We tried to buy tickets for the boat but we only had travellers' cheques, which Otraco would not accept. The captain and the harbourmaster could not be found, but we met a Portuguese who drove us up the hill to his snack bar and changed our money. (Earlier there had been a large Portuguese supermarket in the town. The Portuguese, like the Greeks, Lebanese and Indians were the trading class in much of colonial Africa). When we finally went on board Sparkman and his sons were still with us and we were joined by a couple from Denmark.

We were to spend three days on this boat, the *Major Vangu*. Standards had slipped more than on the train and our first-class cabin smelt musty. The River Kasai is a mere tributary of the Congo but it is huge, with thick tropical forest hanging over into the water on both sides, the trunks of the trees looking almost pink in the afternoon sun. The river steamer pushed along a freight barge, several small barges for local passengers and a brown barge with a roof for second and third-class passengers. We stopped at a

---

22. See the story of the *Liemba* in chapter 12(ii).

number of villages, staying midstream while a fleet of canoes pulled out from the shore, selling sacks of white cassava flour, bunches of plantains, pineapples, fish, goats, chickens and even a live cow from the loaded quayside. From the deck we had a panoramic view over the barges and back upstream and we unhappily watched the cow being slaughtered and cut up for meat. On the evening of the second day the boat called at Bandundu, the only real town on the river and a provincial capital. We went for a walk into the town with its charming brick church framed in palm trees. As we left there was a perfect sunset over the wide river. We thought the River Kasai was wide, but the next morning we joined the Congo river which was wider still, faster flowing and full of clumps of bright green floating water hyacinth, a pest but nonetheless a pretty sight.

We did not spend much time in Kinshasa (which had only recently changed its name from Leopoldville). I had been there twice, in 1963 as described above and in 1967 when Edyth and I had stopped over on the way home on leave. On that occasion we had the chance to choose between two concerts by famous musicians: Le Docteur Nico and Tabu Ley Rochereau. We chose Dr. Nico and it turned out to be the contest, at an open air swimming pool, to choose Miss African Fiesta Sukisa 1967. The women were stunning in their shiny finery with even shinier headwraps and the music was wonderful "classical" *soukous*. We had stayed in a small hotel, La Résidence, which had seen better days. The Belgian lady who ran it explained the way into town: "You turn left at *le Roi Albert*... but King Albert is no longer there." In fact his huge monument still stands today, minus the king.

At the time of our journey there was some kind of stand-off between the governments of Zaire and Congo-Brazzaville, perhaps due to differences between Mobutu, the anti-communist pet of the Americans (although he pretended to glorify the legacy of Lumumba), and President Marien Ngouabi in Brazzaville, a self-styled socialist. Anyway, one result of this was that when we picked up our collection of visas in Lusaka for the former French colonies we could not get one for Congo-Brazzaville. Only French and local people were allowed on the ferry. So we had to take a plane

105

to Libreville, the capital of the densely forested, resource-rich and thinly populated Republic of Gabon.

Libreville seemed smart and clean after Kinshasa and, as we soon discovered, it was one of the most expensive cities in the world. It also rained a lot, but it had one of the best museums we visited. We sat by the palm-fringed beach and had a swim close to where, twenty-two years later, the plane carrying the Zambian football team was to plunge into the ocean. Walking into the city, a procession of motorbikes appeared followed by the car containing President Albert Bernard Bongo. Five fighter planes flew overhead. (The official photo on every wall showed him bedecked with medals, standing with his hand on a gold and leather Bible against a Versailles-type background. Presumably a new photo was taken later when he converted to Islam and changed his name to El Hadj Omar Bongo). Gabon remains one of France's neo-colonies where stability means power handed down from Bongo *père* to his son, Ali, in spite of what claims to be a multi-party constitution. Gabon is a major oil producer and has manganese, iron and tropical hardwood, giving it the third highest average per capita income in Africa. Most of this income goes to the very rich while most Gabonese remain on low incomes with the large population of immigrants, mainly from Cameroon, at the bottom of the heap. French, often in a pidgin version, is spoken by everyone, though in fact when the explorer Mary Kingsley passed through in 1895 pidgin English was in common use along the coast.

Early on day twelve we set off from Libreville in a smart little blue bus named *Grâce à toi* on a good tarmac road through a forest of tall trees with bananas growing beneath them. After the tarmac ended we arrived in a long queue of lorries, cars and buses at the Kango ferry. All the passengers were sheltering under a large tree and there were market stalls and little restaurants. I had a plate of rice and fish. It seems that the wife of a minister was in our bus. She sent a boy across in a canoe with a note to the *sous-préfecture* so that our bus could jump the queue and it got priority. It raced along (mostly tarmac again) and finally descended to the huge Ogoowe River, crossing by another ferry to Lambaréné.

PIC 9) *Dr. Schweitzer's Hospital at Lambaréné, Gabon, 1971.*

This little town is probably the best-known place in Gabon because it is the home of Dr. Albert Schweitzer's pioneering hospital. The bus dropped us outside the pretty but shabby *Hotel d'Angleterre.* We booked in and Edyth had a shower, but a young man who had been on the bus with us, persuaded us that we should really go to *"Chez Choisère,"* meaning Schweitzer's hospital. He accompanied us on *pirogue,* a canoe across the river and introduced us to Dr. Ari, who invited us to dine at a lamp-lit table with vegetarian food. Dr. Ari rang a bell and introduced us to the international staff and volunteers of the hospital. By then it was too late to go back for our luggage and we stayed the night.

Albert Schweitzer was a great celebrity in his day. Born in Alsace when it was German, he was a gifted organist as well as being a pastor, a theologian and a musicologist but he decided to become a medical missionary in Africa. So he went off to study medicine and, having acquired the necessary expertise, he founded his hospital in 1913. As a German working a French colony he was interned a year later when war broke out, but he returned after the war to develop the hospital, funding it with his organ recitals in Europe and with donations from all over the world. He was a paternalist who wanted to cure leprosy, to help Africans rather than befriend them. He wanted the villagers who came as patients to the hospital to suffer no culture shock, so the buildings had to be basic; families would come and cook; the beds were arranged in twos so that patients could have a friend or relative to watch and be with them; there was to be no electricity, except in the operating theatre. John Gunther in his book *Inside Africa* describes his visit to the hospital in 1954 when Schweitzer was alive: he was struck by the doctor's lack of interest in Africa. He had not visited anywhere else, he spoke no African language although he was a gifted linguist. He loved animals more than Africans. He was obsessive about the rule that white people had to wear a solar topi (pith helmet) whenever they were outside. Schweitzer even wore one in the dark. Gunther also found the hospital untidy and careless about basic hygiene.

By the time of his death in 1965 Gabon was independent, prosperous and modernising itself. Schweitzer seemed something of an anachronism, but by 1971 the hospital had already moved a little more with the times. The buildings were still simple wooden constructions with red corrugated iron roofs nestling under the huge trees; and families still came to cook. The place was certainly modest compared to a modern hospital and therefore perhaps, as the *grand docteur* wanted, a place where sick villagers would not feel intimidated. By 1971 there were more Gabonese doctors in Paris than in the whole of Gabon, and none at Schweitzer's hospital. Leprosy was no longer the main challenge and the state covered half the hospital's running costs. The doctor, who received the Nobel Peace Prize in 1952, is still revered today. We watched a candle being lit under his portrait, as was done each evening, followed by prayers, alternately in German and French; we saw his study, preserved as it was in his day – except that his piano had been sent back to Germany; we visited his grave and the grave of a tame deer he loved. His love of animals extended even to ants: he would put a piece of fish in a cage on his desk to attract ants so that his cat could not kill them. His motto was *"respect de la vie"*.

The next morning we returned by *pirogue* to the town, collected our luggage and tried unsuccessfully to change money. We spent our last 1,500 cfa francs on a boat trip up the river to see some lakes and spent the afternoon and night back at the hospital where the accountant kindly changed our travellers' cheques. The next day was 14 January, Schweitzer's birthday, when songs would be sung outside his room, but we left early, crossing the mighty river back to town and on to the first bus north to Bifoun. It was a bossy twelve-seater with notices not to fight, spit, vomit, put your hands out or even touch the windows! It had rained heavily and the main road was a sea of mud, but in Gabon they block the road to heavy vehicles with a *barrière de pluie* until the rain stops and the road dries out a bit.

At Bifoun we got the front seats in a huge Mercedes lorry, driven by a very friendly Monsieur David who owned six lorries and was collecting cocoa from the north of the country. As soon as the barrier opened we followed this well-maintained dirt road, the main – indeed the only – route north, the *grand axe routier,* a red-brown ribbon winding through hills and through the dense tropical forest, with the corrugated iron roofs of the occasional villages strung along the roadside. Trucks carrying huge logs a metre in diameter were coming in the other direction. We had also seen rafts carrying the same hardwood down the Ogoowe river. David was a member of the Jehovah's Witnesses, a sect banned in Gabon and Cameroon. He had been to France and Germany and preferred the Germans. He admitted that when in Paris he had gone everywhere by taxi, imagining that, as in Africa, taxis were the cheapest form of transport! After a long wait at another *barrière de pluie* we passed the monument commemorating a battle between the French and the Germans during the First World War, when Cameroon was *Kamerun*. David wished the Germans had won. Arriving in Oyem we found a hotel, *La Cabosse*, run by a grumpy French couple who offered us *assiette anglaise* (mainly cold meat) for supper. The next morning David took us on to Bitam, the most northerly town in Gabon, and we waited there for any kind of transport to the Cameroon border. A travelling dentist invited us to join him in a shared taxi and he took us to his house to wait. This must be one of the most beautiful of frontiers. The river Ntem is a wide strip of water with the foliage of the dense rain forest hanging over the shore. A few canoes passed along the river, reflected perfectly in the almost still water. There was a car ferry but it would only move if a car arrived. The only way for us to cross was in a small *pirogue* – one of us, plus suitcase, at a time.

Arrived in Cameroon and hoping for a lift, we sat under a tree and had our picnic of bread, sardines, pineapple and bananas. The rainforest was very green and silent. Mary Kingsley, writing in the 1890s, describes it best: *"the vast column-like tree stems in their countless thousands around you… so you get trained to your surroundings, you see more and more, and a whole world grows up gradually before your eyes… what seemed at first to be an inextricable tangle ceases to be so."* The peace was broken by a rattling, smelly, rickety Renault bus taking people to the ferry. It picked us up on the way back. Other passengers scrambled on board at different villages including two men who were teasing a pretty girl, saying they wanted to marry her but the dowry was too high. At the first town, Ambam, our passports were stamped and we found another bus going north to Ebolowa but the driver would not move until the bus was full. We paid a bit extra and the driver, known as *le chauffeur rouge,* drove on and delivered us to the Splendid Hotel, promising to collect us the following morning to take us on to the capital, Yaoundé. The hotel was anything but splendid. It was clean but the door did not lock so we quickly bought some kebabs and doughnuts and ate them in the ballroom, the most splendid – though faded – part of the hotel.

Day 16 and the *chauffeur rouge* came for us at 5.20am but before setting off he had to fill the bus. He circled around the town shouting "Yaoundé, Yaoundé" and the bus began to fill. After three hours of this the driver got news that a soldier at the barracks wanted a seat, so we went to collect him and finally, packed tight, we set off. We reached Yaoundé mid-morning. The city is built on several hills and is quite attractive, though larger and more polluted today than it was in 1971. We walked up towards the white presidential palace and booked in at Hotel Bellevue. President Biya subsequently fenced off the whole area around the palace, so our hotel no longer exists. Later he had a new palace built and the elegant old one has now become one of Africa's finest museums

PIC 10) *Crossing the River Ntem into Cameroon, 1971.*

The German colony of Kamerun had been split into two after the defeat of the Germans in 1918 with a small part in the west awarded to Britain and the rest to France as League of Nations mandates. In the French zone a struggle mainly by the Bamileke and Bassa fought for genuine independence and was brutally crushed by the French, supported by people from other parts of the country.[23] The type of independence prescribed for Cameroon in 1960 was to be the template for the other French territories that became part of the neo-colonial family of *Françafrique*. The southern part of the British zone, Southern Cameroons, was incorporated in 1961 while the northern part voted to stay as part of Nigeria. The French system and language remained and remains dominant. The Anglophones have always resented this and as I write this resentment has grown into a serious rebellion. The policy of bilingualism of course only refers to the official languages. The country has amazing ethnic diversity and many languages are spoken, Ewondo

---

23. The UPC leaders were eliminated: Ernest Ouandié and Bishop Albert Ndongmo were executed, Ruben Um Nyobe and Félix Moumié killed. The great Cameroonian writer, Mongo Beti supported the rebellion and his book, *Main basse sur le Cameroun* was banned in France. His widow still runs a bookshop in Yaoundé.

being the dominant one in Yaoundé. Pidgin English is the street language in the coastal area and in the largest city, Douala. I am fascinated by pidgin and Creole languages and I treasure the copy of St. Mark's gospel that Lois Carter, my colleague at IVS who had been a volunteer teacher at Ndu, gave me later, entitled *De gud news hawe Saint Mark bi ratam* (The good news how St. Mark wrote it.).

My only souvenir of Yaoundé is a *n'gol.* This is a small bronze hand bell made in Chad, perhaps used as a fetish, representing General De Gaulle who was something of a cult figure in this part of Africa which rallied to the Free French during the Second World War. We stayed three days in Yaoundé and needed the rest. In 1971 it was calm and not too crowded. We attended the Presbyterian Church where we were easily the worst dressed people. We found the Nigerian Embassy which had received a letter I had sent from Zambia and they gave us our entry permit. We went to the embassy of Equatorial Guinea, which we thought would be an interesting country to visit. The Ambassador sat us down and told us with the aid of a brochure how beautiful his country was – but that sadly he was not allowed to give us a visa. The brutal first president of this tiny, formerly Spanish territory, Francisco Macias Nguema, was still in control. As I write, the almost equally unpleasant second president, Teodoro Obiang Nguema, is still in power and is obscenely rich due to the little country's huge oil wealth, very little of which reaches any but the tiny ruling elite.

Day 19 and we caught the 6am railcar from Yaoundé to Douala. Food sellers besieged the train at almost every stop with eggs, fish, bread, salad, sandwiches, coconut milk and ice cream. The scenery, as all over southern Cameroon, was lush and varied, forest at first with the tall grass brushing the side of the train, through tunnels and over ravines, with more coconut palms as we neared the coast. We had been given the address of the *Eglise Centenaire,* up on a hill, where the Paris Missionary Society had a guest house and it was all very friendly. We had the idea that we could go on by boat to Calabar or Port Harcourt in Nigeria so we went all round the port, upstairs and down, always being referred to someone else. It finally became clear that very few boats went along the coast and that those that did would not take passengers. We visited the museum, a wonderful collection but very dusty with labels misplaced and probably untouched since Independence. The guide appeared to know less than the labels and at one point he opened a cupboard and tried to sell us some Bamileke pipes and a sculpture which we guessed may have been part of the collection.

A young Swiss couple who were also at the guest house gave us a lift to Kumba where they wanted to visit a farm school. Kumba is in the Anglophone part of Cameroon and everyone was talking pidgin English. We had planned to take a bush taxi from Kumba to Mamfe on the road to Nigeria but we discovered that traffic on this bad, narrow road went north on one day and south the next. So we booked a bed for the following night at the Dynamic Hotel and continued with our friends down through large commercial plantations of banana trees, protected with blue plastic sheeting, coffee, cocoa, rubber and finally oil palms to Victoria on the coast. Victoria (now renamed Limbe) is situated on a beautiful bay with a string of little islands across it. Mount Cameroon, the tallest mountain in western Africa, was hazy in the distance, peeping over some low foothills which had been cleared of their forest cover. Kids shouted "white man" in quite a friendly way. The youth centre where we stayed was run by a bouncy man called Primo, another Swiss. He took us for a swim at the Club, very British, he said – even the meals were lousy. We passed a couple of hotels which, he said, were full of large groups of Germans on package tours, perhaps nostalgic for this former German colony.

Day 21 in the afternoon we drove east along a winding road full of potholes through the palm and rubber plantations and finally, on the only good road we encountered in Cameroon, back to Douala. André dropped us at the station. The train consisted of a big diesel engine and two coaches. It set off at 4pm but after about an hour it stopped and the word went around: "*Machine done die. Dey go fix um.*" After an hour we moved forward again. A bearded man befriended us and wanted to know all about the underground trains in London. At 8pm the machine died again, totally this time. "*Dey go push um.*" The engine driver climbed up the telegraph pole and sent a message for help. This finally arrived and it was midnight when we finally got to our bed in the Dynamic Hotel.

PIC 11) *On the road in Nigeria, 1971.*

The great scholar and explorer, Mary Kingsley described this part of West Africa brilliantly. She wrote that a new road being built by the Germans up to Buea, on the slopes of Mount Cameroon, now the capital of the Anglophone zone, as *"quite the most magnificent of roads... that I have seen anywhere in West Africa... as broad as Oxford Street, on either side of it are deep drains to carry off the surface waters."*[24] The road we took from Kumba to Mamfe seventy-seven years later would have shocked Mary Kingsley. It had once been tarred and there were small bits of tar remaining which the driver of our creaking mammy wagon, a Muslim who sang little songs as he drove, had to dodge. After five hours of hill and jungle we arrived at Mamfe. Our visa was expiring that day and we had hoped to get transport immediately to the Nigerian frontier but nothing was in sight. The Senior Officer at the police

---

24. Mary Kingsley's *Travels in West Africa* was published in 1897 and *West African Studies* in 1899. She quotes many African voices. My favourite is: *"White men are fish not men. They are able to stay a little while on the land but at last they mount their ships again and vanish over the horizon into the ocean. How can a fish possess land?"*

station said that to extend the visa meant going back to Buea. We were rescued by a Land Rover, appropriately named "Who Knows Tomorrow?" which agreed to take us to the Nigerian border for 4,000 francs. The vehicle then had to find some more passengers, mostly Nigerian Igbos, and there was a lot of argument about the fare. It was only 45 kilometres to the border but the road was terrible and there were stops at no less than four customs posts. At the final one we were the only passengers allowed to pass. The border post at Ekok was closed for the night when we arrived. We were very dirty but the kind immigration officer invited us to stay the night and gave us his very comfortable bed. With only 500 francs in our pockets after paying the taxi we had nothing to give him but a map and a large postcard of Trafalgar Square.

Early in the morning of day 23 we walked into Nigeria across the bridge over the Cross River, rather stagnant and not nearly so beautiful as the Ntem. The customs officers wondered how we had arrived so early. We ate our breakfast of bread and sardines with the soldiers performing their morning parade all around us. This area had been part of the breakaway state of Biafra during the Nigerian Civil War which had only ended a year before our arrival – and although this was not part of the heartland of the Igbo people who had created Biafra, there were still a lot of soldiers around. In Ikom we found an Irish priest who was the head of the local secondary school and he kindly changed some money and fed us on tea, grapefruit and Christmas cake.

A mammy wagon took us the 200 kilometres to Gboko. This vehicle was in fact a lorry with high wooden sides designed to carry everything, including people. This was probably our most uncomfortable ride so far, though it was a relief to stretch our legs from time to time at an army road block. We were squeezed in the front cab. I sat between the driver and the gear lever, which was between Edyth's legs. Next was a mother and her baby and finally a policeman who should presumably have charged the driver for overloading. On the back of the lorry was a quantity of plantains and a large number of passengers. It was very hot. Whereas Cameroon had been tropical forest, much of it cleared for cultivation, here we were back in open savannah country, the land of the Efik people. Their houses are rectangular and surrounded by family tombs with concrete statues, memorials of dead relatives, some wearing hats or pullovers. Further north, after passing Ogoja, we entered the country of the Tiv people whose houses are round and tall and thatched – and with no tombs in the garden.

Gboko is the centre of the Tiv country, nicknamed "heavy town" and reported more recently to have been Nigeria's biggest producer of marijuana. We were directed to a hotel called View Point (though there was no view) and we rested here till the following afternoon. Back in the Commonwealth – Cameroon had not yet become a member – breakfast was incredibly British: tea, corn flakes, egg, sausage and soggy toast. The ride to Makurdi, the capital of Benue State, was on the back of a mammy wagon carrying a varied lot of passengers including a man draped in cloth and carrying a dagger, bundles of yams and a lot of enamel basins. On the way there was a sudden bang: a tyre had burst and a woman leaped on to the road in panic.

Makurdi overlooks the wide Benue River, the most important tributary of the Niger, with an impressive iron bridge across it. We still owed 14s 6d – Nairas had not yet been introduced – for our stay at View Point which we duly paid to the owner, Jim Acka'a, at his office in Makurdi. We walked through the market where bald vultures stood on the roof. The government rest house was full but Jim and his wife offered to put us up. The house became a nursery school in the morning and we stayed there all day as the train to the north was due at midnight. In the event it did not arrive until 5am, so we spent the night on the station playing Scrabble. The delay allowed us to see the scenery, still dry savannah country with groups of houses surrounded by woven grass fences. The train climbed up on to the plateau with hazy views over the hills. Arriving at Kafanchan we had hoped to get a local train to Jos. A goods train was preparing to leave and we got a permit to travel on it but it seemed in no hurry to depart so we went to the lorry park[25] and found seats in a mammy wagon instead.

---

25. The West African name for a bus station.

Jos, the local nickname of which is J-town or *Jesus Our Saviour*, has recently been the scene of violence between Christians and Muslims, as have many of the northern cities. It is what was known in colonial times as a hill station, a place with a cooler temperature where the colonial officers could relax. There are many of these places in India – Darjeeling, Shimla, Ootacamund – and in the former German colonies: Lushoto in Tanzania, Buea in Cameroon and Missahohe in Togo. We decided to stop for a few days in Jos, for the climate and for its famous museum. After sweltering for days it was nice to need to wear a pullover in the evening. We ended up staying at the rest house of the Sudan United Mission which was full of evangelical Christians. One morning they suddenly called on me to pray at breakfast. I was not feeling well that day or I might have surprised them with the St. John's College Latin grace.

The National Museum lived up to expectations, though as I write I hear that it is now in poor condition. The Pottery Hall had a collection from all over Nigeria including *terracottas* from the Nok culture, some items from which have been dated to 500 BCE and which were first discovered near Jos by people mining for tin. This culture is the ancestor of the great Nigerian artistic traditions at Ife and Benin which are also represented in the museum – and no African country has a richer artistic heritage than Nigeria. There were also examples of traditional architecture, including a Tiv village with its pointed thatched roofs; beautiful clay and thatch grain stores; part of the Mosque from Zaria and of the walls of Kano, and scattered around the grounds were some ancient cars and a locomotive from the Bauchi Light Railway, which operated from 1914 until 1957 to carry tin from Jos to the main line at Zaria. A small zoo and aviary made use of some large rocks, around which cages had been constructed for the birds and a few small animals.

On February 2 (day 33) the Anglican vicar gave us a lift to Zaria. We passed no less than four overturned lorries on the way. The road went along the ridge of the plateau and the style of the houses became more distinctly northern, with flat roofs and gutters sticking out. Some even had mud domes. Zaria, formerly known as Zazzau and the capital of an Emirate of that name, has been an Islamic city since the 15th century. In fact we only visited the Ahmadu Bello University, now Nigeria's largest and named after the first premier of Northern Nigeria, the Sardauna (Sultan) of Sokoto, Alhaji Sir Ahmadu Bello. There was a demonstration the day we were there in solidarity with Adekunle Adepeju, a student at Ibadan University whom the police had shot and killed. From Zaria we hitch-hiked to Kano and were picked up by an agricultural officer who took us to visit a cotton market. Local farmers were standing around with their bales of cotton but were looking gloomy because apparently the buyers had run out of cash. On the way in to Kano he drove us past the famous pyramids of groundnuts, ready for export, then past the city walls, through a mass of cars, bicycles, scooters, handcarts and pedestrians and dropped us in the Sabon Gari, the non-Hausa quarter, at a small hotel run by an unsmiling Yoruba lady named Comfort. We must have been the first guests, as the bedclothes had to be unpacked, and no "chop" would be served for another week.

Kano is the throbbing heart of northern Nigeria and the largest city in the whole Sahel belt of West Africa. It has over 4 million inhabitants today but less than half that at the time of our visit. Kano had already seen serious ethnic tension in 1953 when the southerners were trying to bring party politics to the north. Then a terrible massacre of Igbos in 1966 helped provoke the civil war. After our visit there has been violence between Muslims and Christians since the 1980s and murderous attacks by Boko Haram in 2012 and 2014.

Rather disorientated after our first night at Comfort's hotel I asked a man the way to the old city. He shouted, "Bos, bos!" and a bus obligingly stopped and took us to one of the many gates through the crumbling walls of the old city. At the central market a young man called Zachary latched on to us and showed us round, through the narrow alleyways, everything built of mud brick. There were robed and turbaned merchants selling saddles, Tuareg and Hausa swords, embroidered saddle cloths, agate necklaces, carved calabashes and in contrast flip-flops, plastic buckets, tin trunks and imported toys. Boys with wide tin trays on their heads – and hurricane lamps for night time sales – sold grilled chicken legs and other delights. We had bought nothing on the trip this far apart from the *n'gol* in Yaoundé but we decided Kano was where we would shop: we bargained for sandals, hand woven and tie-dye cloth and three leather pouffes all packed in a camel skin grip.

We crossed the wide, dusty open space to visit the huge central mosque with its cool carpeted aisles and incense burners. For a small *dash* we were allowed to climb barefoot part way up one of the minarets and get a stunning view over this city of flat roofed mud houses. This impressive mosque, like the nearby Emir's palace, was in fact built during colonial times by the Public Works Department. Later we saw the dye pits where cloth was tied and soaked in indigo and the pit covered with a basketwork cover. Young boys unpicked the cloth and spread it out on the baskets to dry. Then in a house nearby the embroidery on the robes was knocked flat with heavy wooden mallets. We saw the special market selling burnished pots for carrying and cooling water. We watched the municipal "dust donkeys" which collected the rubbish, of which there was plenty, in pannier baskets.

On day 36 we moved south on the train. A shy girl with mountains of luggage got in with us at Kano and we were joined at Zaria by a big, jolly girl with an Afro wig and a huge blue wrap-around dress. She firmly closed the door against any further passengers. "They want me to move up for a soldier. I'm not moving up for any soldier!" She was happy we were going to Lagos. She found the north very "primitivised". We ate pounded yam, pepperpot soup and fried plantain in the restaurant car. We slept well and the jolly girl continued to stand up for her rights. She was disgusted to be offered bread and margarine for breakfast when the menu said toast and marmalade. The waiter clearly thought we were lucky to get anything at all. The afternoon of the next day we got off the train at Ede and found a mammy wagon going to Ile-Ife.

Ile-Ife is probably the oldest Yoruba city. Yoruba tradition says it's the place where the god Olodumare created human life on earth, and it has a very old tradition of craftsmanship. We made straight for the famous university with buildings that were new at the time of our visit. We had an introduction to the historian, Michael Crowder, but he was away, so visited the museum with its fine collection of brass and bronze heads and terracotta and the *Oranmiyan staff*, the sword of the first ruler of Ife. We had nowhere to stay so we hitch-hiked to Ibadan. We got a lift with a large, friendly man who had spent five years in England. We were surprised to learn that, as an admirer of Churchill, he had joined the Conservative Party and was all in favour of arms sales to *apartheid* South Africa!

The Yoruba built towns and the largest of them, Ibadan, was perhaps still the most populous city in Africa at the time of our visit – or it may have already been overtaken by Lagos, Cairo and Kinshasa. It is an immense panorama of brownish corrugated iron roofs. Many of the houses are quite handsome, two storey buildings in the Afro-Brazilian style. After two nights relaxation we arrived at the university, Nigeria's oldest, and found the book-shop with an amazing selection of books about Africa – but no postcards. The manager told us sadly that a million cards had been printed in Ireland but that they could not get an import licence for them. There were, however, some Lenin badges on sale for threepence. We found Dr. Ade Grillo whom I had known at Cambridge and was now Professor of Anatomy. He was most welcoming and drove us around, showing us the evidence of the riot we had learned about when we were in Zaria the week before: broken windows and the Vice-Chancellor's upturned Mercedes. We visited the School of Archaeology at the university and had a preview of an ethnographic exhibit which was being prepared for the museum. Ade gave a running commentary on politics, the cholera epidemic and the students' riot. A father asked his son what they were rioting about. "We used to have three eggs and four pieces of toast for breakfast (in the university hostel). Now we have two eggs and two pieces of toast." The father responded: "When did I even give you even one egg for breakfast?" Students face tougher conditions today.

Our bus from Ibadan to Lagos was a second hand American Greyhound coach. The driving seat was on the wrong side and the driver had to ask his mate when to overtake.[26] Lagos was sultry and humid. We stayed at the YWCA hostel thanks to the fact that Edyth had been Vice President of the YWCA in Zambia. We visited the National Museum and saw the famous 9th century bronze pot excavated at Igbo-Ukwu in eastern Nigeria as well as an astonishing number of other sophisticated artefacts. We visited the Oba's new palace and his rather shabby old one. Each comprised of two courtyards with a box-like shrine in the centre. The guide explained that inside the shrine was a calabash. He opened the door of the shrine and invited us to pray and to put a donation in the calabash. Three drummers played on talking drums and we were requested to put coins on their heads. Afterwards we met Sam Adegbie, a television producer who had known my brother when he visited the NBC studios in Los Angeles. He was wearing a huge pale blue broderie anglaise *agbada* and he took us for a drink at Bar Beach.

On St. Valentine's Day we set off in the rain to the Ebute Metta lorry park to find transport to Dahomey, which would change its name to the People's Republic of Benin a year later. We found an old blue Peugeot taxi which needed another four passengers before it would set off. We sat in the car in the rain and eventually the car filled up and left. The driver stopped to buy a bed and this was loaded on top of all the other luggage on the roof rack. Each time we stopped the car needed a push, and the passengers obliged. Once inside Dahomey the car suddenly turned off the tarmac road, presumably to avoid a customs check, on to a long dirt road through oil palm plantations. The exhaust pipe fell off and we all piled out while this was fixed. We arrived in Porto Novo by the back streets. The bed and a lot of cardboard boxes were unloaded and the car started off for Cotonou, forgetting to drop us in the town. The driver paid a taxi to take us back. We made our way to the *Ecole Evangélique* where we stayed with

---

26. Nigeria, Ghana, Sierra Leone and the Gambia changed to driving on the right a year later. A Nigerian joke: cars changed one day and lorries the next!

Norman Goreham, a Methodist Minister whom we had met in England.

Porto Novo is officially the capital but everything happens in Cotonou. Thus Porto Novo seemed very placid, especially after the hectic pace of Lagos. The houses were modest, many painted pale pink with brown shutters, New Orleans style. The town was full of groups of musicians and dancers celebrating the return of pilgrims from Mecca. In the evening, twinkling nightlights and candles marked the stalls of the roadside sellers of food, cigarettes, razor blades and everything else, giving a magical charm to the warm night. We found the railway station but no trains were running, and we watched fishermen throwing nets into the lagoon. At one point we were surrounded by drummers and dancers and invited to dance. A 100 franc note placed on a musicians' forehead sufficed to liberate us. Norman took us to visit the Methodist Primary School and a hymn was sung to us in each classroom, the seniors piping up with *Enfants du Dahomey debout,* an anthem that must now have a Benin version, and we gave a talk to his theological students about Zambia.

Norman drove us on a visit to the historic capital of the Dan-Homey Empire, Abomey, where each king built himself a new palace. Before the French captured the city in 1892 there were twelve palaces. As the French advanced King Behanzin's men set fire to the city and the two surviving palaces – the word is a bit grandiose for what are quite modest buildings – form the *Musée Historique d'Abomey.* In the throne room there is a stool for each king and behind hangs a remarkable appliqué tapestry showing the animal symbol of each king. One of these represents a buffalo wearing clothes, the moral being that it is very hard to undress a live buffalo – or to strip a strong king of his power. There is also a room full of funerary altars which used to be carried outside once a year to honour the dead kings. The best-known king, Ghezo, who broke away from being a vassal of the Kingdom of Oyo (now part of Nigeria), reputedly had forty-one wives all of whom volunteered to die with him. His throne rests on the skulls of his enemies. Dan-Homey had exported slaves since the 16th century and had grown rich on the trade. The Europeans called Dahomey the Slave Coast as Ghana was the Gold Coast.

Going west from Cotonou we made a side trip to the African Venice, the lake village of Ganvié which consists of a large number of thatched houses on stilts standing in the calm but slightly polluted waters of Lake Nokoué. The Tofinu people lived on the lake to protect themselves from capture and slavery. A boatman paddled us across. The first stop was the bar, a corrugated iron shack selling drinks. The boat went on through the narrow watery "streets" to the "market", a stretch of open water where the main thing on sale was firewood. We stopped at a rather expensive curio shop. All along the way there were children, in or just out of the water calling to us for a *cadeau*. In the lake were brushwood fish traps and some fishermen throwing large circular nets.

We did not stop in Cotonou but caught a glimpse of the ugly, modern presidential palace on the sea shore. Dahomey was politically turbulent in the 1960s with three rivals representing different parts of the country taking turns as president and to live in this palace. Our next stop was at a much more legendary place, the former slaving port of Ouidah, the African home of voodoo, made famous by Bruce Chatwin's evocative book, *The Viceroy of Ouidah*, and the film *Cobra Verde*. The *Relais* where we stayed cooked a really enormous meal specially for us: four eggs followed by steak, chips and salad, cheese and bananas. I had always been fascinated by the story of the Portuguese fort of São João Batista and was determined to visit it. On our way to see it in the morning, we stopped to see the sacred pythons in their rather shabby enclosure. The fort is now a museum showing how the local king granted the trade concession to the Portuguese and how Ouidah became the main port of the Dan-Homey kingdom. It also illustrated Benin's cultural links with Haiti and Brazil where most of the slaves ended up. Despite the fact that it had been cut off from the sea for many years, the Portuguese flag remained proudly aloft until 1960 when Dahomey became independent. Three hundred years of Portuguese presence ended when, seeing the game was up, the lonely governor got in his car and drove off to Lagos airport.

I had seen the coast between Nigeria and Ghana from the air on my flight from Lusaka to Sierra Leone in 1963. Continuing at ground level we passed placid lagoon-side villages and the Atlantic shore thick with coconut palms. A very large lady got into our bush taxi on the way and talked non-stop until we got to the Togo border. Our Togo visas were valid for 48 hours but the country can be crossed in 48 minutes. It is just 50 kilometres along the beautiful coast road. The streets of Lomé were hung with banners. Togo's dictator, Gnassingbé Eyadema, had invited his Zairian counterpart who still went by the name of Joseph-Désiré Mobutu for a state visit. There were banners hung over the streets: *Eyadema et Mobutu, triomphe de la jeunesse africaine; Vive le zaïre, monnaie forte et stable; Mobutu, vous êtes désiré au Togo.* Edith's Inn where we stayed was really a kind of hostel for US Peace Corps volunteers (or "peace corpses" as they were labelled in Cameroon), run by a very jolly African American called Edith. There were monkeys and baby crocodiles in the garden. We went to see the Independence memorial lit up at night, a huge silhouette of a man breaking his chains. We also visited a bizarre private museum, a miscellany of items collected by a certain Hubert Kponton relating especially to the slave trade and to the time when this was German Togoland. The museum recorded the fact that the first shot to be fired in the First World War was by a Gold Coast (Ghanaian) soldier advancing into German Togoland. (Interestingly the last shot was by a Zambian when the German army was finally defeated in the north of what was then Northern Rhodesia.)

A bush taxi took us on to Accra, and Ghana still struck me as being as proudly African as when I had stopped over in 1963, although its outstanding first president, Kwame Nkrumah, had been overthrown in a coup in 1966. The (non-executive) president in 1971 was Edward Akufo-Addo, whose son won the presidency in 2017. Our contacts this time were an archaeologist, Merrick Posnansky and his Ugandan wife, Eunice. We found them celebrating Idi Amin's coup to take power in Uganda which they wrongly thought would lead to the restoration of the Kabaka of

Buganda, to whom Eunice was related. We had a happy couple of days staying at Cosy Inn, looking at Black Star Square, having a swim and applying for a visa to Mali. On February 23 we got up early to catch the "express" train to Kumasi, which wound its way through cocoa country and slowly up the escarpment. Little black and red birds flew in and out of their globular nests attached to the telegraph wires. Pastors came along the train preaching at the top of their voice. Others were doing a hard sell of Thirty Minute Worm Powder, cures for piles and for toothache, talking in Twi but handing out leaflets in English.

Kumasi is a proud place, the historic capital of Ashanti and home of the University of Science and Technology (now Kwame Nkrumah UST) where we found friends whom Edyth had known at Oxford. We visited the museum and the replica of the palace of the King, the Asantehene, with a wisdom tree in the corner of the courtyard "to make sure that everyone considered their words carefully." The fake golden stool was on display. This was the one that was made to trick the British, who confiscated it and returned it after Independence. The real one has always remained hidden and is brought out occasionally on ceremonial occasions.

We missed the train to Takoradi and our friend gave us a lift back to Accra. We took the state bus along the coast to Elmina, home of two of the most impressive of the many castles along Ghana's coastline, their white paint belying their grim history as bases for the export of slaves. The scene was picturesque: finely decorated surf boats filled the harbour, selling fish that they had just landed. The view up to Fort St. Jago with a few tall palm trees was etched against the horizon. We went to see St. George's Castle on the shore which had for many years been the main Portuguese base in West Africa, later captured by the Dutch, and most of which was now a police headquarters. This, like Gorée in Senegal, is one of the key memorial sites to the slave trade and featured in Haile Gerima's prizewinning film, *Sankofa* (1993). A rather stern policeman showed us the dungeon from which the slaves were shipped and the hall where merchants bid for them. The female slaves were cloistered in a dark room with a wooden staircase. The Dutch governor lived above and would look down and choose the slave he wanted for his bed. Any women who gave birth were freed. This resulted in a lot of people in Elmina having Dutch names. We went up the hill to Fort St. Jago which the Dutch built to stop the Portuguese re-taking the castle below. The view down to the harbour and the view of the two castles from the beach below were among the most beautiful memories of this journey. Also memorable were the huge Atlantic rollers pounding the open beach. I tried to swim but this involved trying to stand up and being knocked down by the waves.

On to Takoradi where we stayed in one of Kwame Nkrumah's investments, the cavernous Atlantic Hotel. From there a little blue bus by the name of Jackson took us further along the coast, past another castle at Axim and many coconut palms, and finally off the end of the tarmac on to a very muddy road to Half Assini, Ghana's last outpost and where Kwame Nkrumah lived as a child, just in time to catch an ancient lorry, appropriately labelled Abomination above the windscreen and "Weep not for me" on the rear. This took us, plus the immigration officer, to Jewi Wharf where the little boat across the lagoon to the Ivory Coast charged five times as much for one suitcase as for one passenger. The modern main road which we would take in the reverse direction in 1997 had not yet been built. The only good road from Accra to Abidjan in those days was far in the north via Kumasi.

We slept in an idyllic little hotel beside a rushing rocky stream at Aboisso. From there a good road took us through miles of pineapple plantations and more coconut palms to Abidjan, which was still at the time the capital of the Ivory Coast, now officially called Côte d'Ivoire. This country was reputed to be the success story of French neo-colonialism in Africa. The "moderate" President Houphouët-Boigny encouraged French business and his fairly efficient regime maximised agricultural products for export, notably cocoa – much of it smuggled from Ghana. The economic and cultural divisions between south and north were exacerbated by the huge number of immigrants from Upper Volta (now Burkina Faso) and Mali who were attracted by the economic boom and who harvested most of the crops. Political crisis followed Houphouët-Boigny's death in 1993 and civil war erupted in 2002.

On the day of our arrival a state visit was due. It was General Bokassa of the Central African Republic, the future Emperor. Drummers and school children lined the roadside. We stayed in Treichville, a busy, very African part of the city. Crossing the bridge over the lagoon brought us to the elegant part of town known as Plateau, very clean and smart in 1971 with lots of French people shopping. We found a rather chaotic museum with a good but badly labelled collection, where there was a clear view across the *autoroute* and the lagoon to the white tower of the Hotel Ivoire in Cocody which we visited the following day. *Il n'y a pas de crocodiles à Cocody* is the title of one of the brilliant humorous songs of the Cameroonian singer and musicologist, Francis Bebey. Most African capitals today have a skyline which includes a few tower blocks but Abidjan was the pioneer in West Africa. Seen from the 30th floor of the hotel the towers in Plateau shone in the sun and, looking south, the blue of the lagoon mirrored the blue of the sky. In the distance were the shabbier rooftops of Treichville. Edyth and I returned to Treichville in 1997 after my visit to Liberia and ate *agouti,* a tasty rural rat popular all over West Africa and known in English as grasscutter or cuttin' grass. Treichville had not changed much but Plateau had got shabbier.

Ivory Coast's railway "network" is optimistically called the *Réseau Abidjan-Niger.* It is no network, having just one line – and it never reached the river Niger or the eponymous republic. But in 1971 we found it to be one of Africa's more efficient and punctual railways. Our train was a diesel unit which moved at a fair speed initially through forest which turned progressively into savannah bush. Sellers of bananas, pineapples, bread, plastic toys, baskets, cigarettes, wristwatches and sunglasses moved ceaselessly through the train. The hotel at the country's second city, Bouaké, was booked up for President Bokassa's entourage, but Madame hurried along and kindly gave us a room for a night. After 2002 Bouake was for a time the headquarters of the rebels who controlled the whole of the north of the country.

The next day the bush scenery was very reminiscent of Zambia. The main stop in the north was Ferkessédougou where the platform was a busy market selling tie-dye cloth, golden plastic raincoats, flowery hats, long trousers, *boubous,* not to mention bread, milk and water. The stations here in the north were built in colonial times in the Sudanic style, trying to resemble the traditional mosque architecture.

Across the border in Upper Volta, the station at Bobo-Dioulasso was the grandest of all these stations. Later, in 1984, the great reformer, President Thomas Sankara, changed the country's name to Burkina Faso, "the land of upright people." Bobo-Dioulasso is the second city and it's an impressive place with three long boulevards fanning out from the station. All the official buildings are built in the same mock Sudanic style. People were weaving on huge looms in the street. It was incredibly hot and we had no desire to move. We did, however, stir ourselves to take a taxi to the genuinely Sudanic old mosque, built in *banco* with wooden sticks to reinforce it, but rather spoilt by a restored section built in cement. Edyth and I returned to Burkina Faso in 1997 to attend the Fespaco Film Festival at the capital, Ouagadougou, which is where we were with Djibril Diallo on the cover of this book.

From Bobo Dioulasso we found a little bus which took us on to the Mali frontier where no-one bothered to inspect the expensive visa we had bought in Ghana. We passed Senoufo villages with shady mango trees and tall grain bins which had pointed thatched roofs, through Sikasso and past walled villages complete with little mosques. The bus driver stopped to pray every two hours, getting out his mat and kettle. It was night when we finally crossed the long bridge over the River Niger at Bamako and we ended up in the faded grandeur of the Grand Hotel, next to the station. It was here that the famous *Rail Band du Mali,* originally known as the *Super Rail Band Orchestre du Buffet Hôtel de la Gare de Bamako,* originated only a few years before our trip. It combined traditional music with Afro-Cuban rhythm and modern instruments. The band was based here at the station buffet for many years and produced some of Mali's greatest musicians, most notably Mory Kante and Salif Keita.

FIDELES USAGERS DU RAIL...

SAVEZ-VOUS QUE :

La Régie des Chemins de Fer du Sénégal

vous offre, de nouvelles possibilités de transport sur la liaison **DAKAR-KAOLACK**

— Grâce à l'augmentation de l'effectif de son parc d'autorails, la Régie a judicieusement établi à votre attention de nouveaux horaires des trains - voyageurs qui vous permettront de rallier votre gare de destination à l'heure de votre convenance dans les meilleurs délais. Tous les trains, vous avez la faculté de voyager à votre choix sur les trains et aux horaires ci-après :

21	23	25	27	29	DAKAR KAOLACK	PRINCIPALES GARES	KAOLACK DAKAR	20	22	24	26	28
1re et 2 cl Tr. léger Omnibus	1re et 2 cl Autorail Direct	1re et 2 d Autorail Direct	2 d. Autorail Direct	1re et 2 d. Autorail Direct				1re et 2 d Autorail Direct	2 d. Autorail Omnibus	1re et 2 d Autorail Direct	2 d. Tr. léger Omnibus	1re et 2 d Autorail Direct
6 07	8 45	13.40	16 05	18.45	D	**DAKAR**	A	9 30	13 00	16 56	19 50	22 06
6.51	9 17	14 12	16 37	19.17	A	**RUFISQUE**	D	9 07	12 27	16 24	19 08	21 34
6 53	9 19	14.14	16 39	19 19	D		A	9 05	12 25	16 22	19.06	21 32
7 45	9 56	14.51	17.16	19 56	A	**THIES**	D	8 28	11 45	15 45	18.17	20 53
7 48	10 05	14.54	17 20	20 04	D		A	8 26	11 40	15 41	18 14	20 52
9.05	10 50	15 43	18 49	20 50	A	**BAMBEY**	D	7 41	10 19	14 51	17 01	20 03
9.06	10 51	15 45	18.51	20 51	D		A	7 40	10.18	14 50	16 51	20 02
9 42	11 13	16 12	19.26	21 13	A	**DIOURBEL**	D	7 18	9 34	14 28	16 23	19 40
9.46	11 15	16.20	19 42	21 15	D		A	7 16	9.32	14.26	16 46	19 38
11.08	12 12	17 17	20 58	22 12	A	**GUINGUINEO**	D	6 20	8 17	13 30	14 55	18 42
11.15	12 20	17 23	21 08	22 18	D		A	6 12	8 02	13.22	14 45	18.34
11.48	12.48	17 45	21 30	22 40	A	**KAOLACK**	D	5 50	7.30	13 00	14 13	18.12

VOYAGEZ par LE TRAIN, c'est tellement plus sûr et ÉCONOMIQUE !!

PIC 12) Senegal Railways publicity, 1971.

We did not have time to see Bamako or to hear any music as the weekly train to Senegal was due to leave early the next morning. We bought first class sleeper tickets but when we got on the train all the beds seemed to be occupied. The guard told us not to worry: he would probably find some second class passengers on them and make them move. The heat was intense and we happily sat in the restaurant car all day sipping tamarind juice until the train arrived at Kayes in the evening and some beds had been vacated. The land was dry and parched with occasional large, pinkish eroded rocks. The Kayes area is where most of the large community of Malians in France come from. It was a pity to pass through Mali so fast and not see the ancient cities of Ségou, Mopti, Gao, Djenné and Timbuktu or the extraordinary country of the Dogon people.[27]

We woke as the train approached Dakar, and we noticed crowds at every station. Apparently there was a well-known *marabout,* a holy man, on our train. People waited, singing, and ran towards his carriage with outstretched hands. The crowd at Dakar station surged forward and the *marabout* was welcomed to the city. Although it has grown and modernised itself, much of Dakar was and remains a proud monument to colonial Frenchness, as this was France's first colony in Africa. The elegant dress and topknots of the women, the white robes of many of the men and the huge new mosque reminded us that this was Senegal. There were noticeably more tourists and that meant more hassle from street vendors. I was unwise enough to smile at a huge wooden carving. The seller pursued me through the streets for a couple of hours and I had no Wolof to explain that I could hardly carry it home. We were in a cheerful mood in Dakar as we had finally been able to get mail from our families in England. There had been a long postal strike and my mother had even gone to France for a day to post letters to us. In these days of text messages and instant communication it is hard to believe how dependent we were on the post. The weather was also pleasantly cool after the gruelling heat of Upper Volta and Mali. We visited the island of Gorée which has the unspoilt charm of a small colonial town but, as at Elmina in Ghana, seeing the narrow passage in the *Maison des Esclaves* down which the slaves were hustled into the ships means that you leave the island in a

---

27. Tuareg rebels aided by jihadists from post-Gaddafi Libya occupied the north of Mali in 2012. Some of the ancient mausoleums and priceless manuscripts in Timbuktu were destroyed but a lot have been saved. The government with French support defeated the rebels but the country remains tense, with occasional Islamist attacks.

sombre mood. I visited Dakar and Gorée in 2017 and, while the city had grown and boomed, the island, still attractive, seemed shabbier than I remembered.

March 8, day 67 we returned to the station, a decorated pastiche of a French railway terminus, to take the train to Saint-Louis. The poster exhorted the "faithful users of the rail" to use the improved service of railcars which only took 3 hours 42 minutes. This line was built as early as 1885 but is now closed. The scenery began to look like desert, scattered with bulbous baobab trees. The villages were surrounded by grass fences and we played a game of spotting domestic animals: scoring one for a sheep or goat, three for a cow or a donkey, ten for a camel. The scoring got out of hand when large herds of cattle appeared.

Saint-Louis du Senegal is built on an island in the River Senegal where the river turns south and runs parallel to the sea. A quiet, atmospheric town, Saint-Louis' slightly down-at-heel white painted colonial buildings had the same charm as those on Gorée – and both are now UNESCO World Heritage Sites. The old French cemetery with its tombs of past Governors told many stories, of victims of a yellow fever epidemic in 1881, of children dying young, of wives cut off in *la fleur de l'âge*. We would have liked to stay longer but we had a boat to catch and this involved crossing Mauretania first.

"*Your dreams of sunshine and poetic calm come true*" was the blurb on the brochure encouraging visitors to come to Mauretania, but the slow process of getting a visa suggested they did not really expect many tourists. From Saint-Louis to the river crossing at Rosso it was a ride in a comfortable Peugeot bush taxi, past Peul settlements of domed grass huts looking like small haystacks and a rice project, bright green in the middle of the semi-desert of sand and thorn bushes. Over the ferry as we waited for the frontier post to open, children came rushing to sell us water melons. The over-whelming memory of Mauretania is of the pale blue robes worn by both men and women. The next three hours gave us our only sight of real desert, endless white sand and the occasional camel and nomad's tent.

In colonial times the French ruled both Senegal and Mauretania from Saint-Louis. Nouakchott is a new capital city, a strange modern place, a bit like plonking Milton Keynes down in the desert, filling it with people in blue robes and blowing sand along the streets. The town's name means windy city but there the comparison with Chicago ends. We stayed at the Oasis Hotel, advertised as handy for the movies – in fact it was on top of a cinema. Migration to the city was already underway: a nomad's first step towards a sedentary life seemed to be to build a cement block wall around your tent. And then to build a house.

We had planned to catch the fortnightly boat from Nouadhibou, Mauretania's second city, to the Canary Islands but there was no road there from Nouakchott. We were faced with two alternatives: to fly or to take a bush taxi 430 kilometres north to Choum, where it was possible to ride on the mile-long iron ore train down to the coast. This second option might have been fun but the idea of spending a cold night sitting on lumps of iron ore and then probably missing the boat and having to spend two weeks in Nouadhibou made the decision to take the plane compelling.

Nouadhibou was one of the strangest places on the whole trip. Formerly known as Port Etienne, there was an old fort which housed a supermarket and a pharmacy. There was rubble, barbed wire, broken bottles and the odd hulk of a boat on the wide sandy beach. We walked towards the water's edge and found a little shack labelled *Au Clapotis* ("the lapping of the water"). It seemed to be a bar and we sat down and ordered two orange drinks. Then Madame appeared in her dressing gown and started to chat about her life. She talked at length about the war and the Germans. The word lobster came up in the conversation and she asked if we would like one. Soon we were sitting down to a meal of lobster mayonnaise, cheese, fruit and wine which she refused to let us pay for, while she explained to her turbaned servant how to lay crazy paving. She was an example of the strange, often lonely individuals left like flotsam on the shore at the end of colonialism. The couple who served us with cold meat in Oyem in Gabon were in this category, as was the Orthodox Armenian who lived in Kalomo, Zambia with his icons on the wall.

There was not much to do in Nouadhibou so we took a taxi to Cansado ("tired" in Spanish), the nearby company town housing the staff of the iron mine and railway company, Miferma. Cansado was another modern alien excrescence but much cleaner and tidier than Nouadhibou. We found a small zoo containing local creatures: big-eared desert foxes, monkeys, giant tortoises, warthogs and peacocks.

Spanish Sahara was still Spanish in 1971 and we boarded the little Spanish steamship, the *Leon y Castillo,* and we were able to sleep on board, along with the eager group of young Gambians and Senegalese who were trying to get to Europe, in those days a much easier and safer enterprise than today. Five days passed by on this ship with its coal-fired steam engine and its rather gloomy, dark panelled first-class lounge, complete with the obligatory photo of Generalissimo Franco, still alive and in power. Nouadhibou is on the south side of Cape Blanco and the town of La Gouira on the north side was in Spanish Sahara and our boat docked there the same evening. The next day the sea became very rough and, since the boat had little ballast, it tossed about and was delayed getting to Villa Cisneros (now Dakhla). We had enough time to disembark and wander through this rather nondescript Spanish town with just a few blue-robed people as a reminder that this was still culturally part of Mauretania – and for a few years it did become part of Mauretania when Sahara was briefly partitioned after the departure of the Spanish. Morocco later occupied all of Spanish Sahara and to this day the liberation movement of the Saharoui people face a *de facto* occupation and a population imported from Morocco that far outnumbers the original Saharoui nomads, so that even were the promised UN plebiscite ever held Morocco would be the winner.

After sailing along within sight of the long, dry island of Fuerteventura, the ship called briefly in the evening at Arrecife on the island of Lanzerote. Finally on the Friday we disembarked at Las Palmas. It was a *fiesta* and most things were closed including the shipping agent so we decided not to wait for a boat but to fly on to Morocco. This involved a flight and a night in Tenerife and another plane the next morning to Casablanca. Thence we took a train to Rabat and another train on the following day to Tangier. It was almost like being in Europe.

One more adventure remained: credit cards were a rarity in 1971 and throughout the trip we had used travellers' cheques which were stamped "sterling area only" and we had not been in the sterling area since Ghana. The British Bank of the Middle East could not change our cheques, nor could the British Consul. The only solution was to go to Gibraltar, knowing that the frontier from there into Spain was closed. We therefore boarded a ferry boat to Gibraltar, changed our money, took the cable car to the top of the rock and bought some clothes, laughing at the British currency which had just gone metric. In the morning we flew back to Tangier and then crossed the straits a third time, this time by boat again, to Algeciras in Spain. From there on trains via Madrid and France and a hovercraft over the Channel we finally reached my mother's village in Essex eighty-five days after leaving Zambia.

4
The international voluntary service movement

i) Origins

Since such a large part of my strange and varied career has been involved with the international volunteer movement I thought I should try to explain what it is. My own experience began as a conscientious objector. I was on the staff of IVS from 1971 to 1984. I was briefly as chair of the British Volunteer Programme. I was International President of Service Civil International from 1985 to 1989; Director of the Co-ordinating Committee for International Voluntary Service (CCIVS) from 1992 to 1998 and finally a Vice President of CCIVS. In my retirement I am still active in Volunteer Action for Peace, a small association in the UK.

The international voluntary service, or workcamp movement, was born in reaction to the horror of the First World War at a conference organised by the newly-formed Fellowship of Reconciliation (FoR) at Bilthoven, Netherlands in August 1920. Over 400 people from Scandinavia, the Netherlands, Britain, Germany and the USA met to discuss "How to build peace." After much earnest talk, Walter Koch, a young German Quaker, intervened saying: "*We have now been discussing for two days. That is enough. We must do something now... my brother was a soldier in the German army... he participated in bombing this country – I come here to do my part in order to build, to reconstruct it.*" Pierre Cérésole, a prominent Swiss pacifist who had been elected secretary of the FoR, was enthusiastic about Koch's idea and after a long discussion in a hotel bedroom in Berlin with British Quaker, Hubert Parris the international voluntary service movement was born. Pierre resigned from his post and went ahead to organise the very first international service project, to help reconstruct the destroyed village of Esnes, near Verdun in France. Pierre had become convinced that a mixed group working together on a concrete task was the most effective way of eroding enemy images and building international friendship – not only among the volunteers themselves but also by involving and influencing the local population.

The work at Esnes started well but after a time the villagers showed their unhappiness at the presence of Germans and Austrians in the team and, since the purpose of the project was to reconcile former enemies, it was decided to withdraw. The seed, Pierre said, had fallen on stony ground, but it survived and grew. Pierre went on to help create a movement, Service Civil International (SCI), which began to organise a number of "services" (later known as workcamps) often in response to natural disasters in Europe such as floods and avalanches. *Service civil* in French means civilian service, not the civil service, and from the start SCI campaigned against compulsory military service, but SCI was not only for pacifists. Cérésole's brother, a military man, was an active member. Many people want to work for peace but cannot accept a totally pacifist position.

Having started by working for post-war reconstruction and disaster relief the movement started to develop in new directions. The first social project was in 1931 in the little town of Brynmawr in South Wales, UK where a team of volunteers worked with a community badly hit by unemployment to build an open-air swimming pool and to smarten up the town. A couple of Norwegian volunteers at this workcamp suggested that the houses which were all grey should be painted in different colours as they are in Norway. If you visit Brynmawr today some of the colour remains, though the pool is closed. IVS organised a celebration of fifty years of workcamps at Brynmawr in 1981. The keynote speaker on this occasion was Glyn Roberts who had worked at CCIVS and founded the charity, Tools for Self-Reliance. He described the first workcamp attended by Russian volunteers. Then we all sat down for a picnic beside the empty swimming pool.

In 1934-37 Pierre Cérésole went together with three other volunteers to Bihar, India after an earthquake and a flood. They rebuilt a devastated village and named it Shantipur (Peace Village). A collection of Pierre's letters from India was published with the title *En vue de l'Himalaya.* This was the first volunteer project in the "south." Rajendra Prasad, a future President of India, was enthusiastic: "*The simple fact that European people are doing this type of humble work with Indian people... is astounding for the passer-by*" in the context of the British Raj in India.

SCI's first environmental project was also in Britain. Volunteers worked with wheelbarrows to remove an ugly slag heap outside the town of Oakengates – and this is the site of a story that illustrates for me the potential of international service. One of the volunteers at this camp was a German named Ernst. A few years later, during the Second World War, Ernst found himself in Hitler's air force with the task of bombing... Oakengates. A letter in the local newspaper recorded: *Looking up we saw the swastika on the plane just a few feet above us and the pilot, in his helmet and goggles, looked down and waved.* There is strong evidence that the pilot deposited the bombs in a nearby wood to avoid killing the people he had learned to love when he was a volunteer. Sadly Ernst seems not to have survived the war.

These early services usually lasted for months, with volunteers coming for whatever period they could, as at my camp in Austria. The women volunteers in those early days just did the cooking and cleaning. SCI women soon demanded to take full part in the work and things changed.

The idea of international service survived and blossomed after the Second World War in Europe. The need to reconstruct and to help house the huge number of refugees led to a great expansion of international volunteering in Europe, with many new national organisations[28] as well as revived branches of SCI in France, Germany, Italy, Belgium and the Netherlands. Co-ordination of all these initiatives was badly needed. UNESCO was the UN agency concerned with youth and it helped create the Co-ordinating Committee for International Voluntary Service (CCIVS) in 1948, where I was later to become director.

---

28. Examples are Concordia and *Jeunesse et Réconstruction* in France and *Internationale Jugendgemeinschaftsdienste* (IJGD Germany)

The first workcamps I attended, described in the first chapter, were fairly typical for the 1950s, responding to poverty in Scotland, Austria and India; and helping to build houses for the post-war homeless in France and Germany. As Europe recovered from the war the needs changed, and so did the type of workcamp. Priorities were often to work with deprived children and people with disabilities; to protect the environment; and to preserve cultural heritage. Study themes were often included, usually related to the work undertaken. A project involved with mentally handicapped people might include inputs and discussion on mental health in general. A project to refurbish tools for Africa might study development issues or *apartheid*. Many young people in Europe, not only students, volunteered: workcamping was a popular way of having a cheap holiday and doing something useful.

By the 1960s decolonisation of many countries in Asia and Africa had moved fast. One response from the "north" was to provide volunteer development workers to serve in these newly independent countries and the headline action was President Kennedy's creation of the US Peace Corps. The UK government's response was different. It funded a collection of five voluntary organisations which worked co-operatively as the British Volunteer Programme. Many other countries created similar volunteer programmes, aiming to work for development. West Germany and Denmark had large programmes. This was the time of the Cold War and the Peace Corps in particular was seen by many as a neo-colonial political move to keep the countries which received the volunteers in the western camp. Many also questioned whether these were really volunteers at all as they usually received salaries greater than those of their local colleagues. Some of these programmes still exist as part of aid programmes. When I worked for IVS, the British branch of SCI, from 1971 to 1984, it was a member of the British Volunteer Programme.

In 1971 the United Nations Development Programme (UNDP), CCIVS and others worked to create United Nations Volunteers (UNV) and I remember discussing with the representative in Botswana what level of pocket money the new UNVs should receive. They agreed to set it lower than the Danes and Germans but higher than the British but still well above local salary levels. There was some argument as to whether UNVs were volunteers or junior experts. As time went on the latter argument seems to have won. UNV is still strong and is notable for the fact that 60% of its volunteers are from Africa, serving in other "southern" countries, earning more than they would in their own countries and depriving their own countries of useful skilled people. CCIVS considered that this, even if useful, was not true volunteering and it distanced itself from it. However, CCIVS joins UNV in promoting International Volunteer Day each year on 5 December.

ii) The first workcamp associations in Africa

Meanwhile there was another story. People in the newly independent countries created civil society bodies to respond to their direct concerns such as health, human rights and rural development. These were often linked to existing international organisations such as the Scouts or YWCA. The growth of the workcamp movement was a local initiative but it received much help and encouragement from outside. I am proud to have played a part in providing some of this encouragement, especially in Africa.

Ben Korley whom I met at the workcamp in Worms, Germany in 1955 had been selected to come to Europe by the newly created Voluntary Workcamps Association of *Ghana* of which he remained a leading member. He later became the Chief Medical Officer in the Ghana army. This association, usually known as VOLU, had been the brainchild of Gordon Green, who had been a member of IVS in Britain and was teaching at Mfantsipim School. Together with Ben Korley and others, he organised workcamps where students worked with villagers on small development projects. The idea caught on fast. In its heyday VOLU attracted hundreds of young Ghanaians, mostly secondary school students, who were inspired to go off during the school holidays, often to parts of the country they would otherwise not have had a chance of visiting, to help construct school classrooms or health centres, plant trees or dig pit latrines and trenches for village water supplies. Here the barrier that workcamps bridged was between urban educated youth and rural villagers. A nice tradition in VOLU is that each volunteer is given a camp name, really a nickname – and many have continued using them throughout their lives. My friend Collins was Miniman (he was very short), Francis Donkor, VOLU's long-serving General Secretary, was Osofo (priest), an assistant in the office was Fear God and Work Hard. Sheriff, Headmaster, King Ray, Vapour, Love, Taller, Jess Lee, Benson Burner and Django are all now living in Europe and are nostalgic about their time in VOLU. They are members of a support network that helps support VOLU in Ghana.

In 1957, just after **Morocco** became independent 12,000 young volunteers were brought together from all over the country to build the 31 km Unity Road linking the former French and Spanish zones. This huge national effort led to a strong tradition of youth workcamps still continuing today, with several different volunteer associations and a national co-ordinating body. An exhibition to commemorate this project was held in Rabat in 2018.

In **Togo** the workcamp movement preceded Independence in 1960 and several associations are still active today. Gerson Gu-Konu was the leader of the *Association Togolaise des Volontaires Chrétiens au Travail* in 1956 and he was elected to parliament. When the government of President Sylvanus Olympio was overthrown in Africa's very first coup d'état in 1963, the new dictatorial regime of Gnassingbé Eyadema had Gerson imprisoned and tortured. Lobbying by SCI and Amnesty International resulted in his release and he came to France to work for SCI.

I first met Gerson in 1971. A vivid memory from my short time as London field officer of IVS was a heated discussion in my little office between Gerson and Cephas Munanairi. Cephas, known as Mr. Africa, was a Zimbabwean who had fled to **Kenya** from white Rhodesia where in 1962 he founded the Kenya Voluntary Development Association, which since his death in 1993 has become one of the strongest workcamp associations in Africa. Cephas was a Pan-Africanist who believed strongly that there should be a continent-wide structure for the voluntary service movement. Gerson argued that a Pan African body was unrealistic. By 1971 workcamp organisations, some strong, some struggling, also already existed in different forms in a number of African countries: Sierra Leone, Dahomey (now Benin), Nigeria, Cameroon, The Gambia, Senegal, Uganda, Algeria and Tunisia. Gerson favoured regional platforms such as the one he had set up, the Union of West African Voluntary Workcamp Associations – but this was ineffective due to misunderstandings between French and English speakers and lack of funds. Gerson was later appointed Delegate to West Africa of SCI and he helped develop the volunteer associations in Sierra Leone, The Gambia, Nigeria and Senegal as well as a Women in Development exchange with France and an imaginative partnership between farmers in western France and West Africa. Gerson later went on to work for Amnesty International where he also developed new African sections. Other workcamp organisations were to develop later, mostly in southern African countries.

African voluntary workcamp associations have always welcomed volunteers from Europe and North America – and more recently Japan and South Korea – but they have often become too dependent on the fees that these volunteers pay to participate and, because of the cost and the difficulty of obtaining visas, the north-south relationship has never been equal. Yet this partnership has been positive: African associations have gained ideas and maintained an international profile as well as earning some income. The non-African volunteers have learned a lot. To maximise benefit, SCI created an international commission for solidarity, exchange and education for development. In the UK we called it the Overseas Workcamp Exchange Scheme. There was also a political aspect: enthusiastic about the socialist ideas of Tanzania's President Nyerere, SCI France organised a study visit which resulted in a relationship with the youth wing of the ruling party, *Umoja wa Vijana,* and in workcamps being organised regularly in **Tanzania**.

5
Thirteen years with IVS GB 1971-84

i) London

When Edyth and I returned from Zambia in 1971 we moved into a cottage we had bought in the little town of Holt in Norfolk. It was quite a sunny spring and the hedgerows were in flower. We enjoyed cycling along the country lanes and through quiet villages with their grey, flintstone churches. It was very different from the Zambian bush. Our nearest neighbours seemed friendly. They said they were old colonials too and that we must come in for sherry when we had settled down. After a few weeks we thought we had settled down, but we never got the sherry. Holt was not a good location for finding a permanent job but we did both find temporary work during the summer at a school of English. It was a very bad school. We were lodged at a university hostel in Norwich. The students consisted of young Italians out for a fun holiday – and they got no fun from the tinned spaghetti and other delights of British cuisine they were offered; a few serious Germans; and some Arabs from the Gulf who thought they knew English already. The school was based in a handsome mansion in the town of Aylsham run by a very obese man. He had assembled a bizarre collection of teachers which included a young man called Philby who was related to the famous spy – and us.

After this episode I was happy to find a job back with International Voluntary Service as London Field Officer. IVSP had dropped the word Peace from its title in deference to English charity law which deemed peace to be "political." (Charity law has since changed: Volunteer Action for Peace where I am currently active is a registered charity.) IVS was and is the British branch of Service Civil International. At that time IVS had local groups all over the UK which did useful social support work such as helping elderly people by decorating their homes and digging their gardens, supporting people with disabilities, or running activities for children. I was responsible for supporting and promoting the twenty such groups in London. For this task I was given the use of a car, a mixed blessing as our temporary home was a bedsit in Kensington where I had to get up early to feed the parking meter. I was pleased that one of my first tasks was to accompany two African volunteers on their visits to local projects. Sam Ade Oyewole from the Voluntary Workcamps Association of Nigeria and Paul Dame from VOLU Ghana had been invited to Britain as part of the exchange scheme. My most bizarre memory of them is of a visit to the Lewisham branch of IVS where the main activity week after week was stuffing teddy bears for a Christmas children's project. Sam and Paul looked on with disbelief at this peculiar activity, not a winning idea for Nigeria or Ghana.

The London Regional Office was in a kind of tenement in Macklin Street, near Covent Garden. With my assistant, Mary Ann Acton, I occupied an attic room. Downstairs was the office of the Child Poverty Action Group, the director of which was Frank Field who was to become a well-known politician. I would frequently pass Lord Longford, their chairman, on the stairs.

We settled into a tiny new terraced house in Bermondsey very near the River Thames. A few weeks after moving in a notice was delivered warning residents to move upstairs in case of flooding. The river wall was soon to be raised and the Thames Barrier was built. Bermondsey has not been flooded – yet. Edyth started teaching at a nearby secondary school and we decided to adopt a child. Tom was born in 1973 and this changed our lives. We adopted Sally after we had moved to Leicester. She was born in 1977. We had a very happy family life although I rather regret spending too much time away from the family on field visits for IVS and, later, working in Paris and in Burundi.

ii) Overseas Service Officer

Four months of work with voluntary groups in London was quite a good way of catching up with the changes that had occurred during my ten years away in Zambia. I remember the secretary of Brixton IVS group taking me for a walk, listening to the fairly new sound of reggae. However, I was happy to get back into more contact with Africa when I was appointed Overseas Service Officer in 1972, administering IVS' programme of volunteer development workers. The British Volunteer Programme (BVP), as explained above, of which we were a part was really just a budget from the then Ministry of Overseas Development which supported agencies which recruited skilled British volunteers to work in so-called developing countries, normally for a period of two years or more. The other agencies were VSO, the largest and best-known; the United Nations Association International Service (UNAIS), the National Union of Students (briefly) and the Catholic Institute for International Relations (later called Progressio). The BVP committee allocated countries to these agencies: IVS worked in Botswana, Lesotho, Swaziland, Mauritius, Seychelles, Cameroon and later the Comoro Islands and Mozambique, with a few projects in south Asia. IVS was the most "volunteerish" of the agencies and wanted its recruits to be real volunteers rather than technical assistance personnel. So as part of their preparation we insisted that they take part in an international workcamp in Britain before joining the regular orientation course. We hoped this would give them an idea of the other aspects of the work of IVS. It sometimes led to a volunteer deciding to work nearer home rather than overseas – or falling in love with one of the other workcampers.

The greater part of our overseas programme was in southern Africa, in Botswana, Lesotho and Swaziland. We argued that supporting these newly independent High Commission Territories was a way of showing alternatives to the segregation in South Africa and of promoting eventual reconciliation. The volunteers we recruited tended to be either straight from university or young professionals. Part of my job was to give recruitment talks at colleges and careers fairs around the country – there were no websites or google in those days.

We invited applicant volunteers to attend a selection weekend in a rural hideaway, most often at a freezing cold place in the beautiful woodland near Haslemere in Surrey. A mixture of inter-views and social activities usually gave us a good idea of how the candidates would fit into a new culture and, if not, we hoped they would learn enough to deselect themselves. They had also to undergo a personality test, usually administered by a rather dry psychologist. This process was not always successful. Once we managed to send a motor mechanic to India without discovering that he was allergic to oil! On another occasion a woman who sailed through the personality test turned out to be highly neurotic. Our psychologist's excuse was that she was a smiling depressive and the system could not cope with that.

The final stage before the volunteers departed was an orien-tation course lasting several days which included talks by former volunteers and by nationals of the countries to which the volun-teers were going, plus an introduction to the language and practical information on matters like travel and health. For several years this took place in the palatial Stoke Rochford Hall near Grantham in Lincolnshire. We always tried to invite nationals of the countries to which the volunteers were to serve and they taught the local languages. I have always insisted that at least some basic knowledge of the language is vital for good relations and it was good to hear the sounds of Setswana, Sesotho, siSwati and Pidgin English echo-ing through the building. These orientation courses were enjoyed by all and they created a relationship between the volunteers and the staff in the UK which was valuable once the volunteers were serving overseas. In later years we were sometimes able to organise a further orientation and language course after the volunteers had arrived in their host country.

When I started, IVS' programme was run exclusively from London. One of us would undertake a rapid field visit each year to select requests for volunteers from the governments or other agencies and to support and check up on the serving volunteers. To deal with any problems that would arise in the country and to follow up contacts made on field visits we always asked one of the serving volunteers to act as co-ordinator. This was difficult for the person chosen who also had a full-time job. At that time

VSO used the services of the British Council for this role. CIIR had already pioneered the idea of a Field Officer, appointing Julian Filochowski in Central America. (Later he was head of the Catholic agency, CAFOD.) In 1973 we managed to obtain funding from the Overseas Development Ministry for Tom Franklin to work as a field officer in Cameroon and for Lois Carter to cover Botswana, Lesotho and Swaziland. Later we were able to fund separate officers in each country including the Comoro Islands and Mozambique. IVS was a pioneer in appointing nationals of the country as field officers.

iii) Swaziland (now eSwatini)

My first field visits to IVS overseas programmes were in 1973 and 1974 and the first country I arrived in was Swaziland. It was warm, green and very beautiful. During this time of apartheid, tourists came to Swaziland to do what was forbidden in South Africa: buy books by politically minded black authors or, more often, Playboy – or to gamble at the casino and break the colour bar, which included bathing in the nude in the warm springs nick-named the cuddle puddle. On Friday evenings the dramatic road which winds down from the tiny capital city, Mbabane, to the second "city," Manzini, was lined with Swazi girls waiting to be picked up. The country had attracted investment in hotels, mining and sugar plantations but most of the profits left the country – and the Swazis who benefited most were members of the enormous royal family.[29] Political repression had already begun. In 1973, only five years after independence the aged King Sobhuza II suspended the constitution. Political parties were banned in 1978 and repression continues to this day.

However, the volunteers from IVS did play a positive role in Swaziland's development as there was a serious lack of trained personnel, the case in most post-colonial states. The government officials were good to work with and it was easy visiting the

---

29. One day a minibus full of princesses overturned and it did not even get a headline in the local paper.

government ministries as they were all close together above the shops in Mbabane's main street. The IVS volunteers were working in agricultural research, industrial development and health but the majority were teachers in an education system which was somewhat dysfunctional. Many secondary schools squeezed as many as 60 children into a small classroom and the curriculum was too academic to be helpful for the majority. However, working and living in small rural schools, the volunteer teachers were probably the best integrated into the local community. One school I visited where we did not have volunteers was Waterford KaMhlaba, now one of the United World Colleges and at the time a famous multi-racial boarding school where prosperous blacks and liberal whites from all over southern Africa sent their children as a way of confronting and avoiding *apartheid*.

This was before the advent of AIDS, which has hit southern Africa harder than anywhere. One project we supported in Swaziland was an orphanage for "coloured" children. Swazis explained that any black orphans would always be cared for by their extended family. In recent years AIDS has produced more orphans than the traditional system can bear.

iv) Lesotho

I went by road from Swaziland to Lesotho in 1973, seven hours through the wide, open spaces of what was then the Transvaal and over the Caledon River straight into Maseru which was still the tiny, slightly shabby colonial capital it had been until Independence in 1966. The only intrusion from the modern world was the Holiday Inn with its ugly flashing sign advertising the casino, where, along with South African tourists, numerous poorly paid Basotho gambled away their wages.

Lesotho's beauty is very different from that of Swaziland. The mountains are higher, dryer and rougher, often flat-topped or with a *krans*, a big rock, on top. The soil erosion is dramatic. The rains have cut deep mini-canyons, known as *dongas*. Thousands of tons of soil are washed away by the Senqu River. This river is known in South Africa as the Orange, which is the colour of its water due to the mass of soil it is carrying. As a way of controlling erosion there is a national tree planting day, but the trees often face a losing battle against hungry goats.

With mission schools dating from the mid-19th century, Lesotho had produced more educated citizens than Swaziland or Botswana, but many of these were working in South Africa, and so here also there was a lack of people with skills and qualifications. As in Swaziland the largest number of IVS volunteers were schoolteachers, mainly of maths and science, but some worked in agriculture, at the university, in the remote hospital at Paray, high on the plateau, and in the Flying Doctor Service, which was often able to use a Land Rover instead of a plane as the mountain roads improved. Volunteers were requested for many types of job. An interesting one was from King Moshoeshoe II for someone to work in his garden. I was invited for tea and biscuits in his little palace, the former Resident Commissioner's house, but I had to explain politely that we had development priorities and the royal garden was not really one of them.

On my second visit to Lesotho the very friendly British High Commissioner gave me a lift in his Range Rover from Bloemfontein airport. I was amused when we stopped exactly half way across the bridge which forms the frontier with South Africa and the driver got out and raised the Union Jack on the front bonnet. I was invited to stay the night and I enjoyed a cup of early morning tea with the royal monogram on it. The next night in a village near Butha Buthe with a corrugated shack for a toilet was quite a contrast.

The political temperature in Lesotho had been high since the 1970 elections which the more radical Basutoland Congress Party (BCP) had won but had been denied office in a coup by the governing Basotho National Party led by Leabua Jonathan. In 1974 after an attempted uprising, Ntsu Mokhehle and other BCP leaders fled the country and the Police Mobile Unit (PMU) was very active. To add to this, unemployment had risen fast as many migrant workers had returned to Lesotho after troubles at Welkom mine in South

Africa. The king had returned from exile but had little influence. Odilon Seheri worked in the Ministry of Education and was close to the king. I had known him at the Institute of Education in London back in 1961 and visited him in Lesotho. I was shocked to learn in 1981 that his body had been found by a rural road. He and others were clearly victims of the PMU.

I returned to Lesotho in 1993 when CCIVS organised a training seminar.

v) Botswana

My train journey through the impoverished Bechuanaland Protectorate on my way to Northern Rhodesia in 1961 is described above. The independent Botswana where I arrived on my field visit in 1973 was a very different place. The capital had moved from Mafekeng in South Africa – formerly Mafeking, where the siege was famously relieved during the "Boer War" in 1900 to a brand-new capital, Gaborone, planned like another African version of Milton Keynes. I saw signs that the country's economic development was about to take off with development of the copper and nickel mining town of Selebi-Phikwe, though the biggest resource, diamonds, was still in the future.

Independent Botswana was an easy place for foreign NGOs, too easy perhaps. The small population and lack of well-educated personnel meant that expatriates of all kinds, including IVS volunteers, were badly needed and the administration was welcoming and efficient. Tswana tradition is fairly democratic: the people lived in large settlements, more like towns than villages, such as Serowe, Kanye, Molepolole and Mochudi, each of which had its *kgotla,* a court or council where all the men participated. Cattle are central to Tswana culture and young men traditionally looked after the animals which meant spending time at the cattle posts far from the villages. Girls are therefore often better educated than boys and thus women play a more important role in Botswana than in most African countries. In spite of political freedom and relatively low level of corruption, the ruling Botswana Democratic Party has always remained dominant and the various opposition parties only strong in their own local areas. Surviving on the edge of the Kalahari Desert, rain is important. The national currency is the Pula, meaning rain. I remember Gaositwe Chiepe, the Botswana High Commissioner arriving at the independence party at the Commonwealth Institute in a heavy rainstorm and explaining that this meant the day had been blessed. One bad aspect of Botswana has been its treatment of the minority Basarwa, or bushmen, who live in the Kalahari.

Patrick van Rensburg as a very young man had served as the South African Vice-Consul in the Belgian Congo but resigned in protest at the racial injustice in South Africa. He came to London and was involved in the beginnings of the Anti-Apartheid Movement in London but his main work was in Botswana where he founded the progressive Swaneng Hill School at Serowe, and later also Shashe River and Madiba schools. He also created the Brigades. These were an imaginative type of technical training programme geared to production of goods or services – carpentry, motor mechanics, dress-making – where young men and women learned trades along with school subjects with a practical slant. These projects were coordinated by the Foundation for Education with Production which Patrick founded in Botswana and which is now active in South Africa and elsewhere. He was a very practical man who inspired those who worked with him and the many students who benefited from his work. I think I only met him once but his dream fitted well with IVS' idea of development and our volunteers played an important part at these schools and brigades.[30] We sent a number of teachers to other schools too. We were persuaded that, given that Botswana was likely to develop fast, the need for more educated young people was crucial. Other volunteers were at the agricultural research station; government departments, which included editing the Daily News; the national library and at the hospital at Maun.

Maun is the capital of Ngamiland, the area where the huge Okavango River, fed by rain in Angola, becomes a delta and peters

---

30. A biography of Patrick by Dr. Kevin Shillington is in preparation.

out into the desert. I visited the two IVS midwives at Maun in 1973 and again in 1974. To get there I was offered a seat on the Wenela flight. The Witwatersrand Native Labour Association (Wenela) had been set up by the South African gold mines to recruit labour from all the countries of the region, even as far north as the Congo and Tanganyika. Recruits were brought together for training before arriving in Johannesburg. They were taught a bit about mining and had lessons in Fanagalo, the pidgin Zulu language spoken by migrant labourers in South Africa.[31] Zambia had stopped the flights from Barotseland, western Zambia, at Independence, but Batswana recruits were still being flown from Maun in 1973. Wenela had told me to be at Francistown airport at 5.30am and not to weigh more than 160 lbs. The night porter at the inappropriately named Grand Hotel did not wake me until 5.00. I then had to drive a Land Rover to pick up the driver in the township of jumbled thatched rondavels known as Somerset East. The kind driver, doubting my ability to find his house, had walked nearly all the way to the hotel. I found him on the road and caught the plane, just. The plane resembled a modern slave ship with very basic canvas seats. My fellow passengers had been flown from Johannesburg and had spent the night on the floor at Francistown airport. Some others were waiting to fly to Ovamboland in the north of Namibia or to Malawi.

It was extremely hot in Maun but very peaceful, with just the sound of cicadas and distant barking dogs. The population includes many Herero people who had escaped the genocide perpetrated in 1904-1907 by the Germans in their colony of South West Africa, now Namibia. Herero women still wear the voluminous full-length dresses, with the addition of a "cow-horn" head dress, introduced by the missionaries at the end of the 19th century. They wear it as a silent reminder of their people's tragedy.

The view from the Wenela flight back on my second visit in 1974 visit was of a landscape which had been brown the year before and was now very green. The pilot swooped down low over the

---

31. It was known as Chilapalapa in Rhodesia, or worse, as Kitchen Kaffir.

Makgadigadi Salt Pans above a large herd of wildebeest, much to the delight of the mine workers. This time I was not the only white man on the flight. There was a Swedish family and a Belgian who must have weighed well over the limit.

I cannot write about Botswana without recounting the story of **Marius Schoon**. Less famous than Bram Fischer, the lawyer who defended Mandela at the Rivonia Trial and was then condemned for life and died in prison, Marius was also a proud Afrikaner, one of the very rare ones who was a militant ANC activist. He hated racism. He also loved the Afrikaans language and poetry. He had spent twelve years in prison for attempting to blow up a radio transmitter at a police station in Johannesburg in 1964 – an agent provocateur had infiltrated his group. He could not accompany his African co-conspirator, Mike Ngubeni, to Robben Island because even the prisons were segregated. After his release he married Jeanette who had also been a courageous campaigner against *apartheid*. They were not supposed to meet each other and their marriage was illegal as they were both "banned persons," as was Beyers Naude who performed the wedding ceremony. They skipped the border into Botswana and in 1977 we appointed Marius as IVS Field Officer, though he continued to act as an agent of the ANC. The Schoons and other exiles in Botswana were constantly harassed with death threats and hoaxes. The British High Commission became nervous and put IVS under intolerable pressure to move Marius and his family out of Botswana. I had to fly out in 1983 to try to sort things out. We had no choice but to yield: one option was for them to come and work in Leicester at the IVS office but they decided to stay in Africa. They were both appointed to work at Lubango University in Angola. On 28 June 1984 when Marius was away in the capital, Jeanette collected a parcel from the post. She and their six-year-old daughter, Katryn, were blown to bits. The author of the bomb was the notorious double agent, Craig Williamson. Some years later I stayed with Marius in Johannesburg not long before he died. Peace lover that he was, he told me he could never agree to forgive the killer of his wife and daughter. Williamson went before the Truth and Reconciliation Commission where he showed no remorse. He was controversially given an amnesty after Marius' death.[32] Nelson Mandela paid tribute to Marius, saying *"He destroyed the myth that all Afrikaners were racists and oppressors."*

The fact that we had employed Marius made the South African intelligence take an interest in IVS and we realised afterwards that a young man who had volunteered in our office to help sort out colour slides and had attended one of the orientation courses was probably a South African agent of some kind. We got to know Sholto Cross, another South African activist who had been imprisoned by the regime and who was chosen by the BVP to undertake an evaluation of the work of IVS and the other agencies.

vi) Cameroon and Chad

My first visit to Cameroon was on our overland journey home from Zambia, described above, where we had just been travellers and had no real contact with people. My first visit for IVS was in 1973 after my visit to southern Africa where my passport had numerous South African stamps in it. To enter Cameroon I had to hide my usual passport and present another one. Also, I gave a friend a shirt with a map of Botswana on it. He was stopped by the police for this very tenuous connection with the *apartheid* regime.

IVS had about twenty volunteers in Cameroon, mostly teachers, most of them in the western, Anglophone part of the country. At that time we had no field officer based in the country. Our main agent was the British consul based in Buea This man was not very sympathetic to our volunteers and more concerned about his responsibility should something go wrong. Meeting volunteers on arrival he would immediately raise the possibility of one of them dying in Cameroon, a cheerful welcome to the country. I don't regret never meeting him.

By the time of my second visit a year later the Buea consulate had closed and Tom Franklin had started work as our field officer. He

---

32. In the 1970s Williamson had cheated his way into becoming Deputy Director of the International University Exchange Fund which gave him the data on many South African students.

was already well integrated into Cameroon. Although there were many fields where British volunteers could be useful – training of nurses and teachers, social work, community development (which existed in the west but was unknown among the Francophones), it was not easy developing a volunteer programme here as most projects could not contribute to the costs and our budget was very small. The volunteers, a happy group, came together for a meeting during my visit by the idyllic beach at Londji on the Atlantic coast. Here I picked up some jiggers in the sand, causing great interest at the Chelsea School of Chiropody when I returned home.

To meet our two volunteer teachers at Ngaoundéré and to check on possible new projects in the north of the country Tom and I took the *Transcamerounais* railway from Yaoundé, an exciting prospect for a railway buff like me. The first railways in Cameroon were built during German rule to a one metre gauge. The line from Douala, the port and largest city, to the interior had not extended very far before the country was taken over by the French. It was extended to Yaoundé in 1930. The 653 kilometre-long extension to Ngaoundéré, planned since before Independence, had only just opened. It was a long but fairly comfortable overnight journey with a few stops for the local sellers to tempt us with chickens, bananas, biscuits and everything else. We moved north into dry, rocky terrain, a contrast to the lush forests of the south.

We flew on to Maroua to meet government officials. Airport security has changed since those days. Our suitcases did not appear in the little arrivals hall and we were invited to climb inside the plane's hold where we were able to dislodge them from among the piles of tin trunks and boxes. We continued north by bush taxi through even dryer terrain to Kousseri and over the new bridge to N'djamena, the capital of Chad.

N'djamena, known as Fort-Lamy until 1973, seemed to be a quiet city with handsome arcades along some of the streets as protection from the burning sun. President Tombalbaye swept past us in his motorcade. We met a couple of government officials, people from Swiss Technical Assistance and UN agencies as well as staff from the English Department at the University who would have liked to have volunteers. There were still many French expatriates working in Chad as well as American, Canadian, German and Swiss volunteers. We only spent a few days in the country, not long enough to get any real understanding of the place and its needs but enough to see that there were lots of reasons, including cost, for IVS not to start a volunteer programme there. The British ambassador to Chad was based in London but she was also on a visit to the country and was about to host a party to mark the Queen's birthday where I might have made a few more useful contacts. However, the sudden death of President Pompidou of France meant the party was cancelled. All the flags were flying at half-mast when I stopped in Paris on the way home.

Back in London in 1972 Edyth and I had met and made friends with several Cameroonians who trained as English teachers. When I visited Yaoundé briefly again in 1982 I met Celestin Tcheho and Innocent Futcha again. By the time of my last visit in 2016 Celestin had established an impressive bilingual school in Yaoundé and Innocent was helping establish the *Université des Montagnes* in Bamileke country, the area noted for its steep, pointed roofs and its wonderful wood carvings. We had also remained friends since 1972 with Emmanuel Komguep who had settled in France and in 2016 he and his wife Catherine took me to visit his enormous extended family and many friends in Bafoussam, the capital of the West Region, as well as in Douala and Yaoundé. I was given a second 80th birthday party in Douala. We crossed to Bafut in the English-speaking west of the country to visit a pioneering permaculture project run by Better World Cameroon, a member association of CCIVS. The Fon of Bafut was a keen supporter of this project and we were taken to see him. He is the son of the Fon who features in *The Bafut Beagles* and *A Zoo in my Luggage* by Gerald Durrell. He remembers Durrell's visits to collect animals. On this visit I found Cameroon to be in a rather gloomy mood despite its huge agricultural and mineral resources, perhaps as a result of the 35 years of uninspiring rule by President Paul Biya.

vii) Comoro Islands

In 1974 I set off with Edyth and Tom, aged one, on a field visit which was also partly a holiday to research a possible volunteer programme in the Comoro Islands and to visit the IVS volunteers in Mauritius and Seychelles. We flew on Sudan Air to Nairobi and continued via Dar es Salaam to Moroni, the capital of the Comoros.

The Comoros consist of four islands, three of which, Grande Comore, Anjouan and Moheli, voted in 1975 for independence and one, Mayotte, preferred to stay French. We stayed in the hotel next to the airport. Moroni is a capital city on a small scale with its market, fishing boats, Friday Mosque and a few carved wooden doorways, similar but not as fine as those in Zanzibar or Lamu. Karthala loomed over the little city, a huge presence, an active volcano rising 2,300 metres from the sea and most of the time shrouded in thick cloud. We took a shared *taxi de ville* to the beautiful beach at Itsandra. The whole island of Grande Comore was evidence of Karthala's past eruptions: black volcanic rock and, where it had broken up, very fertile, black soil.

We hired a car for a day and drove north to Mitsamiouli, through a scene of palm trees, bananas and fields of ylang ylang which is Comoro's main export, used for Chanel No.5 and other perfumes, and for aromatherarpy. The scene became bleaker: a huge expanse of broken volcanic rock, like cinders with a few hardy ferns sprouting through them. Karthala and other smaller mountains formed the backdrop. Our memory of this little town was of fishing boats pulled up on the shore, people sitting in the shade of their doorways and numerous goats. On the way back we gave a lift to a farmer who took us to see the *Trou du Prophète*, a beautiful hidden bay guarded by pillars of rock. The next morning we got up at dawn and drove to Foumbouni in the south of the island through several villages of wooden weatherboard houses, each with its little market place and newly painted mosque. The road was winding and narrow, high above the beach. Briefly the whole of Karthala came into view, but soon was again swathed in cloud. At one point there was a hazy view of the neighbouring island of Moheli.

Back in Moroni we noticed signs of political activity and felt tension in the air. Then, as we sat in our hotel we watched the airport as hundreds of eminent looking Comorians lined up in their robes and police took up their positions. School students jeered at the soldiers and a teacher, a member of the opposition, was arrested. They were there to welcome the return of Ahmed Abdullah, the would-be president, a prosperous rice trader, who had returned from France where he had been negotiating independence. The heavy security was a sign that his reign might be brief.

My discussions with government officials were the first step to setting up a small programme of volunteers in the Comoro Islands. We recruited Gill Shepherd, who had already done some research there, to make a long visit, negotiate with the government and look for possible work projects for volunteers. She reported positively, and in 1977 Steve and Carole Davies went out as joint field officers.

This is Steve Davies' story of IVS' brief involvement in the Comoros:

The path towards the volunteer programme had been well laid out by the initial visits described in this chapter. The country was amongst the poorest in the world. The islands were small, even the capital had a population of just 10,000, and the relevant government ministers were very accessible to the field officers. This meant that IVS was soon able to start developing a useful programme: Eric and Sophie were engineers working on water supply; Jean-Paul worked to repair hospital equipment; and Brian was a biologist working on plant disease. France "punished" the islands for declaring independence unilaterally (in 1975) and always retained control over Mayotte, which is still French today and in 2011 voted to become a *département d'outre-mer*, a "DOM."

In the year before we arrived, the Comoros had been hit by an eruption of Karthala, and by the arrival of considerable numbers of Comorian refugees from Madagascar following massacres there. In the face of these events and the underlying problems of poverty and lack of development, the government of Ali Soilih who had taken over from Ahmed Abdallah, embarked on quite radical policies, with splits and controversies of course, but it did mean it was a positive situation in which to develop the IVS programme of volunteers. Left alone by outside forces, we felt that the islands could have made progress…

But they were not to be left alone. Bob Denard and his little boatload of mercenaries were enough to overthrow the government in 1978 and restore Ahmed Abdallah, who declared the country a Federal Islamic Republic. In Europe the mercenaries were portrayed as adventurers, soldiers of fortune and dogs of war but they were clearly acting on behalf of France and French secret services and also on behalf of Rhodesia (as it then was) and with the aim of evading the sanctions imposed on *apartheid* South Africa. Nor was it a one-off "adventure". Bob Denard continued to have considerable power in the Comoros over the years. He was involved in several coups and attempted coups, and in the elimination of more than one president, including Ahmed Abdallah himself! France eventually made an attempt to put Denard on trial in Paris, but they didn't try very hard… The Comorian people were the victims. IVS, while not expelled, could not work in the new circumstances of a government dominated by mercenaries and withdrew over the next months. The IVS programme lasted just a year, but at least it was a footprint and it marked the spot for international voluntary service and co-operation.

Leaving Moroni behind, Edyth, Tom and I flew on to **Madagascar** where we wandered around the picturesque centre of Antananarivo with its steep steps, across the Place de l'Indépendence surrounded by brilliant jacaranda trees and past the grandiose, very French railway station. We climbed up to the Queen's palace, looking down on Lake Anosy. The collection of historic palaces known as the Rova demonstrated the pride of the pre-colonial Merina monarchy. The palaces later suffered serious fire damage but have mostly been rebuilt. I called on the British Ambassador, who was also accredited to the Comoros, to report on my contacts.

He invited us to lunch and we were driven through the suburbs and rice paddies with the flag flying to his large, white residence where we had an excellent lunch and Tom had fun crawling around on the pile carpets. The ambassador's wife was wistfully reading the *Illustrated London News*.

We made a one-night stopover on the French island of ***Réunion***, long enough to admire the houses with their shutters and balconies, a miniature New Orleans, and to hire a car for a few hours to drive uphill through fields of sugar cane, past the remains of the old railway to within sight of the *Piton des Neiges,* Réunion's 10,000 foot-high volcano, before flying on to Mauritius.

viii) Mauritius

Mauritius was devastated by cyclone Carol, the most severe ever recorded in the island's history in March 1960. There were over 1,700 casualties, 42 people were killed and over 100,000 buildings were destroyed or seriously damaged. Over ten percent of the island's total population of 600,000 were in refugee centres. Two IVS volunteers, Patrick Alexander and John Beckett, arrived shortly after the cyclone, helped local people to build shelters and rebuild the houses of cyclone victims. They worked closely with the Mauritius Ministry of Labour and many young Mauritians joined in the work. The upshot was a regular programme of British long-term volunteers and the creation of a local branch of SCI, *Service Volontaire International,* whose first constitution dates from 1968, the year of the country's independence. SVI was not strong at the time of my visit but I met its president, Miko Pottier, and the very active Ayle Duval. SVI supported the local Cheshire Home and the school for the deaf and it organised an annual cycle rally round the island. SVI still survives today.

IVS volunteers had been much appreciated by the Mauritius government and on his field visits Steve Dey, IVS' former Secretary General, had an excellent relationship with the first Prime Minister, Sir Seewoosagur Ramgoolam. But by 1974 the number of IVS volunteers was dwindling, and our host, Tim Blakemore, was one of the last. He worked in the youth department. He took us all over the island in a minibus belonging to the US Peace Corps. The country is a cultural melting pot: whites of French origin; a large number of Creoles of mixed African and French descent; a majority population of Indian descent, mostly of Tamil origin; some Chinese; and a few British. The Creole language grew out of French but educated Mauritians also speak good French and English.

Apart from work we were invited by SVI friends and we visited most of the sights of the island: the Pamplemousses botanical gardens with their huge water lilies and giant tortoises; the varied and lovely coastline with white spray rising as the waves hit the coral reef; the Temple of Shiva; the mountains always in the background; the busy, hot streets of the capital, Port Louis. After a few days Edyth and Tom left Mauritius to visit our many friends in Zambia while I remained in work mode and visited the much smaller island of Rodrigues, politically part of Mauritius and situated 560 kilometres to the east.

As the tiny plane descended I had an amazing view of the coral reefs around Rodrigues followed by a shock as a tyre burst as we landed. It was a frightening experience – but the few of us on board survived unhurt. Rodrigues is beautiful, very rocky, very dry. The island is long and thin and there are dramatic views of the sea from the road which winds along the crest of the island. The population is around 40,000, nearly all of mixed African and French descent with a small Chinese community but, unlike the main island, almost none of Indian descent. At the time of my visit Rodrigues was ruled by a Resident Commissioner, a proconsul of legendary ferocity by the name of Nigel Heseltine who had a passing resemblance to President De Gaulle. I found him pleasant enough and not averse to the idea of British volunteers. The shortage of personnel on Rodrigues seemed mainly to be due to the fact that most Mauritians did not want to work in such a remote place. In fact the two IVS volunteers were just completing their assignments, working on terracing for crops and market gardens, very necessary due to the steep slopes. Their work had been appreciated but they were to be the last. Today Rodrigues is run as an autonomous region with a local assembly, and tourism has grown to be its main source of income.

ix) Seychelles

Seats were only available in first class on the flight from Mauritius to Seychelles and the British Governor welcomed me in the VIP lounge. This little country of 115 islands and less than 100,000 people was not to declare independence until 1976, two years after my visit. The airport had only recently opened and this had created a huge potential for tourism which had already begun to change the quiet ambience of the place. Previous IVS visits by the former IVS Secretary General, Steve Dey, had involved him sailing from Mombasa or Bombay and spending as long or as short a time as the ships' schedules allowed. I think this was the part of the job Steve enjoyed most.

Everything in the capital, Victoria, was on an even smaller scale than in Moroni. Narrow roads led to a central clock tower. I visited the prison, also very small – a dungeon with no facilities. The colonial regime had not trained many Seychellois and most of the nine IVS volunteers in Seychelles in1974 were there to build capacity: one, Janis Tombs, worked at the national library – and joined the staff at IVS after her return; two were at the self-build housing scheme; others included a social worker trainer; an administrator in the hospital; and three teachers at the technical college. The male volunteers lived at La Poudrière, a huge old colonial style house by the sea, falling to pieces and full of cockroaches. Janis recently checked it out on Google and it seems to have been demolished.

Our volunteers' work was greatly appreciated. Not many of Seychelles' new tourists were buying local handicrafts because few were being produced. I was asked for volunteers who could help develop pottery and craft designs. The Governor asked us to send more volunteers with different skills. He considered the needs would continue after Independence. James Mancham, the exuberant Chief Minister, said to me, "Send us fifty"! We did not send many, however, and our programme closed down soon afterwards.

x) Mozambique

Portugal's former colonies were liberated in 1975. Three members of the British Volunteer Programme, IVS, UNAIS and CIIR got together to investigate whether we should try to start sending volunteer development workers to these countries which badly needed skilled manpower after the rapid departure of nearly all the Portuguese. It was decided that IVS should take on Mozambique and in 1977 I made a short visit which sowed the seeds of our programme there. This was an important time in Mozambique's history. FRELIMO, the liberation movement which had just turned itself into a political party and was already present in the north, was establishing itself in the southern part of the country which it had never conquered during the independence struggle. The aim was a socialist state, but the government moved cautiously, encouraging Portuguese people and private companies to stay, keeping trade links with South Africa and even allowing workers to be recruited for the goldmines. Britain's ambassador seemed to have good relations with the government.

However, the country faced enormous problems. Almost all types of job, even taxi drivers and shop assistants, had been done by Portuguese, and there was therefore a glaring lack of skills. The legacy of the colonial regime meant that school curricula, salaries, taxation, the legal system and many other things were inappropriate for a newly independent country; and to make matters worse the Portuguese army had indulged in sabotage as it departed. War was raging in neighbouring Rhodesia and it sometimes spilled over the border. The Cabora Bassa dam had been threatened with sabotage as a symbol of apartheid as it had been built to supply power to South Africa but now that Mozambique was free it was threatened from the other side and on one occasion an important bridge on the road to it was destroyed. The country was also devastated by floods. Mozambique joined in the sanctions imposed on Rhodesia at great cost to itself; South Africa was always ready to destabilise the country. While I was there I made contact with two leading members of the Zimbabwe liberation movement, Henry Hamadziripi, one of the founders of ZAPU who had opposed Mugabe, and Kumbirai Kangai, who later served as a minister in Robert Mugabe's government. I offered them IVS' solidarity for what that was worth.

While I was in Maputo I discussed a lot with the deputy head of the National Directorate for International Co-operation, Lourenço Mutaca, and I remember having interesting meetings with the Director of Agriculture, Jorge Tembe; with the well-known architect, Jose Forjaz, at the Ministry of Public Works and Housing; and the impressive Sergio Vieiro de Mello at UNHCR who was to die tragically in 2003 when the UN headquarters was attacked in Iraq. I also met many of the brilliant group of British socialists working for Mozambique including Polly Gaster, Pam Logie, Julie Cliff, Barry Munslow and Janet, the widow of Frelimo's first leader, Eduardo Mondlane. Polly had been involved in organising Mozambique's first film festival.

FRELIMO had ambitious plans and it was clear to me that Mozambique had a great need for development workers, but these would have to be relatively highly skilled. There was also a political context. The few British and other European workers already in the country had mostly been recruited through the Mozambique, Angola and Guine Information Centre (MAGIC) in London which was part of the movement for solidarity with the liberation struggle. My discussions, especially with Mutaca, led to a draft agreement to recruit mature and experienced *cooperantes* – the Portuguese word seemed better than "volunteers" in the Mozambican context – people who were sympathetic to the aims of FRELIMO, though they did not necessarily have to be socialists. IVS was to work closely with MAGIC, which would be involved in selection and training. In the report of my 1977 visit I noted that development would be based on agriculture, developing state farms, co-operatives and communal villages, learning from the mistakes Tanzania had made with its *ujaama* villages. Big increases were planned in food crops – maize, millets and beans – and export crops, mainly cashew nuts and tobacco. Mozambique, a huge, well-watered country with a small population, had immense potential. Agro-based industry was also to be developed along with the exploitation of minerals. There were also desperate needs for education, health services and basic infrastructure. The Portuguese had built roads to suit their military strategy but not much else.

Within the next two years an IVS programme was established and a field office opened. We had to strike a balance between MAGIC's political line, which we were happy with, and the British Overseas Development Ministry's suspicion that MAGIC was a communist organisation. IVS provided some really excellent *cooperantes* over the years. However, one effect of the type of programme we had in Mozambique, of highly qualified and politically motivated workers, was to create tension with the more traditionally volunteerish, workcamping attitudes in IVS. This was one of the causes of IVS splitting later into two separate organisations, Skillshare Africa running the development orientated overseas programme and IVS retaining its traditional workcamps and local groups. In fact, the main reason for the split was that the overseas programme was well funded by the government and the other work of IVS was not. Skillshare combined with Action Health 2000 and to become Skillshare International. It disbanded in 2015. IVS continues as an active branch of SCI with its office in Edinburgh.

xi) New volunteer associations in southern Africa

African countries mostly have artificial boundaries and contain many different ethnic groups. Fwanyanga Mulikita from *Zambia* had taken part in international workcamps when he was studying in the UK. This experience influenced him when he was appointed Permanent Secretary in the Ministry of Education. He could see that workcamps could be a tool for building national consciousness among youth and reducing inter-ethnic prejudices. His ministry began organising camps for young students from the different provinces. Thus, when I was at Kalomo Secondary School in 1967, students from the Southern Province, which was inhabited by Tonga people, worked together with those from the Western Province (Barotseland), the land of the Lozi. As it happened our colleagues, John and Louise Melbourne, had met on an IVS workcamp on Fair Isle, north of Scotland. John happily took on the leadership of the camp. In general the scheme was not well organised and its cost meant that the government's programme was short-lived, but the basic idea was later taken up by the new Zambia National Youth Service.

My primary role in IVS from 1972 to 1978 had been to run IVS' programme of overseas volunteers, working for development and, in southern Africa, providing a non-racial witness against *apartheid*. But the promotion of the idea of international understanding through workcamps was also high on our agenda. On my first field visit to southern Africa I made contact with James Makoetla who had been trying to establish workcamps in Lesotho and Botswana. His efforts did not succeed, but workcamp associations were soon to be established in Lesotho, Botswana and Swaziland. The process was helped by the presence from 1975 of an IVS field officer for the three countries, Lois Carter. She was later replaced by separate officers in each country. A Swiss volunteer, Augustin Wyss, sent by IVS, had as his main job to support the development of workcamp associations. In **Lesotho** the national leaders were crucial, notably Vincent Mhlakaza and, later, Thabo Marekemane and Kory Masitha. Lesotho Workcamps Association (LWA) has had an impressive record: hundreds of projects including tree planting; making access roads and water supplies to villages; construction of schools and other community buildings., LWA built a hostel in Maseru, with aid from German Agro-Action.

Augustin moved on to **Botswana** where BWA (*Lekgotla la Baithaopi*) began work in 1979 consisting of local groups in the large villages with a main base at Mochudi. It is still active and has organised many workcamps over the years, many of them to support wildlife conservation. An association, SWCA, was started in *Swaziland*, but the movement never took root there. These three southern African organisations pioneered inter-African volunteer exchanges, Boleswa, which involved long journeys by minibus across South Africa. Boleswa grew into a wider regional structure, Southern Africa Workcamps Cooperation (SAWC), described below.

xii) Northern Ireland and other stories

I regretted not applying to be General Secretary of IVS in 1975 as most of us on the staff felt that Geoffrey Hewitt who was appointed was not really in tune with IVS. I took over from him in 1979 which meant I spent less time on Africa and more on the programme in the UK. The conflict in *Northern Ireland* was on our doorstep and IVS had not been active there. Some of our members, stirred on by friends from the Irish branch of SCI, had begun a scheme where children from the two communities went on holiday together, often outside Northern Ireland, where friendship and understanding could grow in a way that was impossible in the segregated towns. An IVS office was established in Belfast in 1972 and Sean Armstrong was appointed as field officer, a very dynamic and charismatic man. Then when we had a terrible introduction to reality in the north of Ireland. A man knocked on the door of the field office asking for John. Sean came downstairs and was shot. He came from a well-known Protestant family but he had taken the Irish name Sean as he identified with the republican movement, so we assumed that the attacker was a Protestant. Steve Dey asked me to go to Belfast to give some support to our shaken colleagues. I raced to Euston station for a flight from Manchester. I had a haircut while waiting for the plane. I told the barber the reason for my journey. He said, "I wouldn't go if I were you!" Sean's murder got a huge amount of publicity as he was a well-known and very popular peacemaker. Unusually no organisation owned up and the perpetrator was never found. Sean had just celebrated his wedding at an open-air ceremony at the Giant's Causeway. His child was born after his death.

Other, stronger organisations took on the children's scheme while IVS and VSI moved on to the idea of *teenage workcamps*. Typically, these were mixed groups selected though youth clubs, usually not the toughest hardliners, who were hosted for a couple of weeks in England, the Republic of Ireland, the Netherlands, France or Germany, doing some manual work and having some "craic." Being together in a strange place made the teenagers realise that they had more in common than they did with foreigners, and a few of the friendships made during the camp survived the return home to Belfast or Derry. The success of this scheme gave us the idea of replicating the formula in England where the focus would be on mixing different communities and reducing racial prejudice. I hoped it would be a major growth area for IVS which would strengthen all our other activities and help to link them. A London group began in 1979 based in Camberwell in south London; then one in Leeds in 1982 based in Chapeltown where most of our volunteers were black; a third group on Tyneside, where there were few blacks but no lack of prejudice, began in 1983. I remember visiting workcamps in West Yorkshire and on the Isle of Mull in Scotland where volunteers from the different groups were happily working and socialising together in the rain. Teenage volunteers from Northern Ireland joined in too. We never found reliable funding for the teenage programme and it had to close down after I left IVS. Perhaps I was too ambitious but I still believe that a similar programme would be valuable today.

As described above, SCI branches, including IVS, had for many years invited volunteers from partner organisations in Africa and Asia to attend workcamps in Europe as part of an exchange programme. Ben and Devinder at my workcamp in Germany back in 1955 had been the first pioneers. The number of exchanges reached a peak in the1970s and SCI created a "commission" to organize this scheme on an international level. In IVS we called it the *Overseas Workcamp Exchange Scheme*, managed by John Telford. People interested in the idea were invited to a Questioning Development Weekend where they were exposed to different views about development, peace building and racism. After this if they were still interested they went to an orientation weekend and then to the country of their choice in Asia, Africa or occasionally Latin America. Some of the many outstanding volunteers who came to IVS this way went on to great things. To mention two, Kari Blackburn became head of the BBC African Service; Michael Jacobs became a well-known expert on the environment, General Secretary of the Fabian Society and Special Advisor to the Prime Minister, Gordon Brown.

Back in 1973 a young Mukesh Kapila was about to start a medical course. He turned up at the IVS office wanting to go somewhere. It happened we had a request for a volunteer to go the remote island of Moudubi in Bangladesh. Mukesh spent three months there, the only outsider on this low-lying island where flood water was a constant presence. Barefoot, he was welcomed by everyone and invited by different families for fish and rice each evening. Fired up by his experience and the needs of this community, Mukesh founded a charity, Friends of Moudubi International. But it seemed better to have a wider remit – and it already had another project in Bihar, India – so he chose the grand title of World Community Development Service. It later changed its name to Action Health 2000 and worked in East Africa as well as in India and Bangladesh. In a strange twist of fate it later merged with Skillshare Africa, the former overseas division of IVS to form Skillshare International.

After his return from Moudubi, Mukesh booked a ticket through Brondesbury Travel, run by Terence Khushal from his tiny flat in Kilburn. Terence had been in charge of tourism at the Indian High Commission. Mukesh met him and together they founded what became North-South Travel, a small agency – what used to be known as a "bucket shop" – all the profits of which go into a trust which gives grants to small projects in "southern" countries. IVS has been closely associated with this from the start and I have now been its chair for many years. Khushal's daughter, the well-known author of children's books, Jamila Gavin, is also on the board. Mukesh went on to be a high flier in the Ministry of Overseas Development and in 2003 was appointed head of UN operations in Sudan. It was he who, at personal risk, exposed to the world the horrific genocide in Darfur.[33]

Another lifelong friendship was the result of a small kindness. Djibril Diallo had founded a workcamp association in Casamance, Senegal and had been to workcamps in Europe. He returned to England to study at Nottingham with fifty pence in his pocket. He managed to convince the immigration officer that if he could get to the IVS office which was then in London, Mr. Watt would pay his fare to Nottingham which of course I did. He never forgot this and he has helped me in many ways. The cover of this book shows him with Edyth and me at Fespaco, the film festival in Ouagadougou, Burkina Faso in 1997. He was later a member of the Africa Centre's Council and he worked for the UN, becoming chief information officer at UNDP and head of UNAIDS for West Africa, based at home in Senegal where I visited him in 2017. In 2018 he became head of the African Renaissance and Diaspora Network and I still hope to work with him to develop volunteer exchanges in Africa.

I made two visits to what were then Communist countries. Poland was changing in 1980 with the birth of the *Solidarność* trade union. While still general secretary I went with Russell Cleaver, IVS Vice Chair, joining SCI's east-west expert, John Myers, who took us to some of the projects of the socialist youth movement, our partner, including teenage volunteers in the steel-making town of Nowa Huta outside Krakow, an international workcamp at Opole, the horrific former concentration camp at Oświęcim, better known as Auschwitz-Birkenau and the Black Madonna in the cathedral of Częstochowa. In 1987 when I was SCI president John Myers and I went on an official visit by SCI to the USSR. A huge wreath labelled "from SCI" was handed to us as we entered Lenin's mausoleum on Red Square. It was uncanny to see Lenin's well-preserved features and we duly laid the wreath. From Moscow we went on an overnight train to Vilnius, capital of the Soviet Republic of Lithuania, where we met our partner, the local youth

---

33. Mukesh Kapila's book, "*Against a Tide of Evil*" (Mainstream 2013) describes his dramatic year in Sudan and is well worth reading.

organization, ate a lot of their traditional Cornish style pasties and drank a great deal of vodka.

I was always keen that IVS should play a full part in the life of SCI, the network of which it was a member, and it seems that this was appreciated, judging by the very warm reception I got at the first International SCI meeting I attended after leaving the IVS staff in 1984. At SCI's international committee meeting in India in 1985 I was elected International President for four years.

I left IVS in 1984 when I was appointed Director of the Africa Centre and I returned to the world of voluntary service in 1992 as Director of the Co-ordinating Committee for International Voluntary Service (CCIVS). In my retirement I have been active in another UK workcamp association, Volunteer Action for Peace.

6
Two more journeys

i) Niger to Zambia

In 1982 after eleven years in IVS I was offered sabbatical leave and unsurprisingly I opted to spend most of it in Africa. In some of the countries I took the opportunity of visiting projects and investigating possibilities for volunteers. My first stop was Niamey, capital of **Niger**, in the desperately dry Sahel belt. As I landed it looked strangely green. Since even by 1982 all the trees within fifty kilometres of Niamey had been cut down for firewood, the green meant just grass and small bushes. The heat hits you like a wall when you arrive, though later I experienced a few cooler hours when a sudden wind got up and blew dust and sand and rubbish in all directions, followed by a few minutes of heavy rain. Henner Hildebrand, my host whom I knew through IVS, was running an orientation programme for a group of German development workers and I was lodged in a flat normally occupied to two such Germans, both sports teachers. So, bizarrely, most of the time I was in Niger I was hearing and speaking German, apart from one evening at a party where, drinking some unpleasant red wine, I tried to tune into the impossible accent of a group of Québecois volunteers organised by Crossroads Africa[34]. I made some contacts to see if there was any demand for IVS volunteers in Niger. There was, but we never followed it up.

Niamey gave the impression of having no centre, just consisting of older houses with *banco* (dried mud) walls or scruffier newer houses made of plaster or corrugated iron. Here and there were taller blocks including a conference hall and hotel on the bank of

---

34. An American and Canadian organisation, still active, which sends young volunteers for short term camps in Africa.

the River Niger near the Kennedy Bridge, the only bridge in the country. I walked across it together with a troop of camels. The *Grand Marché* had been destroyed in a fire a few months before I arrived, so the main market was just an open space with a wall around. I hear it was replaced by a bold new structure in 1987 but this was again badly damaged by fire in 2009. Fires seem to be common at African markets as I found out again in Burundi. For me the most interesting place in Niamey was its remarkable museum, a kind of a park and zoo with examples of the villages of the different ethnic groups, a painted Hausa town house, galleries of costumes, jewellery, dinosaurs and prehistory, and a very amazing tree. This is the *Arbre de Ténéré* which had been found in a particularly bleak part of the Sahara where it had become a landmark for overland travellers. It died in 1972 and the trunk and branches were brought to the museum. A steel replica now stands in its old place in the desert on the route used by many of those hoping to get to Libya and migrate to Europe.

I flew on to Cotonou, **Benin** and stayed with Gideon Akator, the West African co-ordinator for Service Civil International. He had always known me in London in winter where I used to wear a woolly hat, so he took some time to recognize this hatless *toubab*. Gideon had hired an office and we stayed there. A certain Madame Gbogbo lived across the road and prepared us delicious meals and her little daughters ran over and cuddled us! We visited the co-operative workshop for which SCI had paid for an electric planning machine. Several teenage apprentices were producing quality furniture and frames for doors and windows, supervised by Stanislas, the Beninois leader of the project. We also visited Ganvié, the "African Venice" which I had already visited in 1971 – and Madame Gbogbo came too. We passed the huge new sports complex, an early sign of the growing Chinese presence.

Gideon and I left Cotonou in a Peugeot bush taxi labelled "*Qui sait l'avenir?*" (Who knows the future?), crossing into neighbouring *Togo*, through Lomé, the capital, which had sprouted a lot of new hotels since 1971, continuing inland and slightly uphill to Kpalime, the home of most of Togo's many active volunteer associations and the former home of Gerson Gu-Konu (see chapter 4b). In the village of Akata up in the hills we called on Gerson's 88-year old father who had not seen his exiled son for many years. He had been a Lutheran pastor and he could still speak some German from when Togo was a German colony. He had instilled in Gerson a strong moral commitment which first inspired him to promote voluntarism. We also visited the village where a recent international workcamp had been planting orange trees and *College Espoir,* a progressive private school headed by a pioneer from Senegal, Mamadou Pam. Gerson had helped to establish this school and IVS had sent volunteers there.

We left Kpalimé in a very ancient Land Rover labelled "Good Name is better than Rich" which took us across the border to Ho in the Volta Region of **Ghana**, Gideon's home. The road was terrible. We stopped on the way to visit a workcamp as I was carrying some contact lens liquid to deliver to one of the European volunteers. This was the worst period of Ghana's foreign exchange crisis. President Hilla Limann had just been overthrown by Jerry Rawlings. In Togo the roadside stalls were piled high with soap powder, cigarettes, sugar, chewing gum and much else. On the Ghana side of the road there were just a few biscuits and sweets. Other items got snapped up as soon as they were delivered. The shops in Accra were almost empty; the bookshop had nothing but birthday cards; their few books had been confiscated in lieu of tax! There were long queues for petrol and we had to go to five petrol stations to find motor oil. Pepsi Cola was hoarded as if it was gold. The textile factory in Akosombo was working at 10% capacity as they could not import dye. The machinery at the sugar refinery was so decrepit that it could only produce molasses and sugar had to be imported. The efficient state bus service was hopelessly over-crowded for lack of spare tyres, motor oil and brake fluid. There was a serious brain drain – 14,000 Ghanaians were teaching in Nigeria, later to be expelled in the "Ghana Must Go" campaign.

I spent a relaxing weekend at Akosombo with Miniman and his wife, Felicia, whose response to the economic crisis was to make ice lollies with orange squash and send a girl to sell them by the main road. That and tomatoes seemed to be all that was available that day. After that I went to see the powerhouse at the Volta Dam. There was a security barrier and Kojo the driver showed him my pass. The guard brandished his gun and fiercely told us to turn around. Kojo went straight off to the police station to report. Miniman came along and took me back through the same barrier where the guard was now looking somewhat crestfallen. The powerhouse is impressive: water drops about seventy metres and this provides a lot of power when (unlike the time of my 1963 visit) the lake is full. We gazed up at the Presidential Lodge, built by Nkrumah but seldom used by him, where ex-President Limann had been holed up since the recent coup. People were hurrying to sail up the lake on the *Akosombo Queen* and a lot of East German combine harvesters were waiting to be shipped north. A team from West Germany was due to arrive to revive the port and its small shipbuilding industry. During this Cold War time Africa often benefited from east-west rivalry.

A main reason for this visit to Ghana was to maintain relations with the Voluntary Workcamps Association of Ghana (VOLU) described above. Gideon and I met with Francis Donkor (Osofo), the General Secretary (who was later to precede me as a Director of CCIVS) in the shabby old wooden building by the sea shore which housed their office and a hostel for volunteers. The next day Gideon drove me to Aflao, the border town which adjoins Lomé. We jumped the half mile queue of Ghanaians going to Togo to do their shopping. Henner was waiting for us in Lomé, among the street stalls piled even higher with basic goods for the Ghanaians to buy. I flew on to Yaoundé in **Cameroon** where I spent a couple of days with IVS' former field officer, Tom Franklin and Cameroonian friends.

My next stop was a short visit to Bangui, capital of the **Central African Republic**. Getting to Yaoundé airport was delayed by President Kaunda of Zambia who was on a State Visit to Cameroon and I got a glimpse of his famous white handkerchief as he drove off. Bangui was humid and very sleepy. It would fit well into a Graham Greene novel. The wide Ubangui river flowed past the old town centre with a pleasant view across to forest in Zaire (now the DRC). I had diverted here to see if there were any likely openings for IVS volunteers. With this in mind I called on the US Peace Corps, *L'Agence Française des Volontaires du Progrès* (now known as *France Volontaires)* and to the UN Volunteers. We never sent any volunteers to the CAR in the end. It was quite an interesting moment to see Bangui, however, as the Emperor Bokassa's Central African Empire had only recently been overthrown and along the road there were still the remains of some tawdry arches which had been erected for his coronation. The country was at a low ebb – and it was still like that when I next went there for a conference in 1998. At the airport crowds of Muslims were piling into a plane going to Mecca for the Hajj. I had not realised there were many Muslims in the CAR but the violent events of 2014 when there was briefly a Muslim president were a reminder that they were a strong minority, at least in the north of the country. The country is still in turmoil.

After a night in Brazzaville I arrived in **Zambia**. which is always like coming home. I had been back on very brief stopovers since leaving Kalomo in 1971 but this was a longer visit. The airport was friendly and efficient, the breeze cool. The bougainvillea and the jacaranda trees were in flower. I took a taxi to Munali Secondary School where Simeon Kampata who had taught French at Kalomo was now headmaster. Munali was the oldest[35] government second-ary school and still had something of its old reputation.

A visit to Zambia means visiting old colleagues and meeting large numbers of former students. Rodger Majula, who had been a not very humble boarding master at Chizongwe was by now a lawyer running a legal advice centre on Cairo Road, still the main city centre shopping street (and part of Cecil Rhodes' dream of the British Empire linking the Cape to Cairo). He also had several bookshops managed by his wife, Mary. Simon Maonde, who had been head of our sister school at Namwala and whose son, Arthur, lived with us at Kalomo, was now a fairly senior civil servant in the

---

35. Munali was the nickname given by Africans to David Livingstone. Refer to Elias Chipimo's story (Annex 6)

Department of Vocational and Technical Training and was soon to be Ambassador to China.

Our former matron at Kalomo, Agnes Kandeke, was working at the YWCA but politics had hit her. President Kaunda was normally not very vicious but he had unjustly imprisoned Agnes' brother, Goodwin Mumba, along with our friend, the lawyer Edward Shamwana, for an alleged coup plot against him.

The local buses on Lusaka's Great East Road were second-hand double-deckers from Essex which still had details of cheap fares to Braintree and a new service from Southend on Sea plastered all over the interior. After ten days of meeting friends and drinking quite a lot of beer in Lusaka, I took the train south and stayed in the Choma Hotel, always a very modest establishment. The hideous painted pattern on the bedroom walls made it impossible to see the fairly numerous mosquitoes. Room service was "only available in the restaurant" and "continental breakfast" consisted of a bread roll. I asked for margarine but the waiter pointed out that there was jam, so what was the problem? I got a lift down into the Gwembe Valley which is the area on the north shore of Lake Kariba which divides Zambia from Zimbabwe. The lake dates from the building of the giant Kariba Dam during the days of the Federation in 1959. I stayed at the coal mining town of Maamba with one of my favourite ex-students, John Brown Lundu (who when young and slim had played Macbeth at Chizongwe school before joining the army and working on the railway). John drove me to visit my old school at Kalomo where years of budget cuts meant that desks and windows were broken and text books were lacking, but the grounds were well cared for and there were signs of some new equipment.

I headed north to Kapiri Mposhi which is the terminus of the TAZARA railway to Tanzania. I had lunch at the Kapiri Motel which looked as if it had not changed since colonial times – apart from the clientele and they were mostly absent that day as there was no beer and most things were off the menu. This railway was China's first big project in Africa, supporting two left-leaning countries.

The stations are absurdly grandiose, heavy with concrete and more like airport terminals. Kapiri station, a long dusty walk from the little town, was full of villagers with their bundles and bags waiting, for up to a week, for the train. I bought a first-class ticket and had some sleep in the train. Arriving at Mpika in the middle of the night you could be in the station square of Novo Sibirsk, or perhaps Hangchow. A few yards up the road you bump off the tarmac and back into Zambia. I had come to visit Maxwell and Gladys, both former Kalomo students. Maxwell worked on telecommunications and signalling for the railway and had been several times to China for training and still spoke Chinese. Like most Tonga people, agriculture is in their blood and they had started a farm.

ii) A circular tour – and a coup d'état

After leaving the Africa Centre in 1991, I found myself out of a job. I decided I could be useful to the voluntary service movement if I visited and reported on the organisations all round Africa. Djibril Diallo was able to help me with a small grant from UNDP for this work.

PIC 13) Waterloo station, Sierra Leone. The railway is now a road, 1992.

I started in Nairobi and visited **Kenya** Voluntary Development Association where the charismatic Mr. Africa was still active. Buru Buru had been planned as a model suburb and built with British aid funds. I stayed there with Don and Grace Riaroh. We had known Don when he was studying in Leicester and he had become the Kenya government's chief geologist. I travelled west in an express Peugeot taxi. It was large and comfortable but we waited and waited and it did not fill up. One of the other passengers turned out to be Patrick Sang, one of Kenya's most famous athletes. In the end he and I shared the fare for the unoccupied seat in the car which allowed us to move off to Eldoret where I stayed with the parents of my Africa Centre colleague, Wanjiru Kihoro. They were among the many Kikuyu who had settled in western Kenya but were later to move to Nairobi when ethnic tensions became intolerable.

My former IVS colleague, Brenda Eastwood, was working for the British Red Cross in **Uganda** and was living high up on Tank Hill with a view over Kampala. I met the founder of the Uganda Voluntary Development Association (UVDA) Rogers Kamwasi who worked hard to keep it going. Edward Kaweesa would take over the leadership after Rogers' death and promote workcamps at Uganda's World Heritage sites: the royal tombs and the Ruwenzori Mountains. Brenda and I also drove to Masindi. Wrecked tanks beside the road were a reminder of the fairly recent fighting when Idi Amin was driven out. Returning to Nairobi, I found myself in a *matatu* full of young American and German tourists who had been to see the gorillas in Rwanda. At the frontier I took the train as far as Eldoret, entertained by a friendly Ugandan who described how President Obote would start drinking whisky at 10am. From Nairobi I flew to Dar es Salaam, **Tanzania,** and stayed with Eliapenda and Prudence whose wedding we had attended in Leicester. Their plot near the sea was cool and idyllic. There were goats, pigs, cattle, bananas, coconuts, pawpaws, aubergines and peppers. We went to the lovely, crumbling old town of Bagamoyo with its elaborately carved doorways similar to those in Zanzibar and Lamu. David Livingstone's body had been carried to Bagamoyo after his death in what is now Zambia. I also caught up again with John Henjewele who ran workcamps for *Umoja wa Vijana,* the youth wing of CCM, the ruling party.

My second ride on the TAZARA train took me back to **Zambia**. It was comfortable and it kept up a good speed. The evening meal consisted only of Coke or beer and biscuits. After twelve hours and a fairly peaceful night, and a breakfast of tea, bread and eggs, a grey-haired man boarded the train. He turned out to be a former student from Chizongwe, now working as Assistant Controller of Customs. He was certain that President Kaunda, who had been in power for twenty-seven years, would win again in the general election due in a few weeks' time. Kaunda believed this too, but few others I met in Zambia did. It was a free election and, in the event, Kaunda lost. He handed over power gracefully. The Movement for Multi-Party Democracy's slogan, *The hour has come,* often shortened to *the hour,* captured people's genuine desire for change.[36]

The mountains of Tanzania gave way to endless vistas of savannah bush in northern Zambia with plenty of evidence of *chitemene,* the tradition of chopping off the branches of trees and burning them, cultivating and moving on. I stopped again with the friends at Mpika and other ex-students in Ndola before flying on by Royal Swazi Air from Lusaka. The plane was very late as it had just carried the King of **Swaziland** from the Commonwealth Heads of Government meeting in Harare and the VIP seating had to be removed and replaced. The new director of the Swaziland Work Camps Association took me to see a house they were building for an elderly couple along the scenic road to Piggs Peak. Back in Manzini, United Nations Day was being celebrated by the police band, a troupe of semi-nude dancing girls, a school choir and a speech by one of the country's many queens.

Five days in **Lesotho** were spent happily in a thatched *rondavel* at the Lancer's Inn in Maseru. Thabo Marikemane of Lesotho Workcamps took me to the "graduation ceremony" at a nursery

---

36. The new president, Frederick Chiluba, ruled until 2002. He started well but his legacy was to allow the destruction of Zambian industry and greatly to increase corruption.

school that the volunteers had built and where I had to make a speech. The tiny children all had caps and gowns. A group of women dressed all in white performed some songs and traditional dancers stamped their feet.

Thabo drove me into **South Africa** to Bloemfontein. When we arrived at the Boulevard Hotel, the kind of place that would have been *whites only* in the past, it was a pleasant shock to find the gruff-looking Afrikaner lady at the reception being polite to black clients who could then be found drinking cheerfully in the bar, and to hear the ANC and PAC actually being mentioned in television broadcasts. And this was Bloemfontein, the heart of the very conservative Orange Free State.

The forty-eight hour train journey from Bloemfontein to Windhoek, **Namibia** was a lot of fun. I shared a compartment with a funny old white man who told me about his life as an engine driver. From Kimberley, the old diamond town, to De Aar Junction the train was hauled by a beautiful steam locomotive which had been smartened up for the tourists, of which I seemed to be the only one. This train was the *Trans-Orange* running from Durban to Cape Town – but no longer running today. It had a luxurious bar-sitting room car where I sat, watching the occasional ostrich from the train window. At De Aar I had a whisky with the old man and then settled down to sleep in the Windhoek train, which was already in the platform when we arrived at 5pm but was not due to leave until after midnight. The train was clean and comfortable but there was no food or drink. It was morning when we crossed the Namibian border after leaving Upington and the sun shone on a very stony, scrubby semi-desert for many miles with no sign of inhabitants apart from the occasional group of workers' huts by the railway. A few wrinkled hills rose up from the plain like shining islands in the sea. Another night passed before our arrival at Windhoek where I was due to visit the youth ministry. After this long, dry journey, coffee and breakfast at the Thuringer Hof was very welcome. Windhoek was said to be the cleanest city in Africa but I am told that recently its reputation has been overtaken by Kigali in Rwanda.

It was, unusually, cool and wet when I left Windhoek but burning hot when I changed planes in Maun. I was on my way to Gaborone, **Botswana**, where I met the leaders of Botswana Workcamps Association and IVS' former field officer, Francis Johnston, who was running a project producing products from the Kalahari Desert, including devil's claw, a cure for arthritis. I took the excellent air-conditioned train on to Bulawayo[37], **Zimbabwe** and another night train to Harare where I borrrowed a car, and I ended up driving one of the Blacks Unlimited musicians to Thomas Mapfumo's gig. I also met some members of the Real Sounds, a band we had brought to London to play at the Africa Centre.

I had done a deal with **Ghana** Airways to fly me from Harare to Accra, then to Freetown and back, and on to London. The local joke was that this flight to Harare was a special service for the First Lady, Sally Mugabe, who was Ghanaian, to go home for shopping, though she never shopped as extravagantly as Grace, the second Mrs. Mugabe. In Accra I went to the taxi park (*Welcome to the Mother Care chop bar*) and found a Peugeot taxi going right to **Nigeria**, passing through Togo and Benin without too much delay apart from road blocks in Nigeria where the officials tried to earn some *dash* from the Ghanaian passengers who had no passports. One official was fascinated to find I had seventeen visas in mine. In Lagos I found several different volunteer associations and in the end located the Voluntary Workcamps Association of Nigeria (VWAN). I stayed with Sam Ade Odewole in Festac Town, the suburb constructed for the 1977 Black and African Arts Festival of Arts and Culture. He remembered my taking him around the IVS local groups in London in 1971.

On the way back I passed through Benin again without stopping as the taxi was going to **Togo** – and this turned into a dramatic visit. I was tired when I got to Lomé and booked into a comfortable hotel on the sea front and met some workcamp friends in

---

37. On an earlier ride on this line when it was run as part of National Railways of Zimbabwe we found a plastic bag for litter on every seat, inscribed *Pollution is a menace! Keep your countryside clean*. The onboard worker came though the train, picked up the bags and threw them out of the window.

the evening. I was surprised when no-one from the group turned up for me the next morning and I was told that this was due to "turbulence". This was shorthand for a standoff between the democrats who were, we thought, in control and elements of the old one-party state. I went about my business and dined with Edo Amedon, the charming former treasurer of Astovot whom I had got to know on my 1982 visit. He was now Mayor of one of Lomé's neighbourhoods and he lodged me in a smaller hotel. The next morning I woke up to the sound of loudspeakers in the street booming, "*Togolaises, Togolais…*" I assumed it was the Prime Minister telling us that all was well. It turned out to be the army which supported President Eyadema and had taken over the radio station. Shots could be heard. The hotel guests stood around the entrance. Two tanks drove by and others could be seen at the end of the road by the sea. The silence became eerie: there was no other traffic and few pedestrians.

Around midday I chatted with a bearded Frenchman who was also holed up at the hotel. He told me he had to get to Accra for a flight that night. We walked down a side street to buy a banana for lunch. The usual street sellers were not there, or rather their wares were not, but on being asked for a banana one lady rushed into her yard and brought us a huge bowl of them. Walking back, the Frenchman saw a minibus and asked the driver if he could take him to the Ghana border. He agreed and we both jumped in. It turned out he was going inland to Kpalimé and to a border post nearby. We picked up our luggage and another Ghanaian at the hotel and set off. This was amazing luck as no other traffic was moving. As we went north the roadblocks were controlled by young "democrats." The coup was not to touch Kpalimé for some time, but before long Eyadema was back in total control of the whole country – and as I write his son is still in power.

This was the only coup I have lived through and it was quite a tame one, but I was glad to escape from Lomé that day. In Kpalimé I met Kokou Aziki for the first time. He was to serve on the CCIVS executive and became a close friend. Sadly for Togo and the volunteer movement he ended up as a taxi driver in Chicago.

I crossed the border to **Ghana** in a *trotro,* a minibus, stopping as usual with friends in Ho and Akosombo; and I visited Kordiabe where VOLU had built a conference centre with German funding. A large piece of land had been granted for this by the local chief in return for promised training programmes for local people. The centre is a well-designed wooden structure and there are dormitories and other outbuildings but it has not lived up to Osofo's dream. Not many programmes have been run for local people and VOLU has failed to make good use of it. I was to return there for a seminar on promoting literacy when working for CCIVS.

I flew on to Freetown, **Sierra Leone**, where I had been in 1963. Arriving at the airport, passengers had to buy $150 worth of leones, the local currency, a huge brick of banknotes in a plastic bag, which meant they were often prey to young men with sharp knives. I was invited by Edmund Kamara, the secretary of the Workcamps Association of Sierra Leone (VWASL) to stay at his place in Waterloo. The house was one of the lovely old colonial wooden structures, slightly worm-eaten. We ate jollof rice and drank palm wine by the light of a hurricane lamp. Electricity had not reached Waterloo for six months. The next morning, however, there was a crackling noise and people ran out of their houses to see what it was. Amazingly some street lights lit up but the effect was to cause the overhead wires to break into flame. The flames advanced along the wires towards Edmund's highly inflammable house. People started hitting the wires with long sticks until the flames were extinguished – and that was the end of electricity at Waterloo for some time.

VWASL has a plot of land at Mabuveh, a little further inland than Waterloo, which I visited. They used the place for youth training and cultivated some crops. It had been out of bounds during the recent fighting. On the way we stopped at a refugee camp for some of the many Liberians who had fled into Sierra Leone from the troubles there: neat, clean rows of shelters with seemingly happy refugees playing football.

Before finally returning to London I made a short stopover in Abidjan, **Ivory Coast** to see the local volunteer association who put me up in the the suburb of Yopougon Toits Rouges. I had lunch with the country's future president, Laurent Gbagbo, and his wife. We had got to know and like Gbagbo when he had given a speech at the Africa Centre and we had kept in contact. Félix Houphouet-Boigny, the first president, was still in power and Gbagbo's turn was not to come until 2000, by which time the country had become very unstable – and then France did its best to undermine him. He may have made some mistakes as president but I do not believe he deserves to have to face the International Criminal Court where, at the the time of writing, he still languishes. I visited Abidjan again in 1997 on my way to and from Liberia. Edyth joined me there and we went by bus to Ghana, spending six hours at the frontier where every item carried by the passengers in the two buses – clothing, enamel pots and large edible snails – was closely examined. So much for ECOWAS, the Economic Union of West African States.

7

The Africa Centre 1984-91

i) History and politics

The Africa Centre was an attractive, slightly scruffy building in Covent Garden in the centre of London. Its main feature was what had been an auction hall, with a gallery on all four sides at first floor level. The building was listed for preservation on account of this feature. There was a shop at the street front, three floors of rooms which were let to Africa-related organisations and a large basement. When I was on leave from working in Zambia in 1964 and 1967 I had come here and loved the place. What later became the Calabash Restaurant in the basement was at that time like a club room with students playing table tennis, and what became the bar was a cheap little restaurant serving African food. Edyth and I continued to attend events there after our return from Zambia. I remember eating "cocktail" fried ants at a Zambia National Evening and attending Djibril Diallo's wonderfully Senegalese wedding party. When I saw that the post of director was advertised in 1984 I applied for it and was thrilled and slightly surprised to hear that I had been appointed. I wondered why they had not offered the job to an African – and I remember a visiting African American expressing surprise at this. But I was very happy to have the job and I tried to ensure that the other staff were African.

The Centre had been officially opened by President Kenneth Kaunda of Zambia in 1964, at the moment of Zambia's own independence. The first director, Margaret Feeny, had succeeded in creating a unique place: a social space for Africans from all over the continent and their friends, and a venue for a serious programme of talks and conferences, art exhibitions and music. The political context of the centre's birth was somewhat more controversial. The seed from which the Africa Centre grew was the desire of many leading Roman Catholics to show their opposition to Nazism during the Second World War. This had led Cardinal Hinsley and others to create an organisation in 1940 called Sword of the Spirit which opposed extremism on the right or the left. It widened its remit after the war and took a special interest in Africa following Pope Pius XII's encyclical, *Fidei Donum* in 1957 – and the idea of an Africa centre emerged. It would, they hoped, divert Africans from extremism or communism, which they feared would be promoted by the proposal for another centre backed by Ghana's president, Kwame Nkrumah. Covent Garden was not the smart, tourist-infested place that it is today and the building in King Street was purchased at a very modest price and named Hinsley House. The Africa Centre was set up as a charity separate from Sword of the Spirit[38] with Margaret Feeny, a devout Roman Catholic, as Director and a Council of Management consisting of fairly distinguished people, not all Catholics, such as Lord Perth, Sir Philip de Zulueta and Chief Emeka Anyaoku. They were trustees and not closely involved in the management. Africans were not in a majority until the end of my period as director.

Dr. Alastair Niven took over from Margaret as Director in 1978 and in 1984 I inherited from him a very good programme of talks, art exhibitions, music and adult classes co-ordinated by Tony Humphries and Wendy Davies. Down in the basement, an inspired Senegalese chef, Paolo Diop, managed the Calabash Restaurant and also the bar, dubbed *Soweto*, which overflowed up the stairs on Friday evenings. (The restaurant was therefore *Jo'burg* with a somewhat whiter clientele!). The Centre's finances, however, were in bad shape and they have been this way through most of its history. A small piece of land behind the building which, with investment, could have transformed the finances, had sadly already been sold to pay off outstanding debts. It was always a struggle to keep up appearances. The main hall with its slim iron columns supporting

---

38. Interestingly Sword of the Spirit later became the Catholic Institute for International Relations, one of the partners of IVS in the British Volunteer Programme. It later changed its name to Progressio and closed down in 2017 when it lost its grant from the government.

an upper gallery looked splendid, but this impression was sometimes shattered by water dripping through the roof, sometimes onto the head of a guest of honour opening an art exhibition.

The African community in London in the Centre's early days was very different from what it had become by the time I worked there. Back in the 1960s most of the African countries had just become independent and most of the Africans in London were students. Often sent by the new governments or supported by the British Council, most of them were not yet critical of the regimes at home. There was a lot of optimism about Africa's future.

By 1984 a lot of nasty things had happened on the continent – civil war in Nigeria, numerous coups, increasing corruption and misrule in many countries. Many Africans in London were opponents of – or refugees from – their home governments. These included the many exiles from *apartheid* South Africa and Namibia, and had included numerous Zimbabweans, although most of these had gone back when Zimbabwe became independent in 1980. The Centre therefore found itself trying to respond to the needs and interests of its clientele while at the same time trying to remain on good terms with the African embassies and high commissions. The Kenya of President Moi was not happy when we awoke memories of the Mau Mau and worked with Ngugi wa Thiong'o, an arch-critic of Moi, to stage his play, *The Trial of Dedan Kimathi*.[39] We went on to appoint two other Kenyan opposition figures, Wanyiri and Wanjuru Kihoro, as our programme staff.

In 1985 we planned a conference to discuss reconciliation in Sudan but the ambassador refused to share a platform with anyone from the Sudan Peoples' Liberation Movement. The London Committee of the SPLM wrote in *Sudan Today:*

> "The Sudan Ambassador... made attempts to stop this conference by means of a letter to the Africa Centre asking them to deny the use of their facilities to the SPLM, and by approaches to members of the Africa Centre's Management Committee... In response to this the entire staff of the Africa

---

39. The play was written by Ngugi together with Micere Mugo.

Centre threatened to resign if the conference was stopped. They insisted that it was in the interests of Africa as a whole to preserve democratic freedom of expression on the platform of the Africa Centre. It was because of their wise and courageous stand that the conference went ahead... We wish to express our hearty thanks to the Director and staff of the Africa Centre... for standing by their offer in the face of great pressure. We shall not forget their exemplary action."

The conference did go ahead, but without anyone from the government side. The great irony was that a couple of days later the Sudan government was overthrown in a coup and President Nimeiry went into exile in Egypt. Chief Emeka Anyaoku, who was soon to become Commonwealth Secretary General and who had close links with many governments, decided to resign from the Council of Management over this issue.

In spite of such diplomatic storms, most of the African embassies appreciated the value of having an Africa Centre and a few of them gave us small grants. It had become a tradition for three members of the Council of Management to be diplomats. Tunisia, Uganda, Senegal, Ghana, Ivory Coast, Nigeria and Zimbabwe were represented during my time. Herbert Murerwa, the Zimbabwe High Commissioner, who had himself worked in the voluntary sector, was one of the most active and supportive members of the Council. He was to hold ministerial posts under President Mugabe on his return home.

ii) Music and programmes

The Africa Centre opened many doors for me. I had long been a fan of African music and now we were to host some of the musicians whose music I knew, and to discover others I had never heard of. The first concert I remember was with the Congolese star, Kanda Bongo Man, playing for the Centre's 20th Anniversary. Our hall was small and the costs of bringing bands from abroad meant we had to look for grants or tie in the concerts with groups doing a UK tour. We took the risk of twice bringing to London the famous Guinean band, *Bembeya Jazz*, and later also their equally famous sister band, *Les Amazones de Guinée*, a group of ex-policewomen, no longer young but able to put on an electrifying show. Diapy Diawara, the Malian manager of these two groups, produced records and DVDs with the label *Bolibana*. He remains a dear friend and the story of how he met the Guinean president Sékou Touré is recorded in Annex 6. Music at the Africa Centre was almost entirely the work of Toedepi Dangarembizi, aka Wala, backed up by Nish Matenjwa and by our Night Manager, Kwesi Asare. Wala's contacts brought us many good bands from his country, Zimbabwe: *Thomas Mapfumo and the Blacks Unlimited, the Bhundu Boys, The Real Sounds, Jonah Moyo* and *Lovemore Majaivana*. In 1988 we started the Limpopo Club where punters could be sure of finding a live band of the quality *Wala disco* every Friday. The name of the Limpopo Club lives on in different venues. The *African Dawn* were also frequent performers, a brilliant, politically radical group which mixed poetry, music and politics, of which the leading lights were Kwesi Owusu and Ahmed Sheikh. The members of this group performed all the main roles in the production of *The Trial of Dedan Kimathi*. Our hall was often hired out for different activities. We got a lot of extra publicity when Jazzie B used to perform regularly on Sunday nights.

The Africa Centre tried to keep abreast of what was taking pace in Africa as well of wider issues affecting the diaspora. I arrived midway through a series of lectures by Darcus Howe on the history of racism in Britain. Talks and discussions covered subjects as diverse as *the Turkana region, the novel in Soweto, the Non-Aligned Conference, recurrent famine in Ethiopia, the drain of capital from South to North, Botswana as an island of peace, contemporary Tunisia, health in Zimbabwe* and *African textiles*.

The Centre could have played a bigger role in facilitating development on the continent – but we did some useful things. *Bookweek Africa* in 1985 led seventeen publishers to join together as the African Books Collective in 1989. It is still active today. We supported an exchange of art exhibitions between Zimbabwe and Ghana. At the first *Africa at the Pictures* festival organised by Keith Shiri, who had also joined the staff, we brought together film directors to introduce their films and to join a discussion to look at ways of enabling African films to be distributed more widely. Keith continued running an annual London African Film Festival after he left the Africa Centre and continues to play a big role in promoting Africa cinema.

We ran some good programmes focussing on specific countries or on topics where politics, development and the arts were brought together. The *Focus on Southern Africa* included a conference on *South African Militarism*. The *Focus on Zimbabwe* featured sculpture, films, a food and craft market and a visit of the *Real Sounds*, a Congolese band based in Zimbabwe. With them we produced *Harare*, our one and only Africa Centre label LP vinyl record. The *Focus on Uganda* was a big programme and we were enthusiastic (then) about the new government led by Yoweri Museveni. The programme included a conference, *Rebuilding Uganda* and an exhibition, *The Art that Survives*, of work from Makerere University that had survived the use of the university art gallery as a banana store during the time of Idi Amin's rule. We also welcomed a visit by the *Nngaali Ensemble* from Makerere, the brilliant dance and drama group led by the wonderful Rose Mbowe, which toured Leeds, Manchester and all over London. Uganda was always well represented on our staff, especially by our solid, long-serving Finance officer, James Magabo.

In 1987 we organised a *Focus on Angola, Cape Verde, Guinea-Bissau, Mozambique and Sao Tome and Principe* which included an important conference on *The Struggle for Freedom and Development: the role of Culture and Politics,* with visiting speakers from all five countries. The great Mozambican artist, Malangatana Ngwenya, came as our guest. He was the main contributor to our exhibition of paintings by nine Mozambican artists and he painted a mural on the wall of the staircase at the Centre. Some months later, in 1988, we hosted Guinea-Bissau's leading kora player, Queba Galissa, and my house resounded to the sound of the kora.

Malangatana was one of the most memorable characters I have ever met. Instructing us on the telephone how to recognise him at the airport, he described himself as "black and fat like elephant." While his work was on show at the Africa Centre he stayed at my house.

He never stopped doodling and drawing, leaving us with abstract portraits of our children. Later when I was at the UNESCO General Conference in Paris he was a member of his national delegation. He stood up and burst into song, provoking smiles and applause – and some raised eyebrows – among the sober, suited delegates. When I visited Maputo in 1994 he showed me around his house. It was already an art gallery: every wall was covered with paintings. Trunks were filled with drawings and sketches. We then drove off and picked up the Cameroonian Jean Victor Nkolo, an expert on African music who was to be appointed Special Advisor on Africa at the UN and winner of the Legacy on Culture and Peace Award in 2016. We proceeded to a bar on the beach where Malangatana had been asked to be a judge of a competition for Mozambique's best secretary. Apart from looking smart and dancing beautifully, they mostly failed to answer two simple general knowledge questions. To their shame the only male secretary won the prize.

Our *Focus on Zambia* in 1989 marked the twenty-fifth anniversary of the opening of the Africa Centre by President Kaunda. It included an exhibition of the work of the country's first important artist, Henry Tayali. With the help of Mapopa Mtonga, my former student from Chizongwe, we invited the University of Zambia Dance Ensemble and a top Zambian band, *Julizya*. We found them lodgings, but suburban north London looked much the same to them and they spent most of one night being driven around by a minicab driver who evidently could not read a map – and there were no satnavs in those days!

Wanjiru Kihoro's presence on the staff ensured that every year there were outstanding programmes on and for women, and from these a new association was born, *Akina Mama wa Afrika*. These programmes brought us distinguished writers including Nawal el Saadawi, Merle Collins, Audre Lorde, Lauretta Ngqobo, Flora Nwapa and Wangui wa Goro; artists including Nike Olaniyi and Zeinab Abdelaziz; and musicians including the Congolese singer, Mpongo Love; Stella Chiweshe, the *mbira* player from Zimbabwe; and the now celebrated Angélique Kidjo in 1990, her first time in London.

PIC 14) *With the Congolese singer, M'pongo Love and Ben Nganda at the Africa Centre, 1986.*

PIC 15) *With Prince Charles and Keith Shiri at the opening of the Africa Centre's exhibition of Zimbabwe stone sculpture, 1988.*

PIC 16) *Edyth and Nigel with Djibril Diallo at the Fespaco Film Festival, Ouagadougou, 1997.*

PIC 17) *With Susan Odamtten at the old Africa Centre, 2006.*

In 1987 Sokari Douglas Camp came to the centre as our artist in residence. She produced *Sekiapu*, an exhibition of her huge kinetic sculptures and photographs of Kalabari screens. Sokari invited a group of Kalabari masqueraders from her home area in the Niger delta. They performed in the Centre, where they soaked the floor of the hall with generous libations of whisky. The other big event we organised was at the Barbican Centre, an exhibition of Zimbabwean stone sculpture which Keith Shiri put together in 1988. It was opened by Prince Charles, himself an admirer of African art.

I have memories of special moments at the Africa Centre. One was with Tony Humphries carrying a lorryload of wooden platforms to build up a banked auditorium for *The Trial of Dedan Kimathi*. Health and safety rules were less strict then but we were lucky no one fell off the platforms. Then there was the visit by Sally Mugabe, the president's Ghanaian first wife, who had been a member of the Centre's staff during Margaret Feeny's time. There was also the day Jesse Jackson made an impromptu speech when he was still dreaming of becoming president. We organised a literature conference jointly with the Commonwealth Institute and I remember in my opening speech trying to encourage African writers, recalling that my mother sent the manuscript of one of her novels to ninety publishers, never giving up and getting some good reviews in the end. It was at this conference that Ngugi wa Thiong'o eloquently advocated his passionate opinion that African writers should write in African languages and Lewis Nkosi responded with a speech in Zulu to highlight the impracticability of Ngugi's idea. Then there was the day when two great Africans, Ngugi and Sembène Ousmane, met for the first time in our Calabash Restaurant. One embarrassing night of snow and ice we took Francis Bebey, the great Cameroonian musicologist to perform to a nearly empty hall in Brixton. Many other well-known writers came our way – Alice Walker, Taban Lo Liyong, Kojo Laing, Ben Okri, a frequenter of the Centre, Chinua Achebe, Don Mattera – and there were book launches including one that I deeply regret not having sat through, of *Sozaboy – a novel in rotten English* by the tragically famous Ken Saro-Wiwa who was executed on the orders of Sani Abacha.

There were other memorable moments and interesting characters. There was the day when an egg was directed at Lynda Chalker, the Overseas Development minister, which was smartly fielded on to his own smart suit by Bankole Timothy who was chairing the meeting. I had heard many tales about the wild and unpredictable behaviour of the brilliant writer, Dambudzo Marechera[40] – but he had already returned to Zimbabwe before I arrived. The Programme Committee was always enlivened by the arguments between the South Africans, Lionel Ngakane (ANC) and Rakhetla Tsehlana (PAC). There was a bizarre character dressed in a long, black robe who called himself The Lord Justice who would march into any event and occasionally disrupt it. And there were many regulars from all over who came to the bar and loved the truly Pan-African ambience. Katanga, a dear old Nigerian, unpaid, used to collect the glasses in the bar. There were special nights in 1990 when the bar was packed and a TV was installed to watch Roger Milla and *Les Lions Indomptables* playing in the World Cup.

I travelled abroad a few times while working at the Africa Centre: to Egypt where the officials I met seemed not to want to be labelled African; to Somalia where Siad Barre was clinging on to power and to have electricity you needed to live near his palace. (We were in an area where the fan and the fridge would suddenly come alive in the middle of the night); to Kenya to meet artists and to try to get our former colleague, Wanyiri Kihoro, released from prison;[41] and to Zambia to plan the Focus programme. Just before I left the Centre in 1991, Wanjiru Kihoro and I visited the then Chairman of the Organisation of African Unity, President Museveni of Uganda. Wanjiru and Wanyiri were good friends of Amama Mbabazi,[42] then one of the president's closest allies and his prime minister for a time, and he enabled the meeting to happen.

---

40. His best-known work is the prizewinning *The House of Hunger*. His short, chaotic life is recorded in Wikipedia.
41. Wanyiri was tortured in the notorious basement of Nyayo House in Nairobi, described in his book, *Never Say Die*.
42. Mbabazi fell out with Museveni and stood against him for President in 2016 but won less than 2% of the vote.

We found the president reclining in his tent on the hill next to the modest State House at Entebbe enjoying the panoramic view over a bluish Lake Victoria and its green islands and peninsulas. He joked about the Scottishness of my name and we talked about Wanyiri's recent escape from Kenya and of course about the needs of the Africa Centre. Museveni made a few phone calls, I think to Botswana and Nigeria, and our visit resulted in a million pounds from President Babangida. This plugged a hole in the Centre's bank account, though I do not remember any thanks coming to Wanjiru or me for our efforts.

The Centre's Council of Management was often on a different wavelength from the staff. We were happy when Abdulrahman Mohamed Babu[43] agreed to be chairman but he was disappointingly inactive. I left the centre early in 1991. Wanjiru Kihoro, Keith Shiri and some other staff stayed on for a time under the temporary director, George Bennett and the new director, Adotey Bing, but the Centre's later history is not part of my story. Sadly in 2014 a long lease on the dear old building in Covent Garden was sold to a developer and it will probably become another expensive boutique or restaurant like the rest of the street, though the listing of the building will preserve some of its charm. New premises have been acquired and developed in Great Suffolk Street, south of the river. I hope it will again become a lively, popular place and that it will not forget its rich traditions.

43. Babu had been a leading politician in Zanzibar and a minister in Nyerere's government in Tanzania who played a major part in getting Chinese support for the TAZARA railway. He was one of the many accused of the killing of the Zanzibar leader, Abeid Karume, but Nyerere protected him and he spent his last years in London.

8
CCIVS 1992-98

i) History

I moved to Paris to take up the post of Director of CCIVS in January 1992. The Co-ordinating Committee for International Voluntary Service was set up in 1948, as one of a number of NGOs created by or supported by UNESCO in its different areas of competence, including music, literature, cinema, museums and science. CCIVS was for youth and peace. It was, and still is, housed at UNESCO headquarters in Paris. Its role is to co-ordinate and promote international volunteering. This is done through an information service, training, conferences, seminars, publications and the creation of new contacts and partnerships.

My first taste of CCIVS was at its General Conference in 1973 hosted by VOLU at the Meridian Hotel in Tema, Ghana where I represented IVS (GB). We took part in wide-ranging discussions on themes such as *How can Voluntary Service promote International Co-operation and Social Change?* The keynote speaker was Arthur Gillette, of whom later. I dined out with Ben Korley whom I had met at my workcamp in Germany in 1955 and I stayed with Miniman at Legon University. In 1991 I heard that CCIVS was looking for a new Director and I applied for the job, but in the meantime I went off on the tour of Africa described in chapter 6 (ii).

CCIVS was and is a modest little organisation. Our office was in a gloomy basement corridor of one of the UNESCO buildings next to some of the national delegations. We were only three in the office and we had to fight hard to raise enough funds to do our work. Over the years CCIVS had played different roles, responding to the perceived changing needs in the world of volunteering. In the 1940's and 50's it had been the main co-ordinator and stimulus for the large number of organisations working with international volunteers to help rebuild Europe after the war. My workcamps at Metz and Worms in 1955 were typical projects of that era. From the 1960's CCIVS widened its membership to countries in the "south" of the world, an example being a brief flowering in South America in the 1960s with a co-ordinating partner based in Chile. Later it played a very important part, along with SCI, in promoting youth exchanges between Western and Communist countries which enabled many young volunteers to build friendships and learn the realities, both good and bad, of both sides in the cold war. I had experience of this work on my visits to Poland and the USSR noted in Chapter 5. Rao Chelikani, whose long period as president of CCIVS ended just after I arrived, had been very active in supporting this aspect of the work. My predecessor as Director, Alexei Krouglov, had been the nominee of the Soviet member, KMO, the *Committee of the Soviet Youth Organisations*. KMO and the USSR had both collapsed during Alexei's period of office. My colleague, André Neumann, had come from *Freie Deutsche Jugend* (FDJ), the East German (DDR) youth movement, which transformed itself into a more typical volunteer association and is still going strong under the name of *Verband Junger Freiwilliger* (VJF). André was a wonderful co-worker with a great sense of humour.

ii) Lesotho and Namibia

Arthur Gillette, the head of UNESCO's youth division, was a great friend of volunteering. He had worked at CCIVS in his youth and had written the definitive study of the early history of the workcamp movement, *One Million Volunteers,* the whole text of which can be read on line. Arthur procured UNESCO funding for us for two training events in 1993 to which we invited potential voluntary service leaders from different countries. I attended both, together with Mario Carly from Belgium who had been taken on to work with the local partners. The first workcamp seminar was at the village of Ha Makoae in the south of *Lesotho*, where, apart from talking and training, we helped lay a pipe for a village water supply, construct classrooms for a new school and plant a lot of trees on the hillsides. We invited Francis Donkor, the General

Secretary of VOLU Ghana, as the main resource person and we had participants from Swaziland, Botswana, Namibia, Zambia and Zimbabwe. Henry Kabula, who had been selected by Human Settlements of Zambia, the NGO where he worked, went home and founded a workcamp association in *Zambia*.

The second event was in *Namibia* which had successfully broken away from South African control in 1990. One of the *apartheid* rules was that all "native" locations had to be at least 500 yards from any European houses. New houses meant that the rule was broken and all the African population of the Old Location' had to be moved to the new suburb of Katutura, but the cemetery remained. In 1959 the cemetery had been the scene of fierce resistance especially by the women, and forty-four Africans were wounded and eleven killed. At Independence it was declared a site of historic importance. The international team recruited by CCIVS spent a week working there cleaning up the site and camping nearby. Our group then moved off for a seminar in the crazy-looking crenelated youth hostel in the seaside town of Swakopmund, a town where many whites of German origin still live. We all visited Walvis Bay which was then still part of South Africa and attended a rally demanding that this city, originally a British enclave within a German colony, be united with Namibia. When Mandela came to power, South Africa ceded Walvis Bay and its importance as a port has grown rapidly. Our guest trainer for this seminar was "Mr. Africa" who had developed the volunteer movement in Kenya and who appeared earlier in this story. Sadly he died shortly after his visit to Namibia. Two outstanding pioneers who attended this seminar created new workcamp associations which still survive: Innocent Katsiga founded the *Zimbabwe* Workcamps Association (ZWA) – and he later became a Vice President of CCIVS – and Manuel de Araujo[44] founded AJUDE in *Mozambique*. A Namibian volunteer association was also created but it was short-lived.

CCIVS continued to support voluntary service in Africa. We organised a seminar in Uganda in 1997 attended by many African organisations; and we encouraged African members to attend its

---

44. Manuel has subsequently been a university professor. He has been active in politics and has served as Mayor of Quelimane since 2011.

regular general conferences, one of which, in 2004, was held in Nairobi. CCIVS also created a Solidarity Fund which collected donations from better-off members and funded the exchange of volunteers within the "global south" and from "south" to "north".

iii) Mozambique Island

The one thing most people know about UNESCO is it's listing of World Heritage Sites and CCIVS was always interested in promoting volunteer work to help in their preservation. It was in this context that I visited *Mozambique* in 1998. I had previously been welcomed in Maputo by Manuel de Araujo in 1994 when I visited various NGOs, including Skillshare Africa, and government people including Mateus Katupha, the Minister of Culture, all with the aim of strengthening AJUDE. They were already planning to organise workcamps to help preserve and restore the historic *Ilha*, Mozambique Island. So in 1998 I returned to try to make them happen. I travelled from Pretoria on the overnight train which terminated at the frontier. Most of the passengers raced off to take shared taxis to Maputo but I waited for the local train which rattled along slowly into the rather grand old terminus in Maputo. My friends in AJUDE led me to meet key players who could advise on work to be done on the island: OIKOS, an organisation working to preserve the island's heritage, and the National Commission for UNESCO, of which Graça Machel was president. I flew north to Nampula where I was met by the president of the *Amigos da Ilha*. Work on the island was planned: maintaining gardens and public seats, planting and pruning trees, tidying up the ruins of the fortress. Food and accommodation for volunteers was promised.

My visit to the *Ilha* was an exciting and slightly weird experience. The ride from Nampula to the island involved a ride in a *chapa*, a lorry carrying forty passengers, some sitting on side benches, others standing or hanging over the back. On the way we changed onto a Toyota pick-up. This took us over the narrow bridge to the island. I had always wanted to visit this place, the original capital of Portuguese East Africa. It is one of a number of extraordinary historic places in Africa, all of which I have been privileged to visit:

the Stone Town of Zanzibar, Kilwa Island in Tanzania, Lüderitz in Namibia, the castles on the coast of Ghana, the island of Gorée in Senegal, the Zimbabwe ruins and the rock-hewn churches at Lalibela in Ethiopia. The pick-up deposited us at the south end of the island and it was a long, hot walk to the office of the *Amigos*. They found me a bed next door in a large, crumbling mansion belonging to the town council. The bedroom was furnished with large, high wooden chairs and bedheads, heavy red curtains and an old zebra skin mat. The furniture was fragile. The chairs were liable to collapse if you sat on them. There were baths and basins but no water. It was creepy. The Addams Family might have appeared at any moment. The only café I could find provided an extremely boring diet – squid and rice every time, washed down with beer. I admired the architecture of the old town: the white painted hospital, some fine houses, the mighty fortress, the *Fortaleza de Sao Sebastiao,* and notably the governor's palace, the museum of sacred art and the maritime museum. The guide at the palace recited his commentary including the false information that one of the kings of Portugal had visited the place. I met a few local people and a couple of Danish volunteers. After my few days on the island I was told that the weight limit on the bridge had been reduced but the Hi-Lux that took me all the way back to Nampula was apparently light enough to cross. Back in Maputo the plans for the logistics were firmed up and the workcamp went ahead successfully some months later after I had left CCIVS.

iv) Liberia

In 1997 we got a grant from UNESCO for a project in Liberia, country which was for long, together with Ethiopia, Africa's only independent country, though in many ways it was an American neo-colony. The dominant elite had been Americo-Liberians, descendants of freed slaves. They had been an arrogant elite and relations with the majority population were never good. Their dominance ended in a coup in 1980. Many of the elite fled and the country descended into civil war in 1989, a war waged with barbaric cruelty. And there was to be more violence later. Arriving there I saw many buildings in Monrovia badly damaged. The Federation of

Liberian Youth (FLY) was a member of CCIVS which had stopped its activities when the war broke out. Now the country was beginning to recover and our grant enabled us to run a training workcamp to help revive FLY. I was joined by three experienced volunteers to run the project, Abdulai Kargbo from the Voluntary Workcamps Association of Sierra Leone, Mustapha from VOLU Ghana and Kwam from Astovot, Togo. I arrived on a terrible little plane from Abidjan, Ivory Coast piloted by Ukrainians. As we took off smoke appeared to billow out from the wooden luggage rack – but it turned out to be just condensation. The Monrovia city airport was more like a car park. It was crowded with people milling about and asking for tips. Emmersyn and Massaquoi from FLY were there to rescue me and we moved off to call on the founder of FLY, Richmond Draper.

PIC 18) CCIVS training workcamp, Buchanan, Liberia, 1997.

Before going to the town of Buchanan where the camp was to take place I had to register at the American Embassy. It was surrounded by much barbed wire and every form of security. The gruesome killings in the recent war had even been watched from the embassy windows. The road to Buchanan passed though the huge Firestone[45] rubber plantations and patches of thick forest. We were stopped at several roadblocks manned by Ghanaian, Guinean and Nigerian soldiers of the Economic Community of West African States peacekeeping force (ECOMOG). Bailey bridges replaced damaged bridges, the biggest one having been blown up by the future president, Charles Taylor, when he was a warlord.

Our project was at Bassa High School which consisted of two tall buildings that had been occupied by displaced persons during the war. The place was shabby. The classrooms had been used for sleeping and cooking and what furniture was left was broken. Our main job was to paint the exterior walls with limewash. We had a good crowd of Liberian volunteers working with us and plenty of social interaction at work and in the evenings. One day was spent reviewing all the youth activities of FLY; another day was taken up with training inputs from our three friends and me, describing different projects and examples of good practice in our different countries. Some of the Liberians became very enthusiastic about the idea of volunteering and decided to start a local Bassa association. One of the many speakers at the camp's closing session was the Head of Bassa High School. He told us he had been on the road coming back from Monrovia and he was very surprised when a woman congratulated him on the revival of his school. When he got to Buchanan he saw what she meant. The dirty walls had been painted and, although we had not done a huge amount of work, the school staff and the public were inspired by what they saw. FLY never did much to develop youth workcamps but in 2005

---

45. In 1920 Britain and Holland controlled the rubber market and the Americans, wanting an independent source of rubber, established Firestone in Liberia and it became a dominant part of the economy. The country's other main income was, and still is, the sale of flags of convenience for shipping. More recently exports of minerals and hardwood have become important too.

it revived many activities and is now a major player in Liberian civil society.

We returned to Monrovia in a minibus overloaded with volunteers, with a small boy and a Nigerian soldier on the roof along with the leg of an antelope which someone had bought at the roadside. That was one image of Liberia but for me the country provoked mixed reactions. It was sad to see the effects of the war in Monrovia including the derelict former headquarters of the masonic movement which had been very strong among the old ruling elite. On sale on the streets were textbooks and household items looted during the fighting. Liberians speak English with a weird accent – "woykcamp" – a kind of Southern States drawl with the last syllable swallowed. The great footballer George Weah was revered. His house had always been spared, but that did not stop all his furniture from being stolen. People recounted their memories of the conflict. An old woman died of shock when the roof and windows of her house were stolen. A fourteen year old "general" living in Emmersyn's street protected some of his neighbours' houses. Kwam commented on the huge number of churches whose message of peace had clearly fallen on stony ground. We were there in the middle of an election campaign which it was obvious Charles Taylor would win. He was to be president for six years before he was forced to resign. He was in the end sentenced to fifty years in prison for atrocities perpetrated in Sierra Leone. A democratic election in 2005 brought Africa's first woman president, Ellen Johnson Sirleaf to power Liberia and she handed over gracefully to George Weah who was elected in 2017.

v) Asia

CCIVS work took me to India and Bangladesh during the time I was director but I was not to visit eastern Asia until, as Vice President, I visited Japan in 1996 for an executive meeting and a seminar. Shinchiro Kaizawa (Kai) who hosted us had created a very strong workcamp association, NICE, and he went on to help develop a network of new organisations and exchanges in eastern

Asia involving Vietnam, Indonesia, Taiwan, Hong Kong, China, the Philippines, Myanmar, Cambodia, Fiji and Mongolia. Jinsu Yom created a very strong association in South Korea. Both Kai and Jinsu served as Presidents of CCIVS. A training conference which I attended in Vladivostok in the Russian far-east was also organised by us, with participants from South Korea and some from China who were in the movement for Esperanto, a language they favoured as an alternative to English. Vladivostok was a nine hour internal flight from Moscow which had more of the atmosphere of a village bus with women carrying chickens, vegetables and screaming kids. Unfortunately, North Korea was not present at this little conference. However, back in Paris André made contact with the North Korean embassy and we went there one day to make a friendly approach and drank a lot of ginseng. As an East German who felt unhappy with the way the unification process had been handled in Germany, André hoped for something better in Korea. Sadly, even after President Trump's meeting with Kim Jong-un, this still looks like a distant dream.

vi) Palestine

In June 1996 I was invited to a conference in Jordan. This was an opportunity to visit the International Palestinian Youth League (IPYL) which was an active member of CCIVS. I flew to Tel Aviv and took a shared taxi to Jerusalem and stayed in the old city. The next day I took a bus to Amman over the Allenby Bridge over the miserable little stream that is the River Jordan. The conference was about youth and all I remember about it was a brilliant speech by a Jordanian princess and the very impressive participants from the Israeli peace movement. This was the time after the Oslo agreement and there was even some optimism in the air.

Afterwards back in the West Bank the IPYL leader, Adli Da'ana, introduced me to his members in Ramallah, Hebron and also at Bir Zeit University where international solidarity workcamps have been held for many years. I met Hanna Nasser, Deputy Mayor of Bethlehem, where a big event was being planned for the year

2000 and it was hoped young volunteers would play a part in the preparations. I met officials at the Palestine Ministry of Youth and the National Commission for UNESCO. I was also able to get into Gaza and meet IPYL members there. I learned of the many impediments to normal life for Palestinians even during this post-Oslo time. Adli had, for example, to make a long detour to get from his home in Hebron to Ramallah without having to go though Israeli Jerusalem. Palestinians were even able in those days to get in and out of Gaza, but it was often a humiliating experience.

Back in Israel I visited *Neve Shalom* (*Wahat as-Salam*, oasis of peace) the pioneering village where 60 families, half Jewish, half Palestinian, try to live and educate for peaceful co-existence, teaching both languages and trying to overcome the contradictions in the country. International volunteers play a part there too. Trying to see both points of view I also visited *Yad Vashem*, the impressive holocaust memorial in Jerusalem, accompanied by a friend of my former IVS colleague Sara Elkes. Sara was the peaceloving daughter of Elchanan Elkes who had been the leader of the Jewish ghetto in Kovno (Kaunas) in Lithuania, whose memory she kept alive with an annual lecture in Leicester.

I visited the Arab League of Jaffa, a member of CCIVS, which has tried to keep alive the Arab traditions of this old city and welcome international volunteers. They explained to me how Arab owned properties were being systematically acquired by Israeli Jews, as has also happened in east Jerusalem and elsewhere but the community had obstinately survived.

This visit, short though it was, helped me to put the continuing crisis in perspective. It was easier to understand Israel's paranoia about security when, standing in Ramallah, you can see right across Israel to the sea. I could see bullet holes in Ramallah from the recent *intifada* and I heard plenty of evidence of how Palestinians' lives were greatly restricted. Sara always resented the comparison but Israel reminded me strongly of *apartheid* South Africa – and unlike South Africa the situation has subsequently got worse, not better. The voluntary service movement has played and can continue to play a useful role providing solidarity with the Palestinians in parallel with other actions by Peace Brigades International and the Quakers.

vii) National Youth Service

Although it differed from the kind of voluntary service that CCIVS was trying to coordinate, the national youth service which many governments had established was closely related to the origins of voluntarism, civilian rather than military service. National youth services varied greatly. Some countries wanted to inculcate patriotism, closely linked with the military, as in Israel, and in Zambia which had employed Israeli consultants. Others, especially elsewhere in Africa, wanted to harness their university graduates to work as teachers or in other government jobs, often in rural areas where others were unwilling to go. Many saw it as a kind of initiation into adulthood.

With my CCIVS hat on I attended several conferences of this miscellaneous group of organisations, in Rio de Janeiro (Brazil), Port Moresby (Papua New Guinea), Abuja (Nigeria) and Windsor (UK). I learned a little but I do not think I contributed much to the discussions. Liberia, Mali, Gabon, Israel, Germany, France and of course Nigeria were represented at the Abuja meeting but it took place when the grim regime of Sani Abacha was being boycotted by many. Embarrassingly they saw my UNESCO address and began to address me as the UN representative! A leading member of this group was Elisabeth Hoodless, the feisty head of the UK organisation, Community Service Volunteers (CSV), recently renamed Volunteering Matters. In 1962 when CSV started, IVS had already been recruiting medium-term (3-12 months) volunteers but thanks to Elisabeth's dynamism CSV quickly became the leader in this field.

viii) Paris

I left Paris for Burundi in July 1998 when the streets were resounding with the cries of football supporters who were in town for the World Cup. It had been fun living there even though I was only on a volunteer's salary which dried up from time to time. Edyth and the children were able to visit frequently and I spent many weekends in London, happily using the Eurostar train as soon as it started running. UNESCO was a funny place. Some of the staff were impressive, such as Arthur Gillette and Carmen Negrin, the daughter of the Republican Spanish Prime Minister. It attracted a number of interns who were in fact volunteers paid a nominal US$1 for their work. Some were hanging around hoping for contracts such as elderly Indian whom we dubbed Professor Brainstawm who did some occasional translation for us but who was desperately poor, wearing his decent overcoat even in the summer to disguise his rags. My friends in Paris were mostly Africans including my flatmates including Klevor Abo, a Ghanaian musicologist who used to write for West Africa magazine, Laurent Laniel, a French researcher and expert on the drug trade. Florence Ssereo had been an intern in the youth division when I arrived. She has had a career in UNESCO and we have remained friends. She recounts her story is in Annex 9. CCIVS still has its office in Unesco's building. It survives, adapting as usual to the changing world of volunteering. It celebrates its 70th anniversary in 2018.

PIC 19) In Soweto, Johannesburg, 1994.

PIC 20) Planting an indigenous tree in the sacred grove, Kaya Kinindo, Kenya 2010.

9

Angola and Namibia

i) Namibian refugees and Angolan artists

The former German colony of South West Africa had been granted as a League of Nations Mandate to Britain in 1919 who passed it on to be administered by South Africa. This had the effect that the "sacred trust of civilisation" to lead the country towards independence was ignored for sixty years and from 1948 the country also suffered the imposition of *apartheid*. Namibia's lonely struggle for independence got much less attention than that of South Africa. But for the unremitting efforts of Rev. Michael Scott the country might very likely have been annexed by South Africa. Tshekedi Khama invited Scott to Serowe (now in Botswana) and introduced him to some leaders of the scattered Herero people who had fled the German genocide, while those still alive in Namibia were living in conditions as bad as under German rule. Scott managed to meet and befriend Chief Hosea Kutako and, well briefed, took their case to the UN, soon broadening his efforts to include all the African population of Namibia. I went to a talk by Scott at Woodbrooke, the Quaker college in Birmingham, in 1954 and can testify to the passion of this seemingly modest man.[46] Having single-handedly alerted the world of Namibia's case, Scott continued fighting against oppression in South Africa, trying to stop the creation of the Federation of Rhodesia and Nyasaland and supporting the struggle of the Nagas in India. The Africa Bureau, a lobbying organisation backed by David Astor, the wealthy owner of the *Observer* newspaper, was set up to back Scott's work. The Africa Educational Trust and the Minority Rights Group both grew from Scott's efforts. Mrs. Connel Auld Leggatt, a wealthy

---

46. A brilliant biography of Michael Scott, *The Troublemaker*, was published in 2006.

Scottish lady was so inspired by a talk by Michael Scott that she set up a trust for education in Africa of which I am currently the Chair. SWAPO, the principal Namibian liberation movement, was founded in 1960 and the UN with an increasing number of African member states in the 1960s, took increasing interest in the situation, condemning South Africa and, in preparation for eventual independence, sponsoring an Institution for Namibia in Lusaka directed for a time by my former student, Yobert Shamapande.

My first contact with Namibians was with Ottilie Abrahams who was our colleague at Chizongwe School in Zambia and her husband, the popular doctor, Kenneth. Our next contact was in Leicester with Paul, the younger brother of Andreas Shipanga, who had been one of SWAPO's founders but became a critic, was imprisoned and formed an opposition party, Swapo Democrats.

To draw attention to liberation struggle in Namibia the German branch of SCI ran a campaign to convert a military vehicle, a *unimog*, into an ambulance to send to Namibian refugees in Angola, an example of "swords into ploughshares". The *unimog* came to London in June 1988 and parked in Covent Garden piazza. The nearby Africa Centre where I was working organised a photographic exhibition, a discussion forum and a benefit concert. The vehicle was then sent on to Angola where most of the Namibian refugees were based after the end of Portuguese rule in 1975.

In 1986 SCI's east-west commission discussed with SIVSAJ, which was the co-ordinating body for the youth movements in the communist countries, the idea of a joint project which fitted the criteria of both organisations. The plan was to build a training centre for young Namibians in the large refugee complex in Kwanza-Sul province of Angola. As SCI's Africa man I was asked – or maybe I offered – to go to Angola on a joint field visit with Atanas Roupchev, the Bulgarian secretary of SIVSAJ.

In June 1988 I flew to Angola on Aeroflot. The plane was pleasantly empty when it left Moscow. It landed at the scruffy little airport at Simferopol in the Crimea and here a large number of burly Russians filled all the empty seats. These turned out to be fishermen returning from leave for a six-month stint in Angola.

After our arrival in Luanda Atanas and I had detailed discussions about our joint project with Hadino Hishongwa, the head of the SWAPO Youth League, and we visited the grand old man, Andimba Toivo ya Toivo, who, along with Sam Nujoma, Angola's first president, had pioneered SWAPO. He was most appreciative of SCI's donation of the *unimog*.

A day later we met up in Viana, just outside Luanda where a convoy assembled to take us to Kwanza-Sul. There was still a state of unresolved civil war and in places the road was puckered with deep potholes caused by landmines. Military vehicles went ahead of us and followed behind. Our driver put on a soldier's uniform and had a Kalashnikov beside him which was pointing towards me. He assured me it was locked. We stopped for breakfast of tinned beef marked "a gift from Finland." With us in the convoy was Nangolo Mbumba, at that time a teacher at the refugee centre and later to hold many ministerial posts in free Namibia. The landscape was mostly uninhabited and flat with scattered baobab trees and giant euphorbias. We passed through the straggling little town of Dondo with its decaying, colonial villas and crossed the big bridge over the Kwanza River, which had been destroyed in the war and rebuilt by the Cubans, turning off to the small town of Calulo and through hills and coffee plantations to the refugee camp.

I think this was the cleanest and best organised refugee camp I have ever seen, just as Windhoek, Namibia's capital is the cleanest city in Africa.[47] At the camp we were housed in an air-conditioned, pre-fabricated guest house inherited from a Swedish construction firm. We were shown round the well-constructed wooden and concrete buildings. We visited the teacher training centre, the kindergarten, tailoring and shoemaking workshops, the garage, the brickworks, a carpentry project and the Trade Union Centre. We were shown the site of our proposed youth training centre. An architect's drawing had been prepared for three buildings providing for cultural activities, sports, training in various skills, a library and cafeteria. There was land for an agricultural programme too. We drew up a list of possible funding sources including national youth

---

47. Or it was until Kigali (Rwanda) overtook it.

councils, UN and church bodies and, had we been given time, we might have succeeded. In the event the project was not needed because Namibia achieved independence within eighteen months. The whole refugee centre was then handed over to the Angolans as thanks for their generosity towards the refugees.

A special convoy took us back to Luanda as Atanas had to return home. I stayed on for a week making contacts useful to the Africa Centre. I visited SWAPO's transit camp and attended an official party where some of the departing Cubans who had served in Angola were being thanked for their work. In fact, Cuba saved Angola's socialist government at a crucial moment and continued, ironically, to protect American oil interests against US-backed UNITA rebels. Back in London I knew the leader of a small opposition party, Francisco Pedro. His brother showed me around the city, the main charm of which is the bay, sheltered by the *ilha* and some attractive old buildings in the centre. There were a number of uncompleted tower blocks left unfinished when the Portuguese left in haste at independence. One fine old building, the Hotel Turismo where I was staying, was later to be destroyed when war broke out again; another was the Anthropological Museum which I found specially interesting as many of Angola's peoples are the same as those across the border in Zambia. The former director of the museum, Henrique Abranches, had spoken at the Africa Centre and I spent a stimulating evening with him. He was not only a leading novelist but he was also an artist with pen and ink, a maker of model boats and an anthropologist who had fought in the liberation war. He introduced me to Victor Texeira, the secretary of the plastic artists' union, who in turn introduced me to other artists: Jose Zan Andrade, Paolo Jazz and Fernando Caterça Valentim; also to the writer Virgilio Coelho. Virgilio invited me to his flat which was on the eighth floor of one of the unfinished tower blocks with only a bare staircase and no electricity. Water had to be carried up in buckets. It was impressive to find a livelier intellectual scene than would be found in most African countries in spite of the war situation. I visited the British Embassy where they ran a club on Friday nights and attended a party on the roof of the UN building. From Luanda I flew on to Lusaka to contact participants for the Africa Centre's *Focus on Zambia*.

PIC 21) *SCI's Namibia solidarity campaign, 1991.*

Namibia became an independent state in 1990. As a follow up to the *Unimog* the international SCI movement had planned a Namibia Solidarity Campaign in support of liberation. Now the country was free it was nonetheless decided to go ahead and draw attention to the country's inheritance from *apartheid*, its problems and its hopes for the future. A bus was bought in Belgium and fitted up as a small exhibition. I went to Ghent to see it and I rode in it as part of the travelling team in Belgium, then from London to Leicester and again from Belfast to Omagh in Northern Ireland. It went on to France, Germany, Czechoslovakia, Poland, the USSR, which was in the process of falling apart, and Scandinavia. SCI and Indiana University published a small book, *Breaking Free* about the campaign and about the realities facing free Namibia.[48]

---

48. For information on this and other SCI activities visit their excellent archives on line.

My next encounter with Namibia was on my journey round Africa in 1991 when I travelled by train from Bloemfontein to Windhoek and stayed a couple of days[49]. Then in 1993 as Director of CCIVS I took part in the workcamp and training seminar described in Chapter 8 (ii).

ii) Inside free Namibia

In 2003 Edyth and I were in Zambia and we took the coach from Victoria Falls, Zimbabwe into Namibia. The road crosses part of the Chobe National Park in Botswana and numerous elephants came into view. A huge orange sun was setting as we raced across the boring, flat landscape. We had booked a room in Tsumeb and arrived after midnight. The next morning we walked and finally located the town's new station which had been built two kilometres away on the newly built line from Ovamboland in the north of the country. The beautiful rake of coaches making up the tourist train, *The Dunes Express,* was standing in the siding. Our little train, like everything in Namibia, was very clean. Normally in Africa local people sell food at each station. Not in Namibia. The only form of refreshment on this uncomfortable, cold, eighteen hour journey was from a vending machine that sold fizzy drinks and sweets, and we had no small change. So we subsisted on a shared slice of cake and some All Bran until we finally reached Windhoek the next morning. It would have been much quicker by bus but I was of course determined to travel by train. Unsurprisingly this train no longer runs.

Andrew Harris is a housing expert who had been Chair of IVS but had made a new life for himself in Namibia. We stayed with him in Windhoek and then hired a car and drove to see the famous rock engravings at Twyfelfontein in Damaraland, a long drive through mostly deserted, dry veld. This huge collection of 2,000 year-old rock art deserves its fame. The engravings mostly portray animals, including seals and penguins – the sea is not very

---

49. Described in Chapter 6 (ii)

far away across the Namib Desert. Some of the engravings were clearly done by children learning the skill, a lion with a long tail and an eland with six legs.

We stayed overnight at the beautiful Twyfelfontein Country Lodge and the next morning set off to Namibia's other famous site, the *White Lady of the Brandberg*. Matthew, the guide, told us about his 87-year old grandfather who still rode a horse and knew German which he taught to his great-grandson, and about his uncle who killed a leopard with a stick. We climbed up to the cave. The painting got its name after the French archaeologist, the Abbé Breuil, saw a painting of it by a German artist. The South African Prime Minister, General Smuts, invited him to visit the site, which he did in 1947. We found that the white lady did not look very white and was almost certainly a man, but was impressive nonetheless, as are the paintings of animals on the roof of the cave. What we saw was only a tiny fraction of the 45,000 paintings at different sites on the Brandberg, Namibia's highest mountain.

Back in Windhoek our former student, Solomon Mumbi who was the Zambian High Commissioner invited us to tea along with Ottilie Abrahams, who had taught with us at Chizongwe School. We then took the overnight train south to Namibia's second city, Keetmanshoop. I had long wanted to visit the remote, historic coastal town of Lüderitz and we took a taxi to a spot on the road where, the driver said, minibuses stopped. None came but eventually a German-Namibian couple gave us a lift. The scenery started as rocky semi-desert scattered with large crags, then it became thorny scrub and finally a totally sandy desert where we saw a couple of ostriches and some of the feral horses that roam this area. The remains of the railway line could be seen disappearing under the sand. This line has since been reopened.

The Portuguese voyager Bartolomeu Dias sailed into this bay in 1487 and named it *Angra Pequena* (little cove). In the 19th century it became a trading post and the Germans established the town of Lüderitz. The nearby Shark Island was the scene of the barbaric treatment and the death of 4,000 Herero and Nama people during the colonial genocide (1905-7), Germany's first concentration camp. Today the town is small but atmospheric with its art-deco church, the *Felsenkirche*, and some preserved buildings including the Goerke House, the old post office and railway station. We returned the next day to Keetmanshoop in a crowded minibus, then spent a hot afternoon sitting in the hotel before boarding an overnight coach to Cape Town.

My final visit to Namibia was simply a holiday in 2015. Edyth had died in 2011 and I was on my own. I stayed again with Andrew Harris, now married to Priscilla, a Tswana-speaking Namibian. They live in a fine new house with noisy peacocks in the garden. We visited Priscilla's village on the edge of a wide salt pan where we slept in the cool open air. We stopped at Andrew's own ranch where cattle were being corralled on to a lorry to go to the abattoir. It was good to see that the Old Location Cemetery, where we held the workcamp in 1993, was now properly maintained as a national monument.

I met Otille Abrahams yet again, still head of a large secondary school at the age of 79 and eager to chat about our common memories of Zambia,

Namibia, like every country, has political problems and hangovers from the days of South African rule, including still unresolved land issues, but it is stable and generally well governed. Its plentiful natural resources have helped development and reduced poverty. The population of the country is well below three million but there are seventeen languages. Priscilla was working on a project to enable all of them to be used in primary school. Nationally lack of water is normally a problem, but the day I left for Zambia the rain arrived with such force that we had to wade across the road to get into the coach and then to beg the driver to switch off the air-conditioning until we dried off!

10
The Congo (DRC)

i) A personal connection

Fate seems to have involved me in the Congo in many ways. The husband of my mother's half-sister worked at the Etoile mine in Katanga in 1912 and I have two envelopes addressed to her, one from her father, my grandfather, posted in India, addressed to *Mrs Harrison, Star of the Congo, Katanga, Africa – via Cape Town and NW Rhodesia;* the other unstamped and presumably local, addressed to *Madame Mrs Harrison Esqr, c/o Mrs. Hayden Esqr, Lubumbashi River*[50] containing a note dated 1 April 1912 to buy onions, sugar and baking powder. There were no post codes in those days. Then in the 1950s my cousin Pat Wigdahl went to work as an *au pair* with the family of a Belgian planter on the river near to Stanleyville (now Kisangani).

I have several tourist leaflets from the colonial period. Visitors to the capital, then called Léopoldville, were invited to visit the *cité indigène,* the "native quarter," and the Museum of Native Life. The leaflet on Costermansville, also called Bukavu, enthuses about the many possible excursions and the "Watutsi dances." In fact a conference on tourism was held in Bukavu, the centre of "the African Switzerland", just before Independence. There is also a fascinating book full of sepia drawings entitled *Naissance du Congo Belge* describing the country in 1903 in glowing terms when it was still ruled directly and viciously by King Leopold II. The book is available from the Royal Museum of Central Africa at Tervuren, Belgium, which was built as a monument to the imagined past glory of the Belgian Empire. As I write the place is being modernised and hopefully being made more culturally and racially sensitive.

---

50. The name Lubumbashi was given to the city of Elizabethville at Independence.

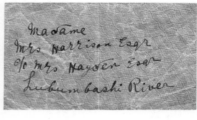

PIC 22) *Letters addressed to Minnie Harrison in the Congo, 1912*

My own concern with the Congo started with anger at the treatment of Patrice Lumumba which I read about while I was working in India. After my arrival in Zambia I felt more anger at the creation of the puppet regime of Moise Tshombe in Katanga, backed by Western, mainly Belgian, mining interests. The UN peacekeeping force had initially failed to stop the secession of Katanga and the UN Secretary General, Dag Hammarskjöld, had lost his life in the process. I went for a day trip to Elizabethville in July 1962 when the Etat du Katanga flag was flying. There were some fairly ferocious road blocks on the way and in the city bullet marks on buildings and other signs of recent conflict. Soon after this visit the UN ended the secession – though Tshombe himself briefly served as Prime Minister of the Congo in 1964-5. When Edyth and I visited the city again twice in 1965 it was looking in better shape. It was a contrast to Zambia to see tree-lined boulevards and the women proudly wearing national dress. When we were working in Mufulira in 1955 I often visited the bar in Mokambo just across the border.

Going home on leave from Kalomo in 1967 we flew on Air Congo using their "limousine service" to the recently renamed Lubumbashi. We were puzzled when, on leaving Ndola, the driver stopped at a local market and bought a huge piece of meat. He explained that the border guards had not been paid for months and this was *chai* to let us over the border. Our plans to go on from Congo to visit a friend in West Africa were blocked by the civil war in Nigeria so we ended up flying on Air Congo to Brussels.

Our next visit was when we crossed the Congo by rail and river boat on our journey home from Zambia in 1971.[51]

ii) CARE International

Much later, in November 2002, CARE International was considering whether to start a programme in the Congo and I was invited to take part in a field investigation. CARE had worked in the refugee camps around Goma after the Rwanda genocide, an unhappy experience, and had pulled out in 1997. Our team of nine members visited different parts of the country. I was named team leader for the west of the country and spent most of two weeks in Kinshasa meeting government people and other NGOs before flying north briefly to Mbandaka, the capital of Equateur Province on the shore of the River Congo. Zimbabwean soldiers had recently left the town. There was little sign of economic activity. I visited a camp for displaced persons, mostly women and children, some who had walked for weeks from the east of the country. The camp was clean and well organised but very crowded. We met inspectors of schools at the provincial Education Department. They had no books or materials and almost no budget. To do their work visiting schools they had bicycles or they went on the occasional boat up one of the rivers which involved weeks of travelling, walking and waiting. From Mbandaka I flew in a very noisy helicopter to Boende over the forest which was so dense that it was hard to spot the few villages along the river banks. The doctor at Boende hospital welcomed us in his white coat. He had almost no medicines, most of the equipment was broken down and he had not received a salary for some months but he continued to try to work.

Our team reported back that conditions throughout the country were appalling and the wars had led to high levels of malnutrition, disease and mortality, and to shocking abuses of human rights. Close to two million people had been displaced, many of them naked – because the clothes they were wearing when they fled had long since disintegrated – and too ashamed or afraid to come out

---

51. Described in Chapter 3 (ii)

of the forest to access food, clothing or medical services. Thirty years of mismanagement had already left health care in the state I found at Boende, It was the biggest threat to people's livelihood. Transport infrastructure had all but collapsed as a result of a lack of maintenance, leaving rural communities totally isolated. For CARE the question is not what needed doing but, rather, where to start. We recommended that CARE should develop a longer-term development programme as well as responding to the immediate humanitarian needs, starting with health care delivery in Kinshasa and economic renewal in Kisangani.

I was back in the DRC early the next year tasked with finding an office and making contacts to start CARE's programme. I managed to find a temporary office, an apartment for staff and a car. I employed a driver, Dodo, who provided many tips on how to survive in Kinshasa. Dodo regretted not noticing in time that one of the men trying to sell us a car was the well-known musician, Madilu of *Madilu Système*. I took a UN flight to Kisangani, the DRC's third city and former diamond capital, to discuss plans for CARE's work there. The roads to this place had been cut for many years and river boats were unreliable. The streets were very quiet. There were almost no cars or motorbikes, just bicycle taxis, many of them carrying what appeared to be bricks. These turned out to be packets of Congolese Franc notes. I stayed in cathedral complex a few doors from the room where, it was proudly announced, Pope John Paul II slept on his visit in 1980 which he apparently enjoyed: they said he had performed a soft shoe shuffle with the teenage girls who were singing his praises.

Then, for part of 2003 and 2004 I was based in *Goma*, the capital of North Kivu province, which hit the headlines in 1994 when it was surrounded by the vast camps for the refugees occasioned by the genocide in Rwanda where CARE had previously worked. I was in Kinshasa in January 2002 when Goma was in the headlines again. Nyiragongo, the mighty volcano which is easily visible from the city, erupted, as it had done at least eighteen times since 1884. A river of flaming lava flowed through Goma's city centre and into Lake Kivu which borders the town on the south side, destroying everything in its path. There were a few human casualties, mostly caused by explosions when the lava hit petrol stations, but the main losses were buildings, roads, housing and cultivable land. Most of the people had managed to flee across the edge of the town into Rwanda or towards the west. When I got there a year after the eruption the main street had been reopened, though not tarred; the thick deposit of lava meant that on either side you could see only the roofs and upper windows of former two storey buildings, and the wrecks of cars, lorries and containers swept away by the flow. The lava, now hard rock, covered half the airport runway which made flights by large planes very risky. Some people's faith in God was reinforced by the fact that the north wall of the Catholic cathedral was almost the only structure that had resisted destruction.

iii) Concern Worldwide

In 2003 I was taken on as the temporary head of the Irish agency, Concern Worldwide, in Goma. One of our main programmes was to work with the national research institute to disseminate public safety information about the volcano. We had a team of *animateurs* who ran workshops in schools and throughout the community to educate the population. Information panels had been erected in each part of town with flags coloured from green through shades of orange to red to indicate the level of risk. The risk was not only from a major eruption but from gas which escapes from cracks in the ground in the town and into the water of the lake. Another of our projects was to support small scale farmers along the road to Masisi with donated goats whose kids were then shared with neighbours, and with tools and seeds for market gardening. Life in Goma itself was quiet as people were slowly rebuilding their houses and their livelihoods. The town centre had regular electricity and running water, the hotels by the lake were reviving and those who could afford it dined out with views over the water. Mobutu's relatively modest palace now housed the provincial governor.

Concern also worked in *Kasongo*, in Maniema province. This had been the capital of the large area ruled by the Zanzibari ivory trader, Tippu Tib, who settled in the town in 1875 but who later returned to Zanzibar and left Kasongo in the hands of King Leopold's Congo Free State. A monument in the little town celebrates Tippu Tib's defeat. The UN flight to Kasongo often did a tour of the south of the country so I got glimpses of Kalemie on the shore of Lake Tanganyika and Pweto on Lake Mweru on the border of Zambia. Concern's man in Kasongo was a rather dour Quebecois who had established an office and a staff house with solar panels. There was a nutrition programme run by the very dynamic Moise Katongo and an agricultural exchange programme in some of the villages run by the equally impressive Christophe Assongwa. Kasongo's airstrip was a grassy space some distance from the town. Just beyond the airstrip was the River Congo crossed by a rusty but functioning ferry. A few kilometres further on was the small town of Samba with its station on the railway line linking Kindu, the capital of Maniema Province, with Katanga in the south.

This line had been out of service for six years. The Anglican bishop of Maniema was in England for the Lambeth Conference in 1998 but he was determined to return to his diocese. He described his journey home to Kindu on one of the last trains to get through in August 1998. It took nine days from Lubumbashi and the conditions grew worse by the day, with no food and little water. Over the next few years a thick undergrowth of bushes and even some fast-growing trees had smothered the rails. People began to believe that the train, the lifeline for their palm oil, cotton, groundnuts and rice, would never run again. They gave up cultivating except for their own family needs. They could not sell their crops. Concern and four other agencies, with a grant from USAID, decided to work to reopen the line, taking responsibility for different sections. Concern was responsible for 112 kilometres. Local villagers were given food aid and pocket money and they cleared the tracks of vegetation. There were huge anthills too close to the line and inside these the queen ant had to be traced and removed to stop the anthill building up again. Drainage ditches had to be dug or deepened. Railway staff who had not been paid for seven years checked the gauge and the clearance and got ready to live normal lives again. The man in charge of the office at Samba station told me that he had to hide for several months as the rebel soldiers thought he had money stashed away somewhere. They smashed the huge safe at the station and found almost nothing.

I chanced to be in Kasongo when the third train since the reopening was due. We went to Samba to witness the scene. It was Sunday morning and word had come that the train was expected at midday. People started pouring on to the station. Children were everywhere. Then with a shriek of its whistle the long train of seven coaches and four goods wagons rolled over the level crossing into the station. Cheers sounded around the sleepy little town. The faithful rushed from their churches. Everyone was at the station. Most of the passengers seemed to be traders bringing all kinds of goods to sell – new and second-hand clothes, shoes, batteries, padlocks, sweets and beer. They turned the station into a huge market. Sadly most of the people had no cash, so some of the fun was just "window shopping." The local mamas were active too. They created a kind of station buffet, setting up tables and selling *ugali*, with chicken and vegetables; others were selling bananas, carved wooden spoons and other local handicrafts. The traders had brought with them as many yellow jerry cans as they could carry which they would fill with palm oil on the return journey, injecting cash into the local economy. A sad footnote to this story is that there was a terrible accident not far south of Samba in 2005. At least sixty people were killed when the train crossed a bridge. In the words of the State Governor, "There were lots of people and goods on the roof. When the train was crossing over a bridge, the beams supporting the bridge swept people and goods off the train and into the river below."

International aid agencies including the UN throw up some extraordinary paradoxes. When needs are properly assessed the work they do is useful and important, but they distort the local economy, creaming off many of the best qualified local people and paying them well – though not as well as the expatriates doing the same work. The aid they bring should lead to sustainability but one often has the feeling that some INGOs would like to continue for ever. They own fleets of large white Land Cruisers emblazoned with a prominent logo and a notice prohibiting casual lifts, especially to people with guns. The arrival of one of these vehicles in a locality raises expectations of some kind of aid. Even if the staff in the Land Cruiser have nothing to offer and are merely assessing the situation, they are quickly surrounded by a horde of children who rush up to stare and practise their French to the extent of asking for a *cadeau*, a biscuit, sweets or money. With patience and a little Kiswahili one or two of them can be persuaded to tell their name and say how old they are and which school they go to, but mostly any attempt at conversation just elicits embarrassed giggles.

iii) Motorbikes and other vehicles

Edyth took great interest in the local transport in Goma and this paragraph is based on her observations. Some things are specific to the Congo but many would be similar in many parts of Africa. The main local transport in Goma was the *taxi-moto*. The *motards* or drivers of these motorbikes are young men who race along the main streets, dodging round more sedate vehicles in a haze of foul smelling exhaust. There was some effort to licence them and make the wearing of a helmet compulsory. The owners of the motorbikes made the drivers pay for the hire of a helmet. There was an outcry when it was proposed that a *gilet* or yellow jacket should also be worn, as that would have been one more expense to meet from hard earned income. The pillion passenger had no helmet of course and no insurance against the risks.[52] At strategic points "*Gadafis*" wait with yellow jerry cans to sell fuel to the *motards*. There are also some minibuses, always full to overflowing, and mechanically unreliable. These jobs are one of the few ways of earning a living.

---

52. By contrast, in Rwanda the rule for the driver and passenger to wear helmets is strictly enforced.

PIC 23) *A chukudu on the Goma – Masisi road, DRC, 2003.*

PIC 24) *The second train in nine years arrives in Samba with cans to collect palm oil, 2004.*

To come into town from further afield, or to travel for trade in food or fresh fish the standard means of transport is by lorry. The passengers sit on top of the sacks of produce, exposed to the dust, the weather and the smell of dried fish. These can also attract the attention of bands of robbers, often causing a small trader to lose his, or more often her, entire stock and be left with nothing but debts to repay. There are other ingenious ways of carrying heavy loads: at worst a woman bent double under the weight with a band across her forehead supporting a weighty package on her back. Lighter loads such as bowls or baskets of produce are balanced on women's heads. Men generally do not carry things but they make up for that by their expert loading of bicycles with at least four cumbersome sacks of charcoal or six crates of drinks piled on the carrier and keep their balance as they make their way into town. There are also roughly nailed wheelbarrows with a single wheel and a flat surface going down to the port with huge sacks of flour, groundnuts or cement. More amazing still is the *chukudu,* a home-made bicycle-shaped object with a wooden front and back wheel but no pedals or saddle which is used to carry sacks for local deliveries. These seem to be unique to eastern Congo. On the road from the Rwanda border disabled people in wheelchairs can be seen carrying large sacks or boxes on the leg rest, while a group of boys push from behind. Disabled people are allowed to cross the border tax free and bring their goods with them.

iv) Observing the election

EurAc is a network of NGOs working in the Great Lakes region which exists to inform its members of the situation in the region and to lobby the European Union and its member states to take action to help resolve problems in the area. In 2011 they sent a team of ninety election observers to the DRC. I went as one of fifteen from Christian Aid, EurAc's only UK member. EurAc worked in solidarity with the Congolese network, *Agir pour les Elections Transparentes et Apaisées* (AETA, Act for transparent and peaceful elections). After a day's induction in Kinshasa four of us, three Belgians, two of whom were born Congolese, and me, flew off to Kalemie on the shore of Lake Tanganyika on the weekly UN flight. On the way the plane touched down at Kananga in Kasai Occidental Province. The airport was crowded with people waiting to greet Etienne Tshisekedi. His plane landed and out stepped the aged opposition leader and the huge crowd swarmed all over the runway. Arriving at Kalemie we could see the coast of Tanzania in the far distance across the lake. We were supported by two local observers who found us a very basic hotel. The smart *Hotel du Lac* shown on the internet was an empty shell with bits of furniture scattered all over the floor. There was little choice of food in the town: we found a little local thatched restaurant or went to the canteen at the UN base. We found several other international observers in Kalemie from the European Union and the Carter Centre, former President Jimmy Carter's excellent organisation.

Our local partners helped us locate polling stations. These are nearly always school classrooms – a large school counts as a polling centre and there can be up to twenty-seven polling offices in one school, each one dealing with up to 500 voters. The lists of registered voters were posted outside the polling station. Due to computer error some did not find their names, and the news that they could vote despite this was only announced two days before polling. Each candidate was identified by a number and most voters memorised the number they wanted to vote for: 1 to 11 for the presidential candidates and from 1 to 116 for the members of parliament. Thus even illiterate people could find the number or the photo of their candidate. Some just said they wanted to vote for the smiling man, meaning President Kabila. The ballot papers were therefore huge and hard to read in the semi-darkness of the polling booths, so the use of numbers really worked.

In the three days before the vote we tried to visit polling stations to see if they were ready. Some were not, but an impressive effort by local officials meant that by election day most of them managed to open on time, yet the ballot papers had only reached Kalemie at midday on the Sunday and the election started at 6am on the

Monday – and transport was short and the roads mostly awful. We moved around during election day, sitting in some of the stations with the witnesses from the different political parties. It was very peaceful. This was an area where Kabila was popular and his score, without any sign of cheating, was around 90%.

Voting ended at 5pm and counting immediately began. My polling station was one of the quickest and the presidential result was counted by 10pm. I did not stay up for the parliamentary count to be finished. The results were then posted outside each office. The witnesses from the biggest opposition party, the UDPS of Etienne Tshisekedi, sent their figures from all over the country to the party headquarters and on that basis he claimed to have won 54% of the vote. A report with the results from each station were then sent to the local electoral commission office to be compiled. In Kalemie this office consisted of four smallish rooms piled up with parcels of voting reports all over the floor and up the stairs. Not an ideal space for calm calculation. The compiled results would then be sent on to Kinshasa. I got the impression that the election officials and the compilers were working honestly and very hard for almost no pay. For the election they had to work from 5am to perhaps 4am the next day, often with no food.

PIC 25) *Election observer at Kalemie, DRC, 2011.*

Election observers cannot easily stay for months but it is a pity that they have to focus on the day itself when most people in fact vote freely. What also should have been taken into account are the period before the election when most of the media would have you believe that nobody existed but Kabila and where his money paid for posters, sunshades, t-shirts and more, and the period after the election when the votes are finally being compiled and there are opportunities for people to provide false ballot papers or destroy ones they do not like. In the event the official results nationwide gave Kabila 49% and Tshisekedi, the main opponent who cried foul, 32%.

We then had to wait for the weekly flight back to Kinshasa. Two of my colleagues had the chance to fly down with the Carter Centre people to Moba, the next town on the lake shore to the south. My other colleague had relatives in Kalemie and we had a huge Congolese meal with them. Back in Kinshasa I was hoping to spend a few days with Bruno Hanses, a friend I had known in SCI who was deputy at the EU mission, but our organisers feared that the contested results would cause trouble and we were all bundled off out of the country after one night's rest. In fact things did not heat up until the results started to be announced some time later.

Kabila was duly sworn in as president. Tshisekedi organised his own parallel ceremony. Whatever the true result – and I suspect that Kabila did win narrowly – half the population did not believe the results and the president's support in parliament was also fragmented. Kabila was greatly weakened. The absence of African leaders, apart from Robert Mugabe, at his swearing in was hardly an endorsement.

v) Congolese Quakers

My final involvement in the Congo resulted from being a Quaker. A school friend contacted me to ask if I was interested in working for the Quaker Congo Partnership, a project set up by Cambridge and Manchester Quakers. This is a relationship between English Friends and the local Congolese Friends' church,

CEEACO. Quakerism in Africa was begun by American missionaries who, as in Burundi, did not worship in silence as in the UK but in other respects it shares the same values including a strong commitment to peace. Abeka is one of a cluster of villages on the shore of Lake Tanganyika in South Kivu province, across the lake from Burundi and backed by a steep escarpment which is the western side of the Great Rift Valley. We raise funds in the UK for three projects: a small hospital, a trauma healing centre and a credit scheme for women. The hospital serves the local area, providing maternity care and dealing with many cases of malaria and anaemia as well as emergencies such as snakebites. Although the well-known massacre at Makobola, down the road from Abeka, was back in 1998 some survivors and their descendants are still traumatised as are many others who have suffered from attacks and often rape by Mayi Mayi rebels and government soldiers. The women who receive small loans are enabled to set up small businesses, trading, producing vegetables or making bricks and tiles. We have also been able to pay for a reliable water catchment high up on the escarpment to supply the hospital and the lakeside villages. This has led a big drop in the number of waterborne diseases. I have visited Abeka three times and have seen the positive effect of this funding but as in any charitable scheme we have to watch against creating dependency. Patients pay something towards their treatment and the Congo government sometimes subsidizes salaries – but sustainable local funding will eventually have to be found.

What hope is there for the Congo's future? The prophet Simon Kimbangu is said to have prophesied what the first four presidents would achieve. For the first three Kasavubu, Mobutu and Mzee Kabila he got it right. His prophesy for the fourth, Joseph Kabila, was that he would achieve great things. Sadly this has not yet come true and the *cinq chantiers,* the five point plan he promised has only produced minor improvements mostly built by the Chinese. The country's enormous potential wealth continues to leak over the borders and into some Congolese pockets. The political structure of the country remains chaotic. Local, mostly ethnic, conflicts continue. Perhaps the country is just too big to control and clearly some regions, notably Katanga and Kivu are pulling away from the weak centre. As I write Kabila has been behaving more and more dictatorially and he has postponed elections way beyond his legal mandate. The powerful Catholic church has turned against him, as has a majority of the population. I have learned much about the Congo from my friend Kris Berwouts, formerly of SCI Belgium, who has researched and written about the DRC. Like him I find it hard to be optimistic.

11
Zimbabwe

When I arrived in Northern Rhodesia in 1961, Zimbabwe was Southern Rhodesia. It was the dominant part of the Federation. When the Federation broke up it was just Rhodesia, illegally independent under the regime of Ian Smith from 1965. When it became clear that white rule had to end, an internal settlement was stitched together and the country became Zimbabwe-Rhodesia. This only lasted from July to December 1979. Negotiations at Lancaster House in London brought back the legal colonial name, Southern Rhodesia for a few months before it became independent as the Republic of Zimbabwe in April 1980. I recently found a letter I had written to the Foreign Secretary, Lord Carrington, in January 1980 to criticise the British government's disregard for the Lancaster House Agreement by allowing the continued presence of South African troops, allowing free movement of Rhodesian troops while the Patriotic Front forces were confined to assembly points and not being even-handed when dealing with the former combatants.[53] The election in February 1980 gave ZANU, led by Robert Mugabe 57 seats out of 100.

The Smith regime and the sanctions imposed upon it had terrible economic effects on Zambia: fuel rationing, shortages and high prices. Zambia suffered from its principled support of liberation, although there were a lot of jokes about Zimbabwean leaders sitting in restaurants in Lusaka eating "chicken in a basket"!

At Kalomo Secondary School we were very conscious of the tension across the border especially when one of our students was imprisoned after he had gone home for the holidays. Edyth and I went into Rhodesia in 1967 and visited the well preserved

---

53. See Annex 5.

archaeological sites at Khami, Naletale and the amazing complex of Great Zimbabwe. On the road north from Fort Victoria was a big sign with the slogan "Rhodesia is super" and on the main road to Bulawayo "Gwelo says thank you South Africa." On our way back to Zambia we stopped at the Kariba Dam and took a boat ride. The white boatman talked non-stop about how Rhodesia had the most stable government in the world. We kept our argument polite in case he tipped us into the lake. The Smith regime was to end thirteen years later.

The Africa Centre had very good relations with Zimbabwe's post-independence government. Herbert Murerwa, the High Commissioner, was a member of our Council of Management and gave his full support to he exhibition of Zimbabwe stone sculpture which had been put together by our Zimbabwean staff member, Keith Shiri. Our DJ and music organiser, Toendepi Dangarembizi (Wala) was also from Zimbabwe and he brought us music by Thomas Mapfumo, the Bhundu Boys and many more.[54]

Innocent Katsiga attended the CCIVS workcamp and seminar which we organised in 1993 in Namibia. By the following year he had created the Zimbabwe Workcamps Association which was to have its first workcamp and seminar in the suburb of Epworth, famous for its balancing rocks. It was a truly international event with participants from Zambia, Botswana and Germany, plus visitors like us from Britain and lots of Zimbabweans. The opening day was a Sunday and we all went for a picnic at Lake Chivero. Apart from the physical work, building teachers' houses at Epworth School, ZWA had a stall at the Harare Agricultural Show where we heard both President Mugabe and Nelson Mandela speak at the opening ceremony. On that day Mandela, the older man, seemed the more sprightly of the two.

Edyth and I then left the camp and went to stay in Bulawayo with Fanuel Mapfuwa, a great friend who had been our student at Chizongwe School. We went up on to the Matopo Hills to see Cecil Rhodes' grave and the fine rock paintings in nearby caves.

---

54. Refer back to Chapter 7.

Fanuel then accompanied us to his home village near Masvingo. The village is surrounded by the huge, smooth rocks typical of central Zimbabwe. We visited the magnificent ruins at Great Zimbabwe a second time. White Rhodesians were unwilling to believe that Africans had been capable of building such a huge complex and they tried to find all kinds of solutions to what they thought was a mystery. Archaeologists and other scholars could see that the pattern of the ruins was similar to other traditional courts in the area but just on a bigger scale and built of stone. It was in fact the centre of a rain making cult. The scholars have won the argument.

We drove east, crossing the iconic Birchenough Bridge over the Save River which was designed by the man who also designed Sydney Harbour Bridge, though it is only two thirds the size. Then the road climbed up through forest fires into the Bvumba Mountains where a friend of Fanuel's had lent us an enormous bungalow with a wide view over the hills, and nearby there was a distant panorama down into Mozambique.

On our return to Harare the workcamp was ending and Innocent asked me to open the seminar which was really the official launch of the workcamp association. There were discussions on issues such as rural development, AIDS and youth leadership. The final party included a church choir, the presentation of all the volunteers to the local people who had come for the ceremony, the treasurer's speech – and a lot of "cool drinks" and beer.

My next visit in 2003 was to help lead another similar seminar organised by Zimbabwe Workcamps Association and CCIVS. We attended the Heroes Day ceremony where President Mugabe spoke at great and boring length about his plans to revive the flagging economy. After the seminar we moved off to ZWA's efficient-looking farm to celebrate the tenth anniversary of the association. There was plenty to celebrate: Innocent had built up a team of active members. They had a strong programme of international workcamps and hosted volunteers from Europe, especially from Germany where they had a partnership with some members of the Social Democratic party. However, as Zimbabwe's political and economic situation deteriorated, it became harder to attract foreign volunteers and funding. Sadly the dynamic Katsiga died in 2011 but ZWA, now led by Ratherford Mwaruta, has survived and is taking the lead in reviving the regional co-ordinating structure, Southern Africa Workcamps Cooperation.

By 2003 Fanuel had moved from Bulawayo to a corner of his home district. After leaving school he had been selected to train as an engine driver when most of them were white. He transferred to Zimbabwe Railways later and managed to commute his pension just before the Zimbabwe dollar became worthless and with this he built his farm house and began to construct a guesthouse for visiting tourists. He was already struggling with lack of fuel and the prospect of no tourists as Zimbabwe descended into economic crisis. In 2012 he was still blaming President Mugabe for all his woes. He died in 2013 and I went for his memorial, joining all his brothers and sisters, his widow, who had gone off to live in her native Zambia, his daughters and sons, including the burly Nigel, named after me and working in Botswana as a motor engineer – and much of the local population.

On my way to Fanuel's memorial I lugged a heavy suitcase full of books published by Books of Africa, They were put on display at the Book Café in Harare, a wonderful social centre for music, meetings, food and books, set up by Paul Brickhill. It was not loved by the regime: Morgan Tsvangirai, the opposition leader, had launched his book there. I also visited the Mbira Centre, the brainchild of Albert Chimedza who has devoted himself to the promotion and manufacture of *mbira,* the iconic traditional Zimbabwean thumb-piano. He has modified the Indonesian gamelan notation for use with the *mbira* which he offers *mbira* to schools and has even introduced to the Zimbabwe Police Band.

12
Burundi 1998-2002

i) Christian Aid

In 1998 I was offered the job of Senior Field Officer for Christian Aid in Burundi, a country which was in a state of low-intensity civil war. I spent nearly four years there and I got to love the country and many Burundian friends. Seeing that there was a total lack of books about the country in English I ended up writing one.[55] This excerpt from the preface of the book provides give some background on the country. "Burundi is Rwanda's twin. Both were kingdoms which retained their pre-colonial boundaries, sharing the same culture, almost the same language and the same division of the population into Hutus, Tutsis and Batwa. They were governed as one mandated territory by Belgium, known as Ruanda-Urundi. There are significant differences between the two countries but events in one always infect the other. Yet, because of Rwanda's notoriety Burundi is often forgotten. . . . On the night of 6 April 1994 an aircraft was shot down close to Kigali, the capital of Rwanda. The plane was carrying two presidents. The death of President Habyarimana of Rwanda, a Hutu, led to the well documented genocide, mainly of Tutsis. President Ntaryamira of Burundi, also a Hutu, was on board also. He had been chosen to be president as a result of events in Burundi in 1993 which were a direct cause of what happened in Rwanda. The fateful date in Burundi was 21 October 1993 when a coup led by elements of the mainly Tutsi army resulted in the death of Melchior Ndadaye, the country's first democratically elected president. This led to a double genocide in Burundi, first of Tutsis all over the country, then of Hutus as the army took its revenge. Seeing what had

---

55. "Burundi, Biography of a Small African Country" (2nd edition Hurst 2016)

happened in Burundi, extremist Hutus in Rwanda wanted to make sure that no Tutsis would survive to take their revenge." In this chapter I am only describing my experiences in Burundi but for fuller information about the country and its history please read the book.

Back at Chizongwe School my colleague had met two Burundian ministers in 1962 on his way to a conference and was amazed at their youth. 1962 was the year of independence, two years ahead of Zambia. That was the first thing I heard about Burundi. Except in Belgium the country seldom got into the news except when there were massacres.

In 1998 Burundi faced an international boycott to protest at Pierre Buyoya taking back power in a coup. To get there I flew to Kigali (Rwanda) and I had to take a little plane to Bujumbura belonging to an embargo-breaking, mineral smuggling company. The destination of the plane was announced as Kalemie (Congo) but to my relief it did land at Bujumbura, descending over the Kibira Forest, the scattered homesteads of Bubanza and the wide valley of the Rusizi River, part of the Great Rift Valley. The very pretty, modern terminal building at Bujumbura Airport is seldom noisy but that day it was totally deserted. I sat and read my book, hoping someone would come for me. After some time a security man appeared and lent me his mobile phone, the big heavy sort that was the latest thing in 1998. Luckily my future colleague, Andy Nicholson, was in the office listening to the BBC news. He came to collect me and we drove into town, along the straight tarmac road I had seen from the air, where the main traffic was bicycles overloaded with grass and leaves, food for the large number of cattle displaced in the city due to the war.

The entry into the city is marked by a magnificent tree towering over a roundabout, the "lovers' tree" much used for wedding photographs. The road then passes through an area of warehouses and moribund light industries followed by the brewery, Burundi's biggest industry. The lively, mainly Muslim quartier of Buyenzi is on the left and the oldest part of town, the *Quartier Asiatique*, on the right. This was where Swahili and Indian traders had settled during and even before the time of German rule (1890-1916) and some are still there.

Burundi had been in crisis since 1993 when the democratically elected Hutu President Melchior Ndadaye was killed and all hell had broken loose. In the rural areas Tutsis were attacked and killed, most notoriously in the petrol station at Kibimba where seventy schoolchildren were burned to death. The mainly Tutsi army was quick to take revenge on Hutus, especially in Bujumbura. Many died and many fled and *quartiers* that had been mixed became mono-ethnic. Tutsis organised strikes that shut down the city, *villes mortes*. By the time of my arrival the worst of the crisis was over but there were still rebel attacks in some areas, usually at night. Villagers were targeted and their houses got burned and their meagre possessions looted. The UN organised a weekly meeting to report on the security situation which all the international agencies attended.

The Christian Aid (CA) office was an old residential house with a leafy garden. The staff were a good mixture. I did not realise at the time how rare this was, as most of the INGOs and UN agencies were mainly staffed by Tutsis. Andy was an experienced humanitarian worker having served in Liberia, the Congo and Rwanda. He also turned out to be the son of a former head of the Friends' School where I was educated. Jean-Marie Badionona, the project officer, was Congolese, fat, jolly and very good company; Serge Ntabikiyoboka was the administrator, a wise and very honest Hutu; Alice Ntibandetse, a Tutsi, the charming secretary is at the time of writing still working there. An aspect of CA that I learned to appreciate was that it always worked through local partner organisations. These could be churches or local NGOs. Where some of the other international NGOs created local partners which could vanish when the agency departed, our partners were real, well-established bodies. They could be maddening but they were genuine, closer to people's reality and would still be there after CA withdrew support.

Our biggest partner was the Council of Churches (CNEB) with which we co-ordinated the distribution of seeds and tools, a vital programme when crops were often destroyed and villagers displaced. Andy worked closely with Jean-Berchmans Rusimbi[56]of CNEB and a team of local co-ordinators, one for each province. We supported many other projects all over the country: housing construction for returning refugees and displaced people with the United Methodist Church; a mobile ambulance service based at the Friends' hospital at Kibimba; and a big agricultural and livestock project at Kimeza in the far north which had been a Belgian aid scheme that had to close due to the embargo but had been rescued by the local Anglican Church. A guiding principle of our work was to promote reconciliation and peace. We tried to ensure that Hutus, Tutsis and Batwa worked together, an example being a women's mat making project at Kibimba where the women became friends as they made straw mats which CA then purchased and distributed to displaced people. I took the initiative to work with the Batwa, as described below. I was also enthusiastic about our small projects fund which supported community initiatives such as a little orphanage and youth workcamps.

I was given a modest Belgian colonial house with a nice big veranda at the back from which you could see Lake Tanganyika and, after the rains, the mountains across the lake in the Congo. Amani, one of the scouts involved in the 1993 exchange mentioned below, and Henry Kabula who had run the workcamp association in Zambia both later shared the house with me, along with Réglisse, the CA dog. Henry was a keen gardener. We had vegetables and chickens. Edyth visited Burundi six times while I was there, and my son Tom twice.

Burundians tend to be reserved, so I was lucky to have six Burundian friends before I even arrived. Back in the summer of 1993 SCI had hosted a youth exchange between East Africa

---

56. Rusimbi was the Legal Representative of the Kimbanguist Church. This originally Congolese church was founded by Simon Kimbangu. The Belgians suppressed the church and imprisoned Kimbangu for 30 years until his death. The Kimbanguists picked up some characteristics of the Salvation Army, notably a fine tradition of music.

and Europe. I had briefly met the African group in Brussels. The European volunteers were to visit Africa in October but at that moment the Burundian President was killed and *la crise* (the crisis) began, so instead of going to Burundi the European volunteers and the Burundians were together in Kenya. I was there with my CCIVS hat on and we drew up a proposal for UNESCO to fund reconstruction work in Burundi. When it became obvious that the crisis was not going to end quickly, we persuaded UNESCO to allow this grant to be used to invite five Burundian youth leaders to visit peace projects in Northern Ireland. They found that the two communities there had less in common with each other than Hutus and Tutsis did but they learned some new ideas about peace building. On their way home the five missed their plane connection in London. I happened still to be at home in London and I picked up the bewildered group at Victoria station and squeezed them into my car with all their luggage. They spent a week at my house, so Edyth and I got to know Dismas and Nepo from the Scouts, Marie-Goretti from the Guides, Aisha from the Muslim Youth and Thérence from the Catholic *Mouvement Xavéri* very well. I had to get back to Paris after several days but Edyth looked after them. Her elderly mother, who had met a number of English-speaking Africans, was puzzled as to why these ones were speaking French. That's how she learned about the Belgian Empire!

Within minutes of my arrival at the hotel in Bujumbura in 1998 Dismas and Nepo called on me, and the next day I attended Nepo's engagement ceremony where imaginary cows – really envelopes full of cash – were handed over to his future bride's family. From then on my circle of friends increased. Looking at my diary I am amazed at my sociability and number of beers and *brochettes* I must have consumed in four years. This enabled me to begin to understand this complicated little country fairly quickly, demystifying the ethnic division – which is not at all like it is in most African countries – and getting some insight into its politics.

My first trip "up country" took me to Kibimba, notorious for the massacre in the petrol station. I was introduced to the mat making women. Kibimba is in fact a mission of the Evangelical Friends' Church, the Burundian version of the Quakers, consisting of a hospital and two schools. The hospital remained under church control and only closed briefly during the first days of the crisis. The primary school and the secondary *école normale* (teacher training college) had been government-run for some years and it was the Tutsi pupils from these schools who had been massacred. In 1998 the petrol station was being converted into a memorial with the words *Plus Jamais* (Never Again) blazoned on it. Sadly it was only a memorial for Tutsis when elsewhere Hutus were suffering the same fate. It could have stood for reconciliation. On this visit I found burnt desks and piles of dirt in the school buildings which had been used to house soldiers and I was told the government planned to turn the place into a permanent barracks. Fortunately some lobbying by the church and the support of a friendly Hutu Minister of Education, backed up with a letter from me promising Christian Aid funding, brought about a change of policy. The teachers' college was able to reopen a year later, with a clear message of reconciliation. Kibimba in fact became a centre of peace building. The Tutsi head of the primary school, Matthias Ndimurwanko, who had through bravery, luck and prayer escaped alive from the inferno, became chair of a very active local peace committee supported by Aloys Ningabira, a nurse at the time and who is today the Legal Representative of the Quaker church.

Another early visit was to the family homestead or *rugo*[57] of Dismas Hicintuka, who had led the group of youth leaders to Northern Ireland. We piled into the Christian Aid 4x4 loaded with beer, Fanta[58] and the whole family. We turned off the tarmac and descended along a track into a banana-filled valley. Traditionally Burundians live on a *colline* (hill) consisting of scattered homes such as this typical *rugo* – his parents' round house thatched with banana leaves, another house for himself and a shelter for cattle,

---

57. Traditionally Burundians do not live in villages but in a homestead, a *rugo*. A collection of these scattered homes make up a "hill", a *colline*.
58. All fizzy drinks in Burundi are collectively known as Fanta.

encircled by a wooden fence. After a lot of greeting and chat we piled back into the car minus some of the bottles but plus jerry-cans of *urwagwa,* home brewed banana beer, with plantains for stoppers. We bumped along for a time and parked in a coniferous wood from which we could descend a steep, rocky slope carrying the crates and jerrycans to the *rugo* of the family of Josephine, Dismas' wife. Here we drank *impeke,* sorghum beer which is rather lumpy compared to the banana version, and we had a second lunch. We then crowded into a hut for the ceremony which had brought us here, the presentation of a cow to Dismas and his children. Josephine's dad, wearing a raincoat and a Homburg in the style of President Kamuzu Banda of Malawi, made his little speech, followed by one from Dismas' dad. All the neighbours were there and much beer, traditional and modern, was drunk, but not by me as I had to drive home on a precipitous road. I was to visit this beautiful spot again for the ending of the mourning period, the *levee du deuil,* of Dismas' grandmother. This is the province of Mwaro where rural life is at its most traditional. It is, unusually, a Tutsi majority area. When Hutus were being killed in 1972 Dismas' father sheltered his Hutu neighbours. In 1993 the Tutsis were being attacked and the Hutu neighbours returned the kindness.

Burundians describe Hutus, Tutsis and Twa as ethnic groups, but these are nothing like the ethnic divisions in most of Africa. They have one culture and speak the same language. Conflict was in no way inevitable, though once it began, fear and sometimes revenge prolonged it. A former American ambassador described the relationship as "a kind of disease like malaria: as long as it remains in the body there is a danger of it breaking out."[59] It is true that Tutsis were traditionally cattle people and drank milk while the Hutus were cultivators. But the Belgians deepened divisions, issuing ID cards showing ethnicity and, imagining the Tutsis were a superior race and educating them as a collaborating class. According to the prejudices of the time Tutsis had long noses, were

---

59. Thomas Patrick Melady, *Burundi, the Tragic Years* (New York: Orbis Books 1974)

tall, good looking and intelligent; the Hutus had squashed noses and were short and stocky; and the Twa were very short pygmies. In reality intermarriage meant that these facile characteristics were not very meaningful. If your father was a Tutsi and your mother a Hutu you were classified as a Tutsi although you might be short and stocky.[60] Strangely, also, it was possible to change your ethnicity. There is even a verb for it! Until you know someone very well you do not ask his or her ethnicity. You often find out through a third party. I was struck when interviewing friends for my book how children usually did not know what they were except at times of crisis. For example, if you lost your father in 1972, the year of Burundi's first genocide, you guessed that you were likely to be a Hutu.

From 1993 for a few years there was residential segregation in Bujumbura, and in the rural areas many Tutsis were settled in "camps" which in time became more or less permanent villages. At the time of my arrival people were starting to move back to their original homes in Bujumbura. The following decade of peace building, added to people's increasing revulsion against war meant that inter-ethnic fear and hatred reduced greatly. Those opposed to President Nkurunziza's decision to run for a third term in 2015 included people of every ethnic group, though the president tries to pin the blame on the Tutsis.

I became especially interested in working with the marginalised Batwa (singular: *mutwa*) of whom there are only around 60,000 in the country. Descendants of the earliest inhabitants, they are related to other communities of pygmies in the Congo and elsewhere. Many of them are not particularly short – and some are quite tall due to intermarriage. They traditionally lived from hunting wild animals and gathering wild fruits in the forests where Hutus and Tutsis feared to go. They were also potters and they still are, but plastic has priced them out of the market so their only options are to obtain land and learn to farm – or to become labourers.

---

60. Some Tutsis said that President Buyoya's appearance meant that he must really be a Hutu.

They used to suffer terrible prejudice. A former missionary I met recalled asking a friend, "What person is that?" and getting the answer, "It's not a man, it's a Mutwa." The situation has now greatly improved due mainly to the courage of a few outstanding Batwa who have organised themselves and now have secondary education and university degrees. They are also now represented in both houses of parliament, notably by an impressive woman senator, Libérate Nicayenzi, and also in the assembly of the East African Community. Vital Bambanze has represented his community at the UN. Christian Aid provided bursaries for Batwa schoolchildren and supported agricultural and fishery projects. However, the reality is that most Batwa are still among the poorest in a country of poor people.

Many of Christian Aid's partners in Burundi were the mainstream Protestant churches that made up the Council of Churches (CNEB). The Anglicans had the reputation of being "the Tutsis at prayer" but in fact, like the others, a majority of their members were Hutus. The Roman Catholic church was much larger than all our partners put together but, as all over Africa, it was the pentecostalists and other very evangelical groups that were gaining ground. As Burundi was 90% Christian these gains were at the expense of other churches. New churches would spring up overnight, usually led by a pastor who decided to set up on his own, sometimes as a way of earning a living. In 2012 Emmanuel Nengo, the Twa member of the East African Assembly, was driving me to one of the bar resorts on the lake shore for a drink only to be told at the gate that the owner of the bar had "found Jesus" and was therefore not selling alcohol any more! There were splits in the Anglican church too: one priest, bitterly disappointed at not being promoted as a bishop, founded his own church; and the former Bishop of Bujumbura, whose extravagant building of a new cathedral, office block and hotel was one of the reasons he was sacked, also set up a new church. At the same time Islam was growing in Burundi where it has a benign reputation. In 1993 Muslims had welcomed displaced families to their homes, Hutu and Tutsi equally, and took no part in the killings.

ii) Politics and peace

The embargo I had encountered on my arrival was lifted in January 1999 when Uganda and Tanzania accepted that President Buyoya was negotiating seriously. It was exciting to see the first international flight, Ethiopian Airways, arrive. Prices went down a bit and the elite were cheerful, at least those that had not been profiting from the embargo. The famous old ship, the *Liemba*, began serving Bujumbura again. Edyth and I were able to sail on her to Mpulungu and visit Zambia. This ship has had a most amazing history. It was built at in Papenburg, Germany in 1913, named *Graf von Götzen* and re-assembled on the lake shore at Kigoma, in what was then German East Africa. The British sank it during the First World War and brought it back to the surface after the war. It inspired C.S. Forester's novel, *The African Queen*, filmed in Zaire (DRC) and Uganda with Katharine Hepburn and Humphrey Bogart, as mentioned above. Since then it has sailed from Kigoma to Zambia serving the villages along the Tanzanian shore and, most of the time, also Bujumbura. We found it neither smart nor especially clean but we had a cabin, good simple food, *ugali* and fish, with Congolese music blaring. After less than a year it stopped serving Bujumbura again and now the only way to reach Kigoma is by minibus. A friend of ours who was visiting Burundi on her journey round the world wanted to take a boat to Kigoma but Henry Kabula, who just sailed on one, faxed to warn her that it would be a nightmare, an open boat with no toilet and liable to held up in the middle of the lake for security reasons.

Security was on and off in 1999. Rebels fired rockets which could occasionally be spotted over Bujumbura. One night it was quite frightening. I was having dinner with friends when the noise began. The others in my house called to tell me not to return home, and a rocket landed not far away. Apart from moments like these, the most worrying things about working for an aid agency in Burundi were anonymous death threats. The motive could be that a worker had been, perhaps unjustly, dismissed, or that a vacancy was filled by the "wrong" person, or that the aid worker had gone off with someone's girlfriend. The director of ADRA, the Seventh

Day Adventist agency, was drowned in the lake. The Action Aid director was shot in a restaurant in Nairobi. I even received a threat late in my stay. I did not fit any of these scenarios and the wording of the threat was fairly gentle, saying I was nice and popular but… maybe they just wanted money. Anyway, CA took the precaution of sending me to London against my will for a couple of weeks before the scare blew over.

Buyoya's government was often heavy-handed. Hutus who had fled from the Kamenge quarter which had earlier been destroyed by the army were driven out of their miserable refugee camps on the edge of Bujumbura. In September 260,000 Hutu villagers were forced to move into *regroupement* sites from which they could not support the rebels, but nor could they carry on farming or living normally. The rebel groups were sometimes very violent. The most shocking action was in October 1999 when they lined up UN officials and others attending a ceremony. They shot the popular head of UNICEF Burundi, the deputy head of the World Food Programme and the director of the sugar company. Incidents like this caused the UN system to panic and send all their senior staff out of the country, after which the work was left to us NGOs who were in fact much more vulnerable.

PIC 26) The march for peace in Bujumbura, 2000.

The former president of Tanzania, Julius Nyerere, was the mediator of Burundi's conflict until his death in October 1999 but we were delighted that Nelson Mandela agreed to replace him. One colleague remarked that it was like God accepting the job. Divine or not, many Tutsis were not happy with either mediator. Mandela tended to see the ethnic breakdown (14% Tutsi, 85% Hutu) in South African terms, equating the Hutu rebels with the ANC and perhaps not understanding that Burundians have more in common with each other than have white and black South Africans. However, his authority could not be questioned and, supported by his deputy mediator, Jacob Zuma, progress was achieved. Mandela could be quite outspoken, condemning the *regroupement* policy in no uncertain terms. "The misery of the Burundian people diminishes the humanity of all of us," he remarked.

In January 2000 Christian Aid was involved in organising a large and successful march for peace through the streets of Bujumbura. At the head marched the band of the Kimbanguist Church, trumpets blaring, followed by the Scouts, many other local associations and individuals. The same weekend the excellent American NGO, Search for Common Ground, organised the Sangwe Music Festival in the stadium, also in aid of peace and reconciliation.

The idea of voluntary workcamps found fertile ground in Burundi. The first camp I helped plan was a collaboration between Christian Aid, the Council of Churches, the Scouts, Guides and *Mouvement Xavéri* to work with families in the suburb of Kanyosha to help them rebuild their homes. Henry Kabula shared the experience he had gained in Zambia. The Council of Churches continued to maintain its interest in the idea and supported workcamps working with the Batwa to build homes and to construct the school at Nyangungu. This school had been started by the Batwa association, Christian Union for the Education and Development of the Underprivileged, and it was unprecedented to see the Batwa community acting as hosts and welcoming volunteers – Hutus and Tutsis from Bujumbura as well as Ugandans and Congolese. After my departure the workcamp tradition was carried on by Phocas Ndimubandi who founded the *Alliance Burundaise du Service*

Volontaire (ABSV). ABSV has played a part in CCIVS and in the East African voluntary service network. It welcomes volunteers to Bujumbura and to their hostel at Mbuye in the centre of the country, They have hosted the "caravan," a rolling workcamp moving through eastern Africa. Even when Burundi is at peace it is hard to attract volunteers as the country is not well known and the cost flying from Europe or Japan is more than to Kenya or Tanzania. The political situation after 2015 has made the task even more difficult.

iii) Life in Burundi

I have always thought it was important – in fact basic courtesy demanded – that a visitor to a country should make some effort to learn the language, even if only basic greetings. In India back in 1960 I learned quite a lot of Hindi. The Colonial Office to its credit made all outgoing colonial officials learn a language, though many countries have multiple languages and you may end up learning the wrong one. Edyth learned Bemba but when she arrived in Zambia she was posted to a Nyanja speaking area. Just before Zambian Independence they offered a prize if you could pass an exam. The one I sat involved translating the report of a Westminster debate. I failed. At IVS we always tried to include language in our orientation courses for volunteers. I was rather shocked in Burundi that the expatriates working for the UN and NGOs, many of whom it is true had to learn French for their work, could not in most cases even greet their colleagues in Kirundi. Fidèle Kanyugu, who taught me Kirundi, helped me and Phocas Ndimubandi produce a phrase book aimed at INGO personnel.

One usually pleasant result of having lots of friends was to attend betrothals, weddings and *levées de deuil*.[61] Burundians love these events and they can be quite fun. Betrothals are small affairs with family and a few friends and some traditional drinks.

---

61. One cause of President Bagaza's downfall in 1987 was his attempt to make people spend less time and money on ceremonies including marking the end of the mourning period.

Weddings involve a civil ceremony at the *mairie*, followed by a Christian or Muslim ceremony and then a party. At the Roman Catholic cathedral ten or more couples are often lined up before the altar in one service. I sometimes managed, with corrections by a friend, to make a wedding speech in Kirundi. The parties can be a bit formal with too many speeches but beer and Fanta flow fairly freely if the couple and their friends can afford it. Photographs are taken by the "lovers tree" or on the beach. Then the day after the wedding is the ceremony of *gutwi kurura* when all the women friends arrive with the typical pointed baskets on their heads filled with gifts of rice, beans and other offerings.

Another spin-off from being sociable and also being something of a soft touch is that I have helped a number of Burundians with needs such as school fees and hospital bills and I continue to receive cries of alarm. One regular payment I make is for Evariste whom I first met as he was leaving secondary school. His mother was a very poor villager but he was highly motivated to go for further education. I paid for him to study in Kenya where he made outstanding progress and quickly became fluent in English. Then suddenly he had a mental breakdown with fantasies about a Tanzanian girlfriend. He was moved to a different campus and had a course of medication but he got worse and in the end there was no alternative but to bring him back to Burundi. He spent a short time in the local asylum and he now lives in quite a happy dream world in Bujumbura. It was disappointing that what I hoped would be an investment in his education became simply a case of humanitarian relief.

Three British Labour Party MPs visited Burundi in July 2000, David Lammy, Des Browne and Tess Kingham. When we passed a certain point on the road where rebels were known to cross into Burundi from the Congo I mentioned this to them. I was mildly reprimanded for making them nervous. They enjoyed their visit nonetheless, as did we. They visited housing and agricultural projects and we met President Buyoya.

In December 2000 the World Bank and UNDP hosted a conference in Paris to encourage offers of funding for Burundi. As I was due to be home in London that week the RESO, the grouping of thirty-seven international NGOs working in Burundi, asked me to go to it as an observer. fifteen countries and six international organisations were represented. President Chirac was delayed so Laurent Fabius, the Minister of Finance, read his speech. Nelson Mandela was present throughout and he played a big role. He paid tribute to his predecessor, Julius Nyerere, and he used his influence to encourage donors to be generous. President Buyoya and some of his ministers found themselves in the same room with some bitter opponents, but the ambience was not unfriendly. I think some of them had been to school together. Many of the donors wanted to be sure that peace really was coming – and the absence of the two active rebel movements at this meeting threw doubt on this – but most seemed to agree that aid could begin step by step as peace came to be established. I was allowed to speak on behalf of the RESO. I pointed out that NGOs had continued to work at some risk when the UN was restricted for security reasons and that we really knew the communities we were working with. While humanitarian aid was still needed, I said that we were entering the phase of reconstruction and development and that security was not a problem in most of Burundi's provinces. The conference ended with pledges of $400 million from a majority of the donors present. Mandela was delighted – clearly his charisma and arm twisting had an effect. I am not sure if all the money was ever delivered.

Christian Aid's policy was to respect the retirement age and I was six months over that in September 2001. I would happily have stayed a little longer even though in the previous months I had experienced the death threat and had also had to fly home for a minor operation. A farewell party was arranged for me on 10 September, a lovely, noisy occasion at the *Cercle Nautique* where in the past I had often sat drinking beer, watching the lake and looking out for the very occasional hippo. It was fortunate that the party was held that day because when I was with Edyth and my son Tom the next morning, a friend phoned saying America had been attacked. Even Burundi television had the pictures and we watched the twin towers, stunned like everyone. Except that Tom who did not understand French thought it was a movie. A couple of days later in English-speaking Nairobi he took in the reality.

iv) CARE International, elections and the President's third term

In August 2002 I returned to Burundi for three months as acting director of CARE International. It was different from life at Christian Aid, which worked with partners with projects all over the country. CARE's work was concentrated in Ngozi province which meant frequent trips there, usually in little Red Cross or UN planes. The flight only took 20 minutes except when it called at other places on the way, a good way of seeing the whole beautiful country from the air. From Ngozi's airstrip along a bumpy road into Burundi's tiny third largest town, we would have a meeting of the staff and visit some of the projects. We went to Tangara where CARE was refurbishing schools, providing school desks, building a new abattoir, a meat market and some new houses; and the next day with colleagues Juma and Rehema to the Ruhororo displacement site for Tutsis, now a huge, permanent village, to visit the households which had benefited from another goat distribution project. At Ngozi we always stayed in a funny little hotel called Sckojet where, as everywhere in Ngozi, the lights and the water went off from time to time. President Nkurunziza comes from a village nearby and it is here that he built his grand football stadium where he plays for his home soccer team, *Hallelujah XI*.

Reading my diary for 2002 my life in Bujumbura seemed to consist of meeting people, usually some of my many friends but often contacts for work, drinking beer at one of the many *cabarets,* bars which usually have a garden, where to get something to eat you call the *vétérinaire* for a brochette, a kebab. This was usually goat meat which tended to be tough so I would choose liver or fish. The choice of beer had to be Primus, known as *ikiyeri*,[62] or Amstel served "hot" or cold. I particularly liked going to Bwiza, a scruffy

---

62. The French word *bière* becomes *ibiyeri* in Kirundi but that is plural so in the singular it becomes *ikiyeri*. Amstel never got a Kirundi name.

but cosmopolitan *quartier* where before the crisis there had been a large West African community. A few Malians remain, running tailoring shops and serving *michopo,* a dish of rather greasy meat with cassava *ugali,* on Second Avenue where you sit listening to Congolese music and watch the moon above the minaret. Round the corner is *Cinq sur Cinq* a very atmospheric little night club with Congolese ambience, especially lively on Mondays. At the time of writing most of these places, if they survive, have to close early due to the tense political situation and the shattered economy.

In 2010, before my experience in the Congo described above, I offered to be an election observer for EurAc. This took me again to Ngozi Province and to the Sckojet Hotel. Before the voting we visited five polling stations to ensure everything was well organised. It was, but the election was something of a farce as the main opposition parties had decided to boycott it. They had cried foul when the governing CNDD-FDD won the earlier local elections. There were a number of other groups involved in monitoring, including the European Union, the UN and church groups. Not only was Ngozi the home of the President but also of Agathon Rwasa, the leader of the other former rebel group which had turned itself into a political party, the FNL. Rwasa was in hiding but we visited his mother in her village. She was sitting with a number of his followers and complaining of harassment by government agents.

I was in Burundi again in 2014, just before Nkurunziza made his fateful decision to stand for a third term. Bujumbura was at its best. The latest fashion for those who had money to invest was to build hotels. Too many were opened – and now there are few visitors. The previous craze had been to open petrol stations: there are no less than six on a short stretch of main road! The *cabarets* were doing good business and FESTICAB, the Burundi film festival, was in its sixth year. This festival is the brainchild of Léonce Ngabo who began as a musician and whose first film, *Gito l'ingrat* (Gito the ungrateful) was for long Burundi's only feature film – and quite a good one. I was given the job of helping to screen English language films from East Africa at a deserted hotel on a steep hillside. Very few people came. Léonce had also organised a training project for young East African would-be film makers and this happened at the same hotel.

Burundi is a country which had strong traditional structures and some of the effects of colonial rule were harmful, notably the sharpening of the Hutu-Tutsi cleavage. The killing of Prince Louis Rwagasore, the country's charismatic leader in 1961 just before Independence, in which the Belgians were complicit, removed the man who might have set the state on a progressive and stable course. Another stabilising factor was lost when the monarchy was abolished in 1966. The country was then ruled by a series of Tutsi military leaders. Burundi has in fact been in a state of spasmodic, suppressed or open conflict for most of its existence. The longest period of crisis followed the overthrow of the demo-cratically elected President Ndadaye in 1993. When it seemed that the crisis was over the exemplary election of 2005 brought Pierre Nkurunziza to power and we had hopes of stability and justice. NGOs and Burundian civil society, working with the government and UN agencies, had succeeded in reviving the economy and in promoting reconciliation. However, Nkurunziza, the new presi-dent, soon showed that he was no angel in spite of his born-again religiosity, but the country was peaceful and the economy was improving. Then suddenly everything was thrown into confusion by the president's decision to stand for a third term. Nkurunziza won a referendum in 2018 which allows him to stay for two more seven year terms, At the time of writing there is no civil war but people are being targeted, beaten and killed, human rights are flouted, the excellent free radio stations are closed, corruption is rife and the fragile economy remains shattered.

Was the work of Christian Aid useful to Burundi? Did I do anything useful in Burundi? I think the many projects and programmes, not just ours, promoting reconciliation had a major effect, part of which is the fact that the divisions post-2015 have become political rather than ethnic: it's not just Tutsis who are against the regime. Otherwise the work of international NGOs to reduce poverty and provide humanitarian relief helped a lot of Burundians to survive but in a context of conflict this could not really be called development aid. In the short period between the signing of the peace accord and the renewal of conflict in 2015 there were signs of development and the government had signed up to quite a good poverty reduction strategy. But there was not much sign that the government leaders had a vision for the country. Rwanda, like Burundi, has few resources and Kagame's regime in is a dictatorship but the man has ideas and Rwanda has developed. Nkurunziza's main focus seems to be to hold on to power at all costs. I think aid can still have a role but it should have the clear objective of enabling the recipient country within a measurable time scale to live without it.

v) Minority Rights

As a follow up-to Christian Aid's work with the Batwa in Burundi I was asked in 2002 to do an evaluation study of the work of the Minority Rights Group (MRG) in the Great Lakes Region, including Burundi. This gave me a chance to visit Batwa communities, sometimes on mountainsides, sometimes deep in the bush, in Rwanda, the DRC and Uganda. MRG's work included training about land rights, human rights, advocacy and capacity building for which its partner organisations received funding and advice from MRG. This included enabling Batwa spokespersons to attend international meetings to raise their profile and fight their corner. The Burundian Batwa were further ahead politically, with backing from the government as explained above. The most effective organisation for training and promotion of economic activities was CAURWA in Rwanda. The most marginalised Batwa community was in the forests of south western Uganda, famous for the mountain gorillas, but even here some advances were being made in education and recognition. In the Congo, as in Rwanda and Burundi, there were tensions between rival organisations. The first pygmy leader, Kapupu, resented the existence of other associations and even dubbed himself the King of the Pygmies. They never had kings or chiefs.

My findings were positive about MRG's contribution, though many felt they lacked enough personal contact with MRG. As with all interventions by outside donors the question arises as to whether the support makes the beneficiaries dependent. The Batwa need to have the confidence to play their full role in society and this requires education and training to be provided and for them to be given official representation as a minority group. They have been able to make their voice heard internationally and raised their profile locally and I think MRG's work has contributed to this.

13
Bermondsey, Leicester and East Dulwich

When I started work with IVS in 1971 we saw an advertisement for a tiny, modern terraced house near the river in Bermondsey, south east London. Edyth and I bought it for £9,000. Here we adopted Tom in 1973 and Edyth gave up teaching for a bit to become a full-time mother. She did not enjoy being shut in the house with the baby and she would go for long walks pushing a rather basic pram. When IVS moved to Leicester in 1976 we moved to a semi-detached house squashed next a pub facing Victoria Park. Here we adopted Sally in 1977 and two years later moved to a large, rambling house with a colossal pear tree in the garden. Here we started to have friends living with us as lodgers: from Zambia, Tanzania and Uganda and also Jagwant and Fo Chaudhary and their daughter Supriya after their return from India. Fo had been an IVS volunteer and Jagwant worked for the Indian branch of SCI. Both joined our staff in the IVS office.

When I was appointed at the Africa Centre in 1984, we bought a large Edwardian house in East Dulwich jointly with Fo and Jagwant. It has a fantastic panoramic view over London and a good-sized garden. A few years later Fo and Jagwant moved out and their place has since been filled at different times by Solvig Starborg, a Swedish friend, who was also a volunteer with SCI India, and friends from Zambia, France, South Africa, Togo, Uganda, Nigeria and Ghana, some of whom came through the workcamp movement. As I write, our oldest co-inhabitant, Ashong Anyetei, has been with us for twenty years. We have two other Ghanaians, Paul and Eric whose wife Marie is from Denmark, plus Supriya, who returned to live in London, and Keith Shiri from Zimbabwe, the expert on African cinema, my former colleague at the Africa Centre. I always liked living in a populated house and I have appreciated it more since my very dear Edyth died in 2011. Sally married Tim Brandon in 2000. They live nearby and they have three brilliant children who seem to be destined for a stage career. Lucy at the age of 11 was praised for her performance in *Much Ado about Nothing* at Shakespeare's Globe and Toby, aged 9, is joining the West End cast of *Matilda*. Tom is happily married to Cheryl, living in Scotland and feeling very Scottish. As a Watt he had the right to a couple of clan tartans at his wedding but we did not find the right one. I have an excuse for a good train ride to see him every few months.

My crazy house also serves as the legal address of Books of Africa and also of Volunteer Action for Peace, of which I am currently chairperson. I also keep busy as chair of the Leggatt Trust[63] and North South Travel[64] and as a director of Just Ghana, a small company set up by the architect, Elsie Owusu with the aim of capacity building and development with an emphasis on the environment and climate justice. I am also a member of the Quaker Congo Partnership[65] and Fighting Poverty in Zambia.[66] Edyth was a great gardener and I try and fail to keep the garden as she should have wished it to be.

Books of Africa

I never intended to go into publishing. In my youth I had helped my mother by proof reading some of her books and 1 followed with interest her experiences of good and bad publishers and their erratic payment of royalties. At the Africa Centre we hosted Bookweek Africa as a result of which the African Books' Collective was launched. Much later when I was working in Paris we met

---

63. Refer to Rev. Michael Scott in Chapter 9.
64. Refer to Mukesh Kapila in Chapter 5 (xii)
65. See Chapter 10.
66. FPZ was created by Francis Makambwe who had been in charge of Scouts at Chizongwe School and become an Anglican priest, eventually a vicar in London. This charity originally supported villages in his home area, Petauke (Eastern Province) with water supplies and it now supports education in the Northern Province.

Dieudonné Gnammankou who was writing up his research on Abraham Hanibal, the African ancestor of the great Russian poet, Pushkin. Neither Edyth nor I were aware of Pushkin's ancestry but were fascinated by the story. Dieudonné's book[67] was published by the venerable African publishing house, *Présence Africaine*, and Edyth translated it into English. At the time Dieudonné found no publisher for the English version and Edyth died without seeing the book in print.

Dieudonné became a publisher himself and in 2008 established Editions Dagan in France. At this time a friend of his, the Ivorian Emmanuel Mah, was moving to London with the idea of starting an English language cousin of Dagan. I got roped in and Books of Africa was born. Having no capital and no premises (apart from storage at my house) we have published several books each year and survived. I had been the literary executor of the Zimbabwean novelist, Wilson Katiyo, and we re-published his well-known novel, *A Son of the Soil*, and his posthumous novel, *Tsiga*, which I edited. Other books came through our French connection: graphic biographies of the early life of two great African footballers, Samuel Eto'o and Didier Drogba; poetry by Gabriel Mwènè Okoundji from Congo-Brazzaville; work by the prizewinning Congolese (DRC) author, Kama Sywor Kamanda who is hugely famous in the French-speaking world but not among Anglophones; and of course *Abraham Hanibal, Prince of Logone* which finally appeared in 2015. Daniel, the son of the great New Orleans jazz pioneer, Sidney Bechet, came to London to launch his book about his father and to celebrate the blue plaque on the house in London where he stayed in his youth. Our most popular titles have been the works of the American scholar, Runoko Rashidi, who has studied the history of the black diaspora in Europe, Asia and the Americas. He has visited black communities all over the world and kept valuable photographic records and he has come and given lectures a number of times in the UK.

---

67. *Abraham Hanibal, Prince of Logone*. The original version, *Abraham Hanibal, L'Aieul Noir de Pouchkine* was published in Paris by *Présence Africaine*.

PIC 27) *With Edyth and Rosemary Mumbi, the founder of Faith and Hope School, Lusaka, funded by the Leggatt Trust.*

14
Last Word

I have had the opportunity and privilege of learning about Africa and Africans from many perspectives. I hope that what I have recorded may be of interest as archival material about the continent. It is hard to evaluate the impact of the many things I have done. Edyth and I started Kalomo School from scratch and it got a good reputation. I think we both also played a role helping to reform the French and history syllabuses in Zambia as the education system was adapting to Independence. I was decorated for contributing to national reconciliation in Burundi and, looking at recent developments, I cannot claim much long-lasting success on that score – the only compensation is that the current fault-line in the country is more political than ethnic. I certainly played an important role in IVS and SCI and in supporting the voluntary service movement in Africa. Along with the support and solidarity of CCIVS and organisations in Europe have backed up the vision and hard work of the leaders of these workcamp associations who have achieved quite a lot in terms of basic development, youth participation, training and international – and in some cases inter-ethnic – understanding. At the Africa Centre the strong team most of whom I recruited produced programmes of a high quality and created an ambience which is still remembered fondly today.

This book does not pretend to try to make general comments about Africa's future, or its past. I have consistently wanted Africans to be in control of their affairs. It is for African governments to determine what role, if any, advice or money or volunteers from outside should play. NGOs and UN agencies do useful things but they tend to distort local economies and often combine ignorance with arrogance. Getting rid of neo-colonialism is a slow and, as yet, unfinished process and new forms of intervention must be on African terms. But Africa is disunited. The African Union falls short of Kwame Nkrumah's Pan-African dream. Most African countries are relatively small with weak economies which makes them easily exploited. The multiple challenges of population growth, environmental degradation and inappropriate agricultural policy mean that there is a real threat of widespread famine and people will continue to try to emigrate, desperately dangerous though this may be.[68] Despite all this Africans have achieved a lot over the past seventy years: in terms of political and economic development but also of art, literature, music and cinema – the positive image that the Africa Centre always tried to promote.

The voluntary service movement I have described struggles to have an impact in today's context. Yet the need for peace, international and intra-national understanding, global justice and human rights has never been greater. At some point the shocking injustice in the world will cause an explosion and I hope there will still be enough idealists and peacemakers around to soften the blow.

London
July 2018

---

68. See "The Famine next Door" by Benny Dembitzer 2018.

Annexes

Annex 1
National Service Acts

Application to local tribunal by a person provisionally registered in the register of conscientious objectors

WATT, Nigel John. Statement:

Nobody denies that peace is a good thing, but many people consider the defence of an abstract thing called "national glory", which involves the destruction of human lives, of cities and of living standards, more worthwhile than a conciliatory peace. The methods of "collective security" have been tried often before and arms races have always led to war. The way of reconciliation has never been tried, and the fact that only very few people are willing to risk it is no reason those people abandoning their faith.

It is alien to any moral standards that one half of the human race should prepare to mutilate the other, which is what modern warfare amounts to, and I feel I must make a stand for reconciliation and human unity which necessitates my becoming a conscientious objector. I have probably been influenced by my education at the Friends' School, Saffron Walden, but the reading of books which oppose the pacifist way has failed to influence me in the other direction. I think that it is quite reasonable to expect everybody to perform some useful service to the human community, but I am perfectly certain that to support the armed forces is to help increase international hatred and to cause war.

The Tribunal was satisfied in this case that there was a genuine conscientious objection to both combatant and non-combatant military service. February 1954.

Annex 2
Letters relating to the Society for the Reinvigoration of Unremunerative Branch Lines in the United Kingdom (SRUBLUK)

The Spectator January 15 1954

LIGHT RAILWAYS

SIR, May we be permitted space in your correspondence columns to draw the attention of your more railway-minded readers to a proposal to re-open privately the Kent and East Sussex Light Railway which was closed by British Railways on January 4th 1954, by means of a Preservation Society such as that which so successfully preserves the Talyllyn Railway in Wales? The Kent and East Sussex line is one of the very few light railways left in Britain and has had a long history of independence which lasted until 1948. We need much support for this project, and we therefore ask any of your readers, if they are interested and would like further details, to write to Nigel Watt, 1 Blenheim Road, London N.W.8.

Yours faithfully,
NIGEL J. WATT

The Society for the Reinvigoration of Unremunerative Branch Lines in the United Kingdom

To Nigel Watt   The Mead
                                                   Wantage
                                                   Berkshire

25 August 1954

Dear Mr. Watt,

I have heard from Mr. Prosser, the founder of the Railway
Development Association, one of whose vice-presidents I am,
and he says that he thinks it is a good idea that I should be president of your Society, since the aims of the Railway Development
Association and your own are similar. But since hearing from
him I have discussed the matter with my friend Lord Kinross,
in whose house I have been staying while in London, and who
has had an invitation from you to be president. We both think
that the most practical arrangement and the best will be the one
which is going to be most useful toward furthering the objects
of the two societies. As we know one another it seems most
sensible that Lord Kinross should be your president and that I
should also be a vice-president of the London Area of the Railway
Development Association, a position which has been offered to
me. In this way Lord Kinross and I will be able to make common
cause when some brutal decision is made by British Railways.
Lord Kinross is an excellent conversationalist and a wonderfully
lucid and vigorous writer, but he asks me to tell you that he is
no good at making speeches from public platforms. He becomes
terrified and tongue-tied. If you want the kind of president who
can make public speeches and is full of knowledge about railways
and in sympathy with our aims, he and I suggest you might care
to approach our friend Sir Arthur Elton, Bt, of 10 Eldon Grove,
NW3. Anyhow, let me know what your Society thinks of the
suggestions.
One point, the title of your Society. Ought the word Unremunerative
to come out? Doesn't it suggest that branch lines always will be
unremunerative?

Yours sincerely, John Betjeman.

(Sir Arthur Elton did become president with Lord Kinross as vice-president. The word "unremunerative" was later removed. The society changed its name to the Railway Development Society and the merged with the Railway Development Association. It now campaigns as RAILFUTURE.)

Annex 3
Article in "The Avenue", the Friends' School magazine, October 1952

The lights went out

High upon a hill a mile away from Thaxted stands a gaunt and hideous building. Within these walls has dwelt a tiny locomotive for nearly forty years. For it was not until 1913 that the railway shattered the old-world atmosphere of the countryside. So the last stretch of railway track to be laid in rural Essex is one of the first to close. The little two coach "flyer" has wound its way between the corn-covered slopes every day (except Sunday, of course) since its opening and early in September it did it for the last time.

Elsenham station was wild with excitement: the platform was thick with local people who had come to see the end "just for the fun of it," railway enthusiasts from distant cities with notebooks in their hands and cameras slung over their shoulders, and press reporters interviewing the ancient guard who had outlived his job. The engine was dressed up for the occasion with a huge wreath hanging at the front of the boiler, another lower down encircling a fire bucket and a large Union Jack waving merrily beside the funnel. A coffin, draped in black, carried by four Thaxtedians dressed in Edwardian costume... was marched in state to the guard's van.

To the shriek of the whistle, the loud explosion of the detonators and the cheers of the crowd, the little engine pulled its heaviest train away up the steep gradient. For once it felt inspired to break the twenty-five miles an hour speed restriction, but before it was running at full speed a Halt came in sight: Mill Road, Henham, Sibleys... at each stop the guard climbed up the battered lamp posts to turn the oil lamps off for the last time. Passengers came and went. In fact, had there been so many passengers every day the line might well have been electrified! Around the last tortuous bend into Thaxted the engine uttered its last shriek. The passengers went and the lights went out. Soon only the hideous engine shed will remain as a memorial to the age of steam.

Nigel Watt and Brian Abbs, Form VI

Annex 4
Letter from R.A. Butler, Lord Privy Seal
in response to a letter from me condemning
the Anglo-French attack on Suez in 1956

Dear Mr. Watt,

Thank you for telling me your views about the Middle East crisis. Let me say at once that I respect their strength and sincerity. And although they differ from yours I hope you will show a similar respect for mine.

The Anglo-French action must, I am sure, be seen in its proper perspective. For past eight years a state of war has existed between Israel and her Arab neighbours. In those eight years there has been sporadic fighting of varying ferocity; in those same eight years aspects of the Arab-Israeli conflict have been before the Security Council no less than seven times. But as a result of this there has been no relaxation of tension; indeed, in the last few months it has mounted, and has been a continuing threat to world peace.

The latest action must therefore be seen as the culmination of eight years of recurring crises in an area of vital importance both to the world and to this country in particular. From this area comes a large part of the oil supplies on which the continued functioning of our – and Western Europe's – industry depends. Not only our factories but our farm tractors must have Middle Eastern oil to keep them going. We could not risk the possibility of their being denied to us indefinitely. And there was a real danger, had immediate action not been taken to stop the fighting, of the whole of the Middle East going up in flames. Had this been allowed to happen, there would have been no knowing how it might have spread. Britain and France were the only two countries able to act immediately to stop the fighting between Israel and Egypt and to interpose their forces as a buffer between the two combatants. So we acted at once. It was not a burden of our choosing: but we believe that because we took a hard decision last week we may well have prevented the need to take an even harder decision in the weeks and months to come.

Our first objective then is to stop the fighting. Thereafter we seek no selfish aggrandisement, but the lasting pacification of this trouble-torn area under the aegis of the United Nations. We have put forward three steps which, in our view, should be taken to secure this aim – an aim which must be shared by all men of good will. We would willingly cease all military operations the moment they are agreed to.

First, that the Egyptian and Israeli governments should agree to accept a United Nations force to keep the peace.

Second, that the United Nations should decide to constitute and maintain such a force until an Arab-Israeli peace settlement is reached and until satisfactory arrangements have been agreed in regard to the Suez Canal, <u>both agreements to be guaranteed by the United Nations.</u>

Third, that pending the constitution of the United Nations force, both Israel and Egypt should accept limited numbers of Anglo-French troops to be stationed between the combatants.

We believe that none can impugn our aim: there can be – and are – legitimate differences about our methods of achieving it. But the dangers were immediate and we felt that our action had to match their speed and intensity. History will be our judge.

As I write this, we have ordered a Cease Fire, and look to the United Nations to act.

(signed R. A Butler).

Israel invaded Egypt on 29 October 1956; a couple of days later Britain and France landed paratroopers along the Suez Canal. The defeated Egyptians blocked the canal. It was later proved that Britain and France had colluded with Israel in advance. The cease-fire that Butler refers to was the result of pressure from the US and the USSR. The attack was a disaster: oil prices rose as it had to be shipped round the Cape; Egypt moved closer to the Soviet Union; The British Prime Minister, Anthony Eden who had tried to paint the Egyptian leader, Nasser, as kind of Hitler figure, resigned in disgrace. Britain's role as a major power was greatly diminished. It also gave the Russians a green light to invade Hungary.

Annex 5
Letter to the Foreign Secretary as Zimbabwe was attaining independence

---

Lord Carrington,   22.1.1980
The Foreign Office,
London S.W.1.

Dear Lord Carrington,

I should like to congratulate you and your officials on the remarkable achievements at Lancaster House.[69]

At the same time I wish to express dismay, which I know is shared by many others, at the apparent disregard by the British authorities now in Salisbury of the provisions and spirit of the agreement, in particular of the following:

– the continued presence of South African troops on S. Rhodesian soil in spite of a clear undertaking on your part that this would not be permitted. It would appear to me that there might be as much need to defend the northern end of Beit Bridge against South Africa as against anyone else.

– the continued free movement of the forces of the former regime while Patriotic Front forces are rightly confined to the assembly points.

– the actions being taken against ZANU-PF. I accept that some ZANU guerrillas are still active but feel that a much greater use be made of Patriotic Front personnel in helping to bring the remaining guerrillas in and that this difficulty does not justify

---

69. This was the independence agreement with the former rebels led by Robert Mugabe and Joshua Nkomo. Margaret Thatcher had evidently opposed this until the last moment and our friend, Simon Maonde, who was involved in hosting the Commonwealth meeting in Zambia, considered that the Queen had played an important role along with President Kaunda of Zambia.

the Governor in acting in a manner that appears to show a clear bias against one party in what everyone wishes to be a genuinely free election.

The British have a reputation for "fair play" which is being rapidly undermined in the eyes of Africans and many others.

I write with experience of ten years in Northern Rhodesia and Zambia and in the hope that steps can be taken to rectify these matters before it is too late.

Yours sincerely,
Nigel Watt

A civil servant in the Rhodesia Department replied: "It was kind of you to set out your thoughts on this issue and we have taken note of your views."

Annex 6
Elias Chipimo's story

Elias Chipimo Senior was my colleague at *Chizongwe School in Zambia* and we remained friends until his death. I recorded this interview with him in 2011.

We had no kindergarten. We learned as we grew up from seeing what our parents were doing. I would have grown up pretty much like my father. I would have known how to till the soil, how to hunt, how to live. But something happened. I could not exactly tell what. I was about nine years old, and you could only go to school when you were old enough to walk twelve kilometres and back the same day. You were limited as to the age you could start school in the first place. I began going to school. My place was to sit underneath a tree and write my first alphabet on the sand. When the teacher came to inspect what you were doing the sand had already dispersed and you had to do your ABC again. It happened that my father's youngest brother had actually gone to school, was educated and was a teacher, and when he spotted me aged eleven he took a fancy to me and took me with him to school where he was teaching, at Nangulu then to Chibote. And then he fell ill. He was suffering from dementia and I had to walk him back to my village which took three weeks on foot. When I got back to the village it struck me that I didn't belong in the village any more.

So I walked thirty kilometres to a mission school but I had made no application. An uncle of mine lived at the mission. There I was admitted and I went on until what we call now grade six. Then I was stuck. I couldn't raise the money, 17 shillings or something, but an opportunity was offered to me. The missionaries had established a seminary school sixty kilometres from my village and a cousin was already enrolled there and had mentioned this to me – and again I had made no application but after the holidays

I walked back to the seminary and they enrolled me in a lower class because we had to do Latin and I had to start from scratch. I later realised this was a great opportunity. I was not going to sit for the normal Standard 6 exam. I had already done that. I only had to do Latin, so I only attended the Latin classes and little else. So I had all the time in the world – there was a big library – to read as much as I could. That's when I really first came in contact with English literature. I read many books and then just when I had finished the seminary term, something happened. The rector at the time just decided that I had done something that was not "seminary-like" and he dismissed me and my cousin. In fact we had gone to the village and we were late because we had a promise of a lorry coming and it did not come. We were afraid of walking because there were lions about but eventually we did make it but we made it too late and the rector said we had to go.

I was left roaming with nowhere to go. I was about sixteen. Fortunately, a cousin of mine had already done Grade 7 and he brought me an arithmetic book… and I had nothing to do in the village. I just sat there doing arithmetic on my own. With the reading I had been doing when idle at the seminary I brought myself up to two grades ahead. We sat there and did nothing, my cousin and a lot of other boys who never imagined school as anything… but one day we said, "Look, we must leave the village," and we walked for something like five weeks on foot and eventually towards the end we boarded a lorry and got ourselves to Mufulira. When we got there all my colleagues, there were 4 of us, looked for work as kitchen boys or garden sweepers but I was focussed on one thing: I wanted to go to school and so I applied to the nearest school, Ibenga. One of the Ibenga students looked at my letter and listened and said I should go straight into Grade 8 upper and I did and was accepted. It was a boarding school but I was so poor and my cousin who helped me with school fees could only afford half the school uniform I needed. So I was forced to choose either the shorts or the shirt and I naturally I chose the shorts and for the rest of my life at the school I was wearing a singlet. That was all I could afford and as you can imagine I was washing it at night. And for food we used to grow sweet potatoes and looked for wild fruit – we survived.

The next year I was lucky. I came top and was awarded a government bursary to go to Munali Secondary School but I was concerned about the state of affairs in my village – my father poor, my mother poor, my young brother not going to school. I don't know what got my fancy: I said I will not go to secondary school. I will go and take a course so I can start work quickly, help my parents and educate my brother. I went to do medical training at Lusaka and there I saw everything I didn't like: people killed, people coming for treatment, sexual diseases or wounds received from brawls and fighting. The one thing that I remembered particularly was a woman with fibroids. We took out one huge one weighing 14 pounds. There was also a girl who had after-birth problems. It was my first time in the female ward. It struck me how important women are. The next ward I saw was the male ward, with syphilis cases and, comparing the two, I said to myself: here are women suffering from diseases connected with birth and procreation and what are the men doing? Spreading their sperm and having children without care. I looked at the world of the animals and I said it's the same everywhere: the male leaves the care of the babies to the bitch. My perspective had become very different. From then on I have had more respect for women as a biological factor than I have for men. I felt depressed. We had a sitting room, we had newspapers, magazines depicting colleges, universities and students playing football and I suddenly said to myself I am stuck here. I don't want to be stuck in a rut and I must get out somehow and I decided to go back to secondary school.

By that time the rules had changed and I had lost my bursary. An uncle of mine who had been at Ibenga was proud of what I had done there and in the meantime I started to work as a caddy on the golf course, to raise money for going to secondary school. I raised enough to buy myself my first shoes and my first trousers. Eventually I did go to Chikuni School[70] and on the way I passed through Lusaka where my uncle was, and he simply said, "You're going to secondary school. I'll pay your fees." I did not waste my

---

70. Chikuni was run by the Jesuits. It was, along with Munali one of the two best boys school in Zambia.

money. Instead I used it to pay fees for my cousin whom I took with me and we were both admitted.

I decided to continue with Latin at Chikuni and eventually did so well that I was given my bursary again to join Munali Secondary School but because of what I had gone through I pocketed my bursary and went back home for the first time since I had left when I was about sixteen. This time I was ready to get married and to get a job. I made an application to work in Mufulira as an assistant council secretary. In those days if you did Grade 8 or secondary school you didn't look for jobs. Jobs came running after you. So I made up my mind: I'm going to marry; I'm going to educate my brother and I'm going to serve my parents. Then Mr. W.C. Little, the headmaster of Munali, sent me a telegram that I had been offered a bursary, and the experience I had gone through having lost one before compelled me to forget everything and I ended up at Munali. I did well at the end of it but again the same thought that had gripped me when I finished the Grade 8 came back, to educate my brother. (I had sisters but they were all older than me.) And it so happened actually that I had a friend, a Jesuit who was teaching us religion at Munali who said he would arrange for me to have a place in Ireland to do law. I found myself not doing Form 6 and not going to Ireland but teaching as a pupil teacher, which is how I met my future wife. She was waiting to go overseas for studies and we happened to be pupil teachers at the same place... and so I took a job as assistant labour officer on the mines and studied at home. It was all very well knowing all about the miners, the trouble they cause and the copper they produce, but I was still anxious to go to study. I was about twenty-four by then. I had started school late. And things went wrong with the Form 6 project at Munali: only three or four students remained for the sixth form so they closed the class for a time.

I got an envelope shortly after that from my old principal of Munali, Mr. Little: "You have been offered a scholarship to go to Fort Hare." I began to unwind everything I was doing in order to go to Fort Hare university college in South Africa. I delayed, organising a passport, a visa and also a pass because you could not go to South Africa in those days without a South African pass. To get from one town to another I also needed a pass. When it finally arrived – I was doing English as well as French and Latin, politics and philosophy – on one of them I was described as "a foreign native!" It was just one of those things that make you think what must have been in the Afrikaner mind. Anyway, I finally majored in Latin and English. (*Here Nigel mentioned students inspired by my teaching of Latin.*) There was a judge, since retired, who whenever he meets me, greets me as *Magister* and recites some of the Latin I used to quote to them. Latin inspired me in many ways.

Anna. my future wife had studied at Bath, UK during the time I was at Fort Hare. She had been engaged to get married to a man who had been a colleague of mine at school, and I had been engaged to be married to a girl whose education I was able to help. Suddenly everything went wrong. Anna was about to get married to this man, she had bought a dress and the banns had been announced in church. She came back the week following the banns and they would have got married the following Sunday, but she discovered to her dismay and she got an authentic message from her brother that this man had been misbehaving and had even had a child with one of my wife's own nieces. She scrapped everything all at once. And here was I face to face with her, an already mature, well-educated woman, and I had this girl whom I was struggling to bring up to the level… the choice was open and I couldn't resist it. So we decided to get married. I was to teach at Chizongwe which was to be a co-educational school. They thought they could expand it with one wing for girls in the east near Kaizore's village. When they tried to expand, Kaizore rose up in anger and said, "You cannot build here. That's where all my ancestors are buried." Today they have actually extended the school to the grave site but that is why my wife ended up teaching across the river at Walela Primary School. We got married in December 1959 and I went straight to Chizongwe.

Then the students had this strike. I was very worried about that. It put me to tears because I had just been teaching for the first time in my life and loved the children and I just couldn't bear it; I tried to talk to them, but they would not listen. UFP (pro-Federation) MP Gabriel Musumbulwa was the Minister of Education. There was an atmosphere, a resentment of anything pertaining to Federation. The politicians had brewed it up and the students were burning with it in their hearts. The Monckton Commission was going to sit at Chizongwe Secondary School and the students would not accept that. I was the one up in front to try to contain and control the whole strike thing even though I was a fellow Zambian and a promising young teacher respected by all the students, but they still did not heed me. They all were expelled and went to different schools in the country, and some found their education in other countries. When the school reopened – it must have taken three months – some of the students, especially those in the lower forms, came back. But now there was a very accelerated spirit of change because that's when the *chachacha* (agitation for Independence) started.

When I went to Chizongwe Alf King was headmaster. I remember once when Kaunda and his political colleagues, Arthur Wina, Sikota Wina and Dingiswayo Banda were campaigning in the area, they visited my house and according to our tradition I gave them a meal and talked with them but we really didn't in my recollection talk politics as such, but the language was political anyway because the atmosphere was political. King cautioned me and he used Latin saying it's bad for you entertaining a *persona non grata*. I said that according to our tradition we treat our guests without regard. During Mr. King's leave I took over briefly as acting principal. I left late in 1963 and I went to work as a civil servant as they were looking desperately for educated people to replace the colonial administrators.

I always give credit to the British in the sense that whatever they did they were in many ways restrained, as compared to what white Rhodesians would do. I think from the start the British were just exploiting the resources. They wanted to leave the people alone. Indirect rule. If they had a vision they did not do much to prepare for it. I came to the UK once as a visitor – I was a banker by then – but I had entertained the Lord Mayor of London the time he visited Zambia. (After we re-introduced multi-party democracy there was a gap which I filled as acting Mayor of Lusaka). When I came to see my children in England the Lord Mayor invited me for lunch but then he gave me a tour. There were golden chalices and golden this or that donated by previous Lord Mayors or other people. You looked at it like all the gold in the ground in Africa was still less than the gold I could see collected in one place. So the colonial administration's first interest was simply to collect resources for themselves and to collect ivory for piano keys and for decorations of one kind or another. In all other respects they wanted to leave the Africans alone. When they needed it they carved out a piece of land for themselves: in Zambia along the line of rail from Livingstone to the Copperbelt where there was rich soil and then pockets in Chipata and Mbala where the soil was also good to grow something that they would sell or eat. About 3% of the land was taken up and the rest was in African hands as "trust land". On trust land the chiefs, although they are now losing it fast, had control. And the only other people allowed to settle on trust land were people who were doing something for the "natives" such as missionaries. Land in Zambia was owned communally.

PIC 28) *Elias Chipimo, then Zambian High Commissioner in London, with his wife Anna and Kaye Whiteman.*

The British developed no real education system, no hospitals, no clinics – only the missionaries were able to start the beginnings of education and health care. West Africa was generally way ahead. If I look at the architecture, compared to what you find in Zimbabwe, Angola or South Africa where the white man came to settle they built memorable structures which are still of some architectural value, but Zambia and Malawi were simply staging posts. They built only three good buildings in Zambia, the Old Secretariat, the Governor's house and the High Court. The only things we built after independence which were comparable were our National Assembly, a lovely structure, and the Anglican cathedral.

I was Zambian High Commissioner in the UK in 1968-69. The first High Commissioner had been Simon Katilungu. But I took over from Ali Simbule, who had described Britain as a "toothless bulldog". We are all in the Commonwealth and all High Commissioners owed allegiance to the head of the Commonwealth who happened to be the Queen. So when we went to each other's countries we did not have to present credentials to begin working. Technically Simbule was High Commissioner the moment he landed at the airport but formally he was not. When he landed the journalists asked if still thought of Britain was a "toothless bulldog" – and by the way it was not Simbule's invention – and he repeated it at the airport. The British did not accept him and he did not stay long, not one week. They sent him to the UN for a conference and he was brought directly back to Zambia. I was appointed in his place. Later I used to drink at the Flying Club with Simbule[71] and others. It so happens that we had earlier had differences when he was High Commissioner in Tanzania and I went to work there as fuel coordinator for Zambia. I worked from his office and he thought I was going to take over from him. The irony is when he was High Commissioner in London I did take over from him! In the end he worked under me when I was Minister for the Central Province. Eventually our two families inter-married and we ended up as friends.

---

71. He was nicknamed "Toothsome"!

Annex 7
Diapy Diawara talks of his encounter
with Sékou Touré

I was 13 years old when I first met Sékou Touré. I had an uncle living at Kankan in Guinea and I decided to go and visit him. It was December 1961. My dad gave me 1,500 cfa francs to go by boat but I took some bananas and mangos and cycled the 380 kilometres from Bamako. When I arrived in Kankan I was surprised that there were crowds of people lining the road. I continued on my bike and people laughed. Sekou Toure approached waving his white handkerchief and the people were shouting "Prési, Prési". I had no idea who this man was. "Who is it?" I asked. Sékou Touré overheard this and asked me who I was. "I am Diapy Diawara", I replied. "You must be Malian. Have you come to see me?" "No," I replied, "I've come to stay with my uncle." The President responded, "Inshallah we shall meet again". Then I was directed to my uncle's house by the policeman who had said nothing in the President's presence.

A day later I was in my uncle's garden playing ludo. Someone knocked on the door and my auntie opened it. It was Sékou Touré. Terrified, she slammed the door in his face and called her husband. He opened the door and, equally terrified to see who it was, slammed the door again. Thinking better of it, he invited Sékou Touré into the house. He must have wondered if was this how Malians welcomed their guests. The President explained how he had met Diapy and the boy was invited into the room. Touré spoke of how Guinea and Mali were united by the Malinke civilization. Then he went back to the road and to his bodyguards and the crowds who were still shouting "Prési!"

My uncle was really frightened. Sékou Touré had said that all traffickers must be killed and my uncle was a major trafficker of diamonds as well as being the head of the Malian community in Kankan. He met his friends and they agreed that all the diamonds must be removed from the house at once. And I was hastily driven back to Bamako.

But Sékou Touré never forgot me and would call me when he was in Paris and send a note with his visiting agents. Through this connection I was invited eventually to manage the two great Guinean bands, Bembeya Jazz and Les Amazones, both of which I brought to the Africa Centre.

(Interview with Diapy Diawara at L'Hay-les-Roses, France 2012.)

Annex 8
Letters from Jozef Muwanga

Jozef was a good friend during my year at the Institute of Education (1960-61). His comments on Uganda just before and after Independence are interesting.

(1961)

I got home only to find we were still as under-developed as ever... I had forgotten what it feels like riding on earth roads, seeing people carrying water on their heads etc... However, there have been some changes: Kampala even has traffic lights! What has impressed me is the larger part the Africans are increasingly playing in the affairs of the country. Every government department has quite a few Africans in high posts... Asians are still as prominent as ever but are gradually getting into the background... Things don't change in African rural life. But oh! The towns! Bars are open throughout the day and night life starts at 4pm and ends at 6am. A rather significant change is that now football, at least at the national level, is played in boots!

(1962)

We have become the 110th UN member. The Duke and Duchess of Kent have just returned to England after "giving" us our Independence. Uganda's politics are most unpredictable. The Uganda People's Congress, my non-Catholic left-wing party, has joined hands with Kabaka Yekka, an extreme rightist group, to form the first government... Personally I am not too happy with the set up but it was the only answer in the circumstances. Thus power is balanced between the Baganda and the Nilotics. The Minister of Justice is a drain-pipe clad youth of 27 and a class-mate of mine, as is the Minister of Information. These last two make me think that either there is a serious lack of trained and experienced personnel or I am a failure! The celebrations went off very peacefully... The Asian community were surprised by this. Many had sent their wives to Kenya for fear that rape might take place!... We are still the old people we were before Independence, illiterate, half-starving, slum-dwelling etc. but the "better offs" are even getting better off. For example King Freddie[72] has added a Bentley and a Mercedes to his collection which includes some six Rolls Royces. No doubt taxes will go up and we shall be urged to work even harder!

---

72. Kabaka Mutesa II of Buganda, in full Sir Edward Frederick William David Walugembe Mutebi Luwangula Mutesa, died, according to a press report after a visit by "a beautiful girl" who may have poisoned him, in1969 near where we were to live in 1971 in Bermondsey, south east London. He had been deposed in 1953 by the British and again in 1966 by Milton Obote, the first president of independent Uganda.

Annex 9
Tedson Rukundo's story

Rukundo was born in Kabale, Uganda and lived with his mother. He knew his father only later. When his mother moved to Kampala he remained with his half brothers and sisters and went to primary school in Kabale. His brothers did not get on with him and they had fights, so at the age of nine he became a street kid in Kabale. He survived by earning a little money bricklaying and taking tourists to visit Lake Bunyoni.

After two years of this he moved to Kampala and spent eight more years as a street kid and he helped carry stuff for the *kadogos* (child soldiers). He visited Rwanda in 1994 where he joined an association for street kids called Kiddo which was run by an ex-army man. One visitor to the Kiddo house was Lieut. Guma, who asked Rukundo to look after his brother who was dying from AIDS. He died in Rukundo's arms in Mulago Hospital in Uganda. Guma was the personal secretary of my friend Tajudeen Abdul Raheem, the director of the Pan African Movement (PAM) and a former member of the Africa Centre's council. Rukundo was invited by Guma to help him in his office. This is how he met Tajudeen who was impressed by this bright-looking boy and who started to pay his school fees so that he could finish primary and begin secondary education, though he never knew that Rukundo was still sleeping on the street.

Through his connection with Tajudeen, Rukundo met most of the movement's well-known visitors including Gamal Nkrumah (Kwame's son); Betty Shabazz (the wife of Malcolm X); Bob Marley's mother; the Zanzibari leader and Tanzanian minister, Abdulrahman Mohammed Babu (later to be Chair of the Africa Centre); the Sudanese leader, John Garang; various Palestinians and others struggling for liberation. He also began to read books by

Gandhi, Malcolm X and others. Another visitor was Prof. Horace Campbell, author of *Rasta and Resistance* who gave Rukundo some advice which he always followed: "Opportunity comes once." Tajudeen was always considerate towards him: when Lucky Dube had his concert in Kampala, his first outside of South Africa, sponsored by the Pan African Movement, Taj told his staff: "Don't forget Teddy!" Rukundo used to look after the office during weekends while the Ugandan soldiers sat around drinking, or he stayed in the house when Taj was away. I also stayed in that house as the guest of Ahmed Sheikh who was the PAM's Cultural Commissar, so I may have met Rukundo earlier than I realised.

When there was a robbery at the PAM office. Guma was blamed and jailed for it. Staff were not getting their pay and were discontented and here was this street boy getting special treatment just because he was Guma's protégé, so he took the term's fees and set off on his own, but he could not complete the remaining two years to "O" level.

In 1996 he returned to see his mother in Kabale and found that his half-brothers were not helping her at all. He said to her, "Mum, I will build you a house." She did not believe him. Then he continued to Rwanda where he survived by repairing vehicles for the RPF army. He had no formal training in mechanics but learned just by watching people repairing vehicles. In Kigali he also started by sleeping rough but later some Ugandans gave him a bed. Then tensions got bad between Uganda and Rwanda and one Ugandan friend was shot by a policeman. Rukundo was briefly thrown into gaol for refusing to take part in a night patrol and he was forced to carry dead bodies after a grenade attack. With a risk of being imprisoned again he decided in 1999 to move on to Burundi.

Rukundo found a mechanic friend to stay with in the Avenue de l'Université in Bujumbura and he found a job as a bouncer at the Hippo Club (a rather good pizza restaurant which I used to frequent, so I may have seen him there). He linked up with some other Ugandans: the singer Bernard Katende whom he knew from gigs in Rwanda, Henry, the DJ at Havana Club and Chizzo Lubega, also a singer. I met him when he became a bouncer and later a driver and sound engineer at Havana Club. My son Tom visited Bujumbura and played in the band with Chizzo at Havana and when I was away in England Rukundo looked after my house. By about 2001 Havana had become a a dodgy place for drugs and money and Rukundo left. He was in contact with Salim, an Indian who had opened a cyber café, who offered him a pool table and he paid a deposit on this. The Koromboka Bar gave him some space for the pool table and this is where he was when I left Burundi the day after 9/11.

In 2002 Rukundo decided to leave Burundi. He had arrived in Burundi with no passport but as his home language was Kifumbira, which is very similar to Kinyarwanda and thus to Kirundi, he now spoke perfect Kirundi and convinced the authorities to give him a Burundi passport. He sold the pool table for US$200 and a friend gave him another US$200. He visited his mum in Uganda and told her he was going to South Africa and he set off to Dar es Salaam. On the roadside he found Robert, the former manager of Havana Club who was broke and being pursued by Bujumbura money changers. Rukundo helped him with his bus fare to Dar where Robert had his wife and other contacts. Robert wanted to go to Malawi. He gave Rukundo a lift there but the police raided the hotel in Blantyre where he was lodging. He was carted off to prison where he stayed for ten days, after which the police came and drove him to the Tanzanian frontier. He was not allowed to go back to the hotel to get his passport and his belongings including all his photos of the Pan African Movement, his school and life in Burundi.

By chance he had met a group of Norwegian backpackers in Tanzania on their way to Malawi. They said they were going later to Zanzibar. He chatted them up and they gave him the bus fare to Dar es Salaam. Again he met up with Robert who said, "You are a personable guy and you speak good English and Swahili. Why not go to Zanzibar where there are lots of tourists? You should be able to make a living." Robert gave him the boat fare. Once on Zanzibar in February 2003 he chanced to recognise a back-packer who had helped him at the Malawi border. He visited the

Norwegian group and there he met Maria, who fell for him. She was to leave for Norway in April and they quickly got married. She paid for him to get a passport and visa and introduced him to the Norwegian embassy in Dar. Back in Zanzibar he was doing quite good business helping to show tourists around. Maria had rented a house for him for a year and left him a computer. Then the embassy called to tell him he had a visa. Maria had sent him money for the ticket. He sold the computer and set off.

On 22 June 2003 he was nervous with excitement and dressed for the cold North. It was his first flight. He sat up all night gazing at the flight map and getting free drinks. Arriving at Amsterdam he tried to look cool like a regular traveller but immediately got his shoelace caught in the escalator. A cheeky cleaner could see he was a novice and exclaimed: "Welcome to Europe!" It was 10pm when he arrived in Oslo and he kept asking people the time, unable to believe that it could still be light in the night time. The next hurdle was immigration. He had been led to believe that only criminals had tattoos, but the immigration officer had a big tattoo. He froze and asked the woman behind him if it was safe to give his passport to a criminal. She managed to convince him that the man was no criminal. Next there was a man with a fierce dog. Past that and he finally found Maria and was in Oslo.

The relationship with Maria did not last long but he managed to stay on in Norway, marrying Hilde, having baby Noah and getting more training and a job as a mechanic with Oslo city transport. He kept the promise to his mother, using his earnings to build her a house in Kabale with a built-in toilet and bathroom which she describes as "heaven on earth." She rents out the servants' quarters and is now a landlady! He is also building two houses in Zanzibar – and when Rukundo builds it is not just a matter of sending money. He is out there mixing cement and laying bricks. When I visited Zanzibar in 2018 the houses were not finished but I stayed nearby and saw him at work.

Annex 10
Florence Ssereo's story

When I arrived in Paris in 1992 Florence was an intern in the Youth Division of UNESCO, which was the department CCIVS had relations with. We became friends while I worked in Paris and have kept in touch ever since. Her life is an interesting and inspiring African story. These are the notes of my interview with her in 2015.

I was born with the name Elvira Florence Sereo in April 1960 in Moyo, in Madi District (now Moyo District) in the West Nile Province of Uganda. My father was Mzee Erminio Vuru, my mother Mama Santina Asobasi, usually known (by the name of the first born) as Mama Iya. I was the sixth of seven children – Philipo, Zackeo, Dominica, Natalina, Thereza, me and Judita. Dominica and Natalina died very young. When I was three years old my parents split up. Mzee had been a teacher since the age of 18 and was already retired after 25 years' service. He had grown up with Catholic missionary priests, who trained him as a teacher and sent him all over the district to found primary schools and work as a headmaster in rural areas where the missionaries worked and established Catholic parishes. He also farmed and produced food for the extended family and for the many visitors that came to our home. However, for someone who started to work at the age of 18 he retired too young and was soon drawn into a reckless life: he drank a lot of home brew *waragi* (gin) in wrong company and he frequently beat my mother.

One day she could take it no longer. She departed. It was a day's walk to her parents' home with baby Judita on her back. She set off early one morning, determined to find peace and calm with her own mother. It must have been 1962: Philipo was away studying at a seminary and Zackeo was at Teacher Training College, both far from Moyo. Thereza was in her first year in primary in the girls' parish school. Mzee could not cook and my elder sister and I were too young to cook for ourselves. We ate dried beans soaked in salted water. No-one offered to look after us girls. Thereza had told Mzee that our mother had gone to hospital. Believing that she must have been admitted to hospital, he searched for her everywhere but did not find her. He decided to look for her at my grandmother's, and indeed he found her there but failed to persuade her to return to Moyo. He had mistreated her and her relatives were not amused. He was beaten up by her brother and cousins. My mother's sister, my eldest aunt, came to visit us, unaware that my mother had left and, finding us in a worrying situation, she decided to take me with her. Thereza went to stay with a paternal cousin who was a policeman until Zackeo completed his training and was posted to teach in a primary school near my father's home. Thereza then went to live with him. Coming home for holidays and not finding Mama was bad news for Philipo. He eventually decided to quit the seminary to help Zackeo look after his sisters, who they both believed needed to go to school. This must have been a good decision for us girls in a socio-cultural context hostile to girls' education. At the age of about six I was sent to help look after the young children of a cousin who was a primary school teacher with two young children. I was badly treated. My cousin and her husband were always fighting and I was very unhappy living with them. One day on a visit to the nearby hospital when I was sick I had noticed there was a bus to Moyo. I noted which days of the week it passed by and one day I took a bucket so they would think I had gone to fetch some water. I got on the bus with no money and no idea where I was going except to escape from this horrible household. To my (and his) surprise, Zackeo was on the same bus. He took me to his home and I joined my sister there.

Mzee was furious when my cousin reported me missing. He came to tell Zackeo but found me. Zackeo refused to return me to my cousin's. When my cousin came to plead with my father I hid until she and her husband had left. I wanted to go to school like my sister. Zackeo agreed to pay my school fees and he sent Thereza to a boarding school. Judita had joined us but unfortunately Judita and I had to go and stay with Mzee, who was not in favour of girls being educated. Luckily my brothers wanted educated sisters. All three of us joined the Xaverian movement and through its activities we learned life skills. When she successfully completed her primary education Thereza was awarded a bursary. She was a bright girl and the local government was implementing affirmative action for girls' education. She went on to the Sacred Heart Secondary School in Gulu, 100 miles from Moyo. I would follow her several years after, as would Judita. This was a boarding school with nearly 1,000 girls (to be targeted in the mid-90s by the Lord's Resistance Army). Mzee finally apologised for his attitude and supported our ambitions and insisted that we trained as teachers.

Towards the late 1970s my mother eventually returned to live with us but quite briefly because she died in January 1980. Mzee did not remarry, and when he fell sick Zackeo brought him to stay in Kampala with his family until his death in 2003.

I recall vividly that I was in the last years of primary education when Idi Amin came to power in 1971. He seemed popular at the beginning, sending the Asians away, putting the national economy into the hands of Ugandans, condemning neo-colonialism and praising Ugandan patriotism. Coming from West Nile himself he was said to favour us people from this province when reallocating former Asian businesses and property, which they then did not run successfully as they were not well educated. He also gave advantages to Muslims, causing many Christians across the country to convert to Islam. During his eight-year rule he cooperated with Arab countries: the Saudis built a new public hospital in Old Kampala; Gaddafi built the biggest mosque in East Africa in Kampala and a Libyan Bank was established.

In April 1979 Amin was facing defeat by Tanzanian forces. Some of his soldiers, the disintegrating national army who were deserting the war, tried to capture my brother Philipo on his way by car to Moyo, but he would not stop, so they shot at him and ended up killing my sister-in-law instead. Baby Augustine was in the car but survived the shooting and Philipo drove to the nearest military

Institution in Gulu looking for help. After the burial of his wife Philipo was very bitter and went to join some of his friends who had fled into Sudan. I had also fled briefly after the funeral of my sister-in-law. The new government that was formed after the fall of Idi Amin was calling Ugandans to return to work. Not finding my brother in Moyo, I went to look for Philipo in Sudan, in a small town called Kajokeji, walking 40 miles. I went to convince him to return to his job and informed him that the Comboni missionary priests in Moyo could take him back to Kampala. I stayed on in Kajokeji overnight but a friend of Philipo's took advantage and raped me. (This man, "George" later became District Commissioner of Arua). When I discovered that I was pregnant I went to see him, but he was very harsh and arrogant. He insulted me and told me how my brother was proud of me, boasting that I was a serious, intelligent girl but that with a baby in my tummy I could not continue with my studies at secondary school! In fact he had sought to ruin my future and frustrate my brother's efforts to educate me. This realisation would later fuel my intellectual ambitions and determination. At this time Father Adelmo, the chaplain of the Young Christian Students Movement and of Moyo Senior Secondary School, sympathised with my situation and he had found me a temporary teaching job in the school. I was earning some pocket money, hoping to return to school after the war. There was no way I could accept having a baby forced onto me through violence, so I insisted on having an abortion. One of Thereza's friends, whose husband was a nurse, arranged for me to travel to Arua, the provincial capital, where a competent medical doctor could help me. At that time abortion was illegal. I had to undergo a "spontaneous miscarriage." A senior midwife, another friend of my sister, took me to George's house to explain the situation and the consequence of his actions to him but he would not listen. He insulted us and chased us out of his house. Thereafter I returned to Moyo and continued teaching until I was able to return to school.

In the meantime Philipo had returned to his job in Kampala and settled down. In Moyo I "stole" Augustine, my young nephew, from his aunt's home, where he was staying after the loss of his mother. I took him to Kajokeji in Sudan to stay with one of my cousins. I eventually fetched Augustine and took him to his father in Kampala, who was happy to be reunited with his son. I returned to complete my secondary education, aiming at university entrance. Thanks to Fr Adelmo I was able to complete my advanced secondary education and go to Makerere University. He shared my vision and determination, paid my school fees and gave me moral support. Thereafter he became my adopted brother, friend and later uncle to my children whom he loved dearly.

During my time at Sacred Heart Secondary School, I had joined the Young Catholic Students movement and soon became its President both at school and at diocesan levels. I became the deputy national leader when I got to Makerere University in 1982. I studied chemistry and biochemistry and upon graduation I enrolled on a post-graduate diploma course in education and trained as a teacher. I took study leave after qualifying and volunteered to work for the Pan-African Young Christian Students coordination office in Nairobi, Kenya. I was elected co-Secretary General of African Young Catholic Students (YCS) and worked in Nairobi from 1984 to 1986. The 1986 World Council of the International YCS elected me to its international team and in 1987 I left Nairobi for the Secretariat of the IYCS in France where I worked till 1991.

During this period I discovered UNESCO through its link with the youth NGOs Consultation. I was to serve as a youth volunteer in the Youth Division at UNESCO from 1991 to 1993 and I have remained with UNESCO ever since, working in various capacities. I served as Education Specialist in Ethiopia 2004-09, in Tanzania 2009-10 and since 2010 at UNESCO Headquarters in Paris. I pursued advanced studies and obtained a Ph.D.in social sciences, post-doctoral diplomas in curriculum design and development, in comparative education and in education policy and planning as well as an MA in pluri-disciplinary research and the sociology of defence. During my time in UNESCO in the education sector, I have contributed to the development and implementation of education programmes in Ethiopia and Tanzania. I have advocated for girls' education and gender equality and in this context coordinated the production of a publication called *A guide for gender equality in teacher policy and practices*. I have initiated and supported the integration of peace education and intercultural intellectual cooperation across the curriculum in schools using UNESCO's General History of Africa. I am part of a team working to help implement teacher-centred curriculum development and educational reforms. I have always respected principles of professionalism in my relations with colleagues and given the best of my knowledge and skill but the work environment in UNESCO is often far from stimulating. Neither professional ethics nor the ideals of the organization seem to guide its day to day operations. Certain factors seem to block professional advancement for a black, intelligent woman. There is hidden discrimination in practice: some staff who are known to be performing well do not easily get promotion and are marginalized or isolated, either because they are perceived as potential threats by their bosses or have cultural origins that are negatively perceived.

I had first met my future husband, Dominic Lulu, at my cousin's house but his family had for long been closely linked to mine. His mother was my mother's godmother and "matron" at my parents' wedding. Dominic had two sisters and seven brothers, but all seven brothers died young due to various causes, including alcohol abuse. Dominic and I had a civil wedding in Kampala in October 1986. He was initially an art teacher but was offered a post in the Ministry of Internal Affairs after taking a political training course. He took study leave and came to join me in Paris in 1989, where he continued to study while working part time at a hotel. As a husband Dominic was pleasant during the early years of our marriage but turned violent, especially after the birth of our first child. As he grew up our firstborn, Guy-Clement, imitated his behaviour, even beating up a small girl at his nursery school. By 1995 Guy-Clement and his brother Kevin were experiencing a very unhappy family life. As separation by mutual agreement failed and I filed for divorce to protect the young children from this violence but Dominic resisted the idea and the court process took several years. My elder brother Philipo, a traditionalist, tended to support reconciliation on the argument that children must grow up with their father, which was also Dominic's line, while Zackeo, who was more pragmatic, supported my position that a violent home where children and parents do not love and respect each other is more destructive for children. They spoke of what other people might say rather than my happiness and that of the children.

My situation in 1997 brought to mind my eldest sister Thereza's experience. She was badly treated when her first relationship did not end up in marriage. She had a child during her first year in the law school at Makerere. She experienced severe psychological problems and dropped out of the law school. She would later have three children from different relationships. but because she had traditionalist attitudes and respected her brothers' authority although their rejection of her was a cause of her mental problems, she failed to live her own life. By contrast my younger sister Judita became totally independent through her membership of the Baha'i faith. She worked at their centre in Haifa, Israel and Baha'i friends who lived a community life were like a family to her. She unfortunately died young in 2008. Thereza's situation encouraged me to build my own house in Kampala, which I did secretly. When my brothers learned of it they were angry at not being informed or associated with my plans. I managed to remain independent of my brothers through sheer determination. My mother has been my role model. She was not educated and she signed a document with a coloured thumb print but she knew her own limits and when to take a decision when it came to stopping the domestic violence she suffered.

Looking back I find what has happened to me amazing, so much self-discovery and professional growth. I have come to know many people through the various events in my life. I am a single parent, my two sons have grown up and are studying. I am fortunate to have a stable job and to enjoy my work. UNESCO has empowered me through my job. Making it possible for me to live comfortably be it in Ethiopia, Tanzania or Paris and to pay for the education of my sons.

Interviews with Florence Ssereo and notes by her in February and March 2015

Glossary

apartheid – the South African policy of separating the races

brochette – kebab (French)

bush taxi / taxi de brousse – long distance shared taxi or minibus

cabaret – bar (Burundian French)

cadeau – gift (French)

chai (Swahili) – tea, or a bribe

chitemene – Zambian practice of cutting and burning trees for cultivation

fanta – any soft drink (Burundi)

ilha – island (Portuguese)

INGO – international non-government organisation

masokono – scones i.e. bread rolls (Zambia)

mbira – thumb piano (Zimbabwe)

motard – motorbike taximan (Congo French)

muzungu, mzungu (Swahili, Kirundi, Zambia) – white person

NGO – non-government organisation

obruni – white person (Ghana)

oyinbo – white person (Yoruba)

rondavel – round hut or house (southern Africa)

rugo – homestead (Kirundi)

taxi-moto – motorbike taxi (Congo French)

toubab – white person (West Africa)

trotro – minibus (Ghana)

ugali (Swahili), nsima (Zambia), sadza (Zimbabwe) – maize porridge (staple food)

Bibliography

(Many of these books are out of print but can sometimes be found through Amazon or second-hand booksellers)

Bennett, Frank: *Under an African Sun* (The Radcliffe Press 2006), memoirs of a young Colonial Officer in Northern Rhodesia 1959-61.

Berwouts, Kris: *Congo's Violent Peace* (Zed Books 2017).

Betjeman, John: *Letters Volume Two 1951 to 1984* (Methuen 2006).

Bolam, David W.: *Unbroken Community, the Story of the Friends School* (1952).

Caute, David: *Under the Skin, The Death of White Rhodesia* (Penguin 1983).

Cérésole, Pierre: *En Vue de l'Himalaya* (Lausanne. Editions La Concorde 1936).

Dembitzer, Benny: *The Famine Next Door. Africa is Burning. The North is Watching* (Ethical Events 2018).

Gillette, Arthur: *One Million Volunteers* (Penguin 1968) – available on line.

Gnammankou, Dieudonné: *Abraham Hanibal, Prince of Logone* (Books of Africa 2015).

Gunther, John: *Inside Africa* (Harper Brothers 1955).

Hall, Barbara: *Tell me, Josephine* (Andre Deutsch 1964).

Hall, Richard: *The High Price of Principles, Kaunda and the White South* (Hodder & Stoughton 1969).

Hegnauer, Ralph: *A Lifelong Volunteer* (SCI Archive1999).

Hughes, David: *The Man with the Stick and other tales from a bar in Botswana* (Books of Africa 2016).

Jeans, Angela: *Condemned to Life* (Sylvan Press 1949).

Jeans, Angela: *The Man who was my Husband* (Vision Press 1964).

Kapila, Mukesh: *Against a Tide of Evil* (Mainstream 2013).

Kapuscinski, Ryszard: *Another Day of Life* (Vintage Books 1976) – Angola in 1975.

Kashita, June: *This was my Africa – Living with Changes* (2018) available from Amazon.

Kaunda, Kenneth: *Zambia shall be Free* (Heinemann African Writers 1962).

Kihoro, Wanyiri: *Never Say Die* (Nairobi, East African Educational Publishers).

Kingsley, Mary: *Travels in West Africa* (1897 but many reprints and kindle edition).

Marechera, Dambudzo: *The House of Hunger* (2nd ed. Heinemann).

Melady, Thomas Patrick: *Burundi, the Tragic Years* (New York, Orbis Books 1974).

Morgan, Bryan: *The End of the Line* (Cleaver Hume 1955) – my bible of little railways in Europe.

Musée Royale: *Naissance du Congo Belge* (Brussels, Didier Hatier 1989).

Obe, Ad'Obe: *Yunhouse* – a novel which echoes life in the Africa Centre.

Paye, Peter: *The Saffron Walden Branch* (Oakwood Press 2017).

Reynolds, Reginald: *Beware of Africans* (Jarrolds 1955).

Rosenstock-Huessy, Eugen: *Planetary Service* (Vermont, ArgBooks 1978).

Short, Robin: *African Sunset* (Johnson 1973).

Snelson, Peter: *Educational Development in Northern Rhodesia 1883-1945* (Lusaka, Kenneth Kaunda Foundation, revised 1990).

Various: *The School on the Hill, 300 Years of the Friends' School* (2002).

Watt, Nigel: *Burundi, the Biography of a small African Country* (Hurst 2016).

Whiteman, Kaye: *Lagos, a Cultural and Historical Companion* (Signal Books 2012).

Williams, Susan: *Who killed Hammarskjöld?* (Hurst 2011).

Wilson, Richard: *Titanic Express* (Continuum 2006) – about Burundi.

Yates, Anne and Chester, Lewis: *The Troublemaker. Michael Scott and his Lonely Struggle against Injustice* (Aurum Press 2006).

Young, Peter: *A Disgrace to her Country* (Lewes. The Book Guild 1997) – the story of a Russian teacher in Zambia.

Index of countries

A

Aden, 47, 81
Afghanistan, 43, 45
Algeria, 143
Andorra, 32
Angola, 50, 105, 152, 154, 165, 192, 212, 213, 214, 215, 283, 301
Austria, 29, 34, 139, 140

B

Bangladesh, 170, 206
Belgium, 23, 31, 79, 139, 200, 216, 220, 234, 239, 240
Benin, 100, 103, 119, 123, 124, 125, 143, 174, 183
Botswana, 52, 104, 140, 146, 148, 150, 151, 152, 154, 155, 167, 183, 191, 198, 201, 212, 217, 236, 238, 300
Bulgaria, 213
Burkina Faso, 103, 128, 130, 171
Burma, 17
Burundi, 10, 145, 174, 209, 233, 239, 240, 241, 242, 243, 244, 245, 246, 247, 248, 249, 250, 251, 252, 253, 254, 255, 256, 257, 263, 289, 290, 299, 301, 302

C

Cambodia, 207
Cameroon, 99, 108, 111, 112, 113, 114, 115, 116, 117, 118, 119, 126, 143, 146, 148, 155, 156, 157, 176
Central African Republic, 129, 176
Chad, 114, 155, 156, 157

China, 77, 178, 179, 207
Comoro Islands, 146, 148, 158, 159
Congo-Brazzaville, 107, 261
Congo (DRC), 177, 220, 223, 228, 229, 231, 234, 248, 257, 261
Cyprus, 34

D

Dahomey (Benin), 100, 103, 123, 124, 125, 143
Dubai, 37

E

Egypt, 32, 33, 190, 197, 272, 273
Equatorial Guinea, 114

F

Fiji, 207
France, 29, 30, 31, 41, 108, 111, 113, 132, 136, 137, 139, 140, 142, 143, 157, 159, 160, 169, 177, 186, 209, 216, 259, 261, 272, 273, 285, 296

G

Gabon, 108, 109, 110, 111, 134, 209
Gambia, 123, 143
Germany, 19, 23, 27, 29, 31, 34, 57, 110, 111, 137, 139, 140, 141, 169, 176, 199, 207, 209, 216, 219, 236, 237, 248
Ghana, 30, 46, 48, 99, 100, 102, 123, 125, 126, 127, 128, 130, 132, 136, 141, 142, 145, 175, 176, 183, 184, 185, 186, 188, 190, 191, 199, 201, 203, 204, 259, 260, 299

Index of people